SMART BUSINESS

SMART BUSINESS

WHAT **ALIBABA'S** SUCCESS REVEALS ABOUT THE FUTURE OF STRATEGY

MING ZENG

HARVARD BUSINESS REVIEW PRESS
BOSTON, MASSACHUSETTS

HBR Press Quantity Sales Discounts

Harvard Business Review Press titles are available at significant quantity discounts when purchased in bulk for client gifts, sales promotions, and premiums. Special editions, including books with corporate logos, customized covers, and letters from the company or CEO printed in the front matter, as well as excerpts of existing books, can also be created in large quantities for special needs.

For details and discount information for both print and ebook formats, contact booksales@harvardbusiness.org, tel. 800-988-0886, or www.hbr.org/bulksales.

The web addresses referenced in this book were live and correct at the time of the book's publication but may be subject to change.

Library of Congress cataloging-in-publication data

Names: Zeng, Ming, author.
Title: Smart business : Alibaba, the future of strategy, and what it means for you / by Ming Zeng.
Description: [Boston, Massachusetts] : Harvard Business Review Press, [2018]
Identifiers: LCCN 2018006877 | ISBN 9781633693296 (hardcover : alk. paper)
Subjects: LCSH: Alibaba (Firm) | Business planning—Technological innovations. | Strategic planning—Technological innovations.
Classification: LCC HD30.28 .Z425 2018 | DDC 658.8/72—dc23 LC record available at https://lccn.loc.gov/2018006877

ISBN: 978-1-63369-329-6
eISBN: 978-1-63369-330-2

The paper used in this publication meets the requirements of the American National Standard for Permanence of Paper for Publications and Documents in Libraries and Archives Z39.48-1992.

*To my wife Qing Tan, my sons Andy and Tommy,
and my daughter Tina, for their tireless support all these years.
Even as I have had to take so much precious time away
from my family, they have encouraged and
sustained my efforts.*

*And to all the AliRen, who have worked at and contributed
to Alibaba, a miracle beyond anyone's imagination.*

CONTENTS

PART THREE

HOW SMART BUSINESSES RUN
Organizational Implications

FOREWORD

In 1995, I traveled to America and saw the internet for the first time. When I searched for "China beer" on the internet, I found nothing. Seeing the lack of results, I decided to go back and start a company to bring the internet to China, and to bring China to the rest of the world. Back then, there was no online business in China. Now, the internet is everywhere. I cannot believe how far the world has come.

Alibaba has also come a long way from the eighteen people gathered in my small apartment back in 1999. We had a dream of transforming the poor business practices around us using new internet technologies. Today, we serve hundreds of millions of consumers and millions of businesses all over the world. We have grown large by helping others do business better. The world around us has changed, and we have done our little part.

Businesses drive progress in society. To make it easy to do business everywhere in the world, Alibaba has developed a unique business model. We have never been a simple business-to-consumer (B2C) firm. We are a business ecosystem with millions of players that range from sellers to software service providers and logistics partners. Today, I see our dream from 1999 coming true, as the internet helps solve problems for billions of people.

Yet this is all just the beginning. By 2036, Alibaba hopes to serve 2 billion customers, create 100 million jobs, empower 10 million firms to create profitable businesses linking online and offline commerce, and become the world's fifth-largest economy. Our goal is to globalize e-commerce so that small businesses and young people all over the world can buy and sell globally. My hope is that conducting business over the internet becomes the norm and that the term *e-commerce* becomes moot. E-commerce is just commerce, connecting and empowering people all over the world.

After the first and second industrial revolutions, the dominant players were the factory and the company. Today, the dominant economic players are the platform and the business ecosystem. They will drive the evolution of the digital economy and of global society. Platforms and business ecosystems provide the vehicles for the little folks around the world to get on board and succeed.

Ming Zeng joined Alibaba in 2006 as our "Zong Canmouzhang," a military term similar to chief of staff and strategy adviser. We have worked closely together since then. When I first invited him to join our company, I promised him that Alibaba would be one of the most exciting cases that he could someday write about.

And here it is! With deep knowledge of Alibaba and a strong academic background, Dr. Zeng has written an insightful book. The book describes the evolution of Alibaba since its inception and, more importantly, the new strategic framework it pioneered and what that framework means for everyone in the future. The book has achieved an excellent balance of conceptual rigor and practical relevance. Readers will find it a valuable guide as they venture into the new digital economy.

Back in 1999, we saw opportunities. Now, we see challenges. There are so many problems we need to fix in the world, but I am optimistic— as you should be. Great entrepreneurs are optimistic by nature. They ask what problem they can solve or how they can solve an existing one better. In this new era of data technology and smart business, we should enable others, not just ourselves. In this process, we make the world a better place. Dr. Zeng's book and Alibaba's story will show you how to do that.

The digital economy is part of the great future that the human race will build together. I am very glad that Alibaba has contributed to this important progress. But there is so much work left to be done. Hold on to your idealism and ambitions, and don't get complacent. As I often say, today is hard, tomorrow will be worse, but the day after tomorrow will be beautiful. I cannot wait to see the beautiful world that you will create.

—Jack Ma

WHY YOU NEED TO KNOW ABOUT ALIBABA

November 11, an otherwise ordinary day in China. Because of the ones in the date (11/11), young Chinese humorously dubbed the date Singles Day near the turn of the century, and the tongue-in-cheek holiday was celebrated as a time for single people to meet. In 2009, Singles Day was reimagined as an online shopping festival. Today, the holiday is the biggest shopping event in the world.

The original conceit, created by employees of Tmall, the Alibaba Group e-commerce site for large brands, was to turn Singles Day into a shopping occasion emulating the frenzy of a post–Thanksgiving Day Black Friday or a Memorial Day sale in America. Little did the Tmall team know that the ersatz holiday would grow into the largest one-day sale in history.

Just before midnight on Singles Day Eve, November 10, 2017, I waited anxiously in Alibaba's command room. There, a bank of computer screens flashed figures, charted trend lines across multiple dimensions, and assessed network speed and responsiveness. In 2016, Alibaba had

Alibaba stories, facts, and figures (unless otherwise cited) are a product of internal research by my team throughout my decade-plus tenure within the company. Many observations and stories from the growth of our main e-commerce marketplace, Taobao, have never appeared in print in English-language media before the publication of this book.

facilitated 120.7 billion RMB (about US$15 billion) in sales on its platforms in one day to consumers from more than two hundred countries.[1] That number blows the American Black Friday and Cyber Monday out of the water—in 2016, those two days each saw less than US$3.5 billion across the United States. How far would we go in 2017?

In China, where access to an abundance of consumer goods is still a relatively recent phenomenon, Singles Day is a nationwide event. The average Chinese consumer will spend weeks before the holiday comparing deals, planning expenses, and adding items to virtual carts. But exciting customers is only part of the challenge. In the first few years of the sale, the deluge of traffic caused Alibaba's servers to break down, bank payment channels to collapse, and fulfillment networks across the country to grind to a halt. Since 2012, when a trebling in transaction volume nearly paralyzed the system and delayed package deliveries by weeks, Alibaba and its many partners had worked steadily to improve the logistics system's capacity and efficiency. At its peak in 2016, the platform handled 175,000 orders and 120,000 payments in one second. A year later, a major marketing push and a live television event broadcast across China brought high hopes for the sale. What would be the impact of the additional advertising this year? Would our technology handle this year's deluge?

Midnight approached, and the fingers of users across the country and around the world hovered anxiously above their phone screens— the event is a largely mobile experience in China. The command room music swelled as the countdown began—five, four, three, two, one.

The magic unfolded in front of my eyes. Within eleven seconds, our platform facilitated 100 million RMB (US$15 million) in sales; seventeen seconds later, we reached 1 billion (US$150 million), with 97 percent of transactions made on mobile devices. Consumers snatched up the best deals; those who waited precious seconds before checkout found that the products they had chosen over the past month had sold out.

Soon after the three-minute mark, 10 billion RMB in sales (US$1.5 billion) had been transacted. It took only one hour to reach the total sales volume of Singles Day 2014—and there were still twenty-three hours to go. At its peak, Alibaba's technology platforms processed 325,000 orders and 256,000 payments every second.

FIGURE I-1

Alibaba's e-commerce processing capabilities, compared with Visa's, 2009–2017

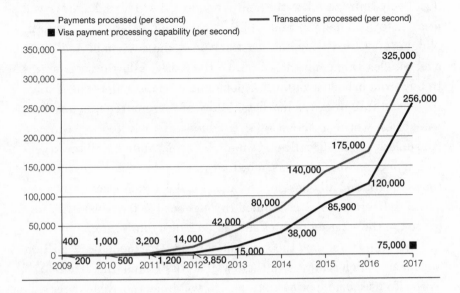

In offline terms, every person in St. Louis or Pittsburgh would have to check out in a single second. Compare these numbers with the second-most powerful payment processor in the world, Visa. Its stated capacity as of August 2017 is 65,000 payments per second globally— one-fourth of Alibaba's (figure I-1).[2]

By seven minutes and twenty-three seconds, 100 million transactions had cleared, approximately the same number in the twenty-four hours of Singles Day 2012. Nike's official storefront on Tmall made a record-setting billion RMB (US$150 million) of sales *within a minute*. Not to be outdone, Adidas quickly followed its competitor's lead. Both brands surpassed their sales volume from Singles Day 2016 within the first hour of Singles Day 2017. By day's end, both storefronts saw over one million new online consumers make purchases. HSTYLE, an online-only apparel brand founded on Alibaba's platforms, watched sales data surge, breaking 50 million RMB (US$7.5 million) in just over five minutes. (For more information on HSTYLE, see chapter 6.) The "We're sold out" cry began resounding across the country at the headquarters of online sellers transacting on the platform.

Open Sesame

Just twelve minutes after the midnight start, the first package arrived at a customer's door in Shanghai. Three minutes later, a woman in Ningbo on China's Pacific coast received the first imported package. Singles Day connects China to the world, allowing consumers to buy from brands around the globe and offering sellers the chance to expand into overseas markets. Many of these purchases are from categories whose international products are coveted by Chinese consumers—almost 3 million Canadian shrimp and 1.6 million Argentinian prawns were purchased by four in the morning; more than five thousand tons of milk powder and a billion disposable diapers by nine. The purchasing frenzy continued throughout the day. Just after one o'clock in the afternoon, sales surpassed 2016's total.

Throughout the day, the e-commerce geyser expelled 812 million packages, which had to find their way across China and around the world. To use some spatial analogies: if you lined those packages side by side, they would circle the globe twelve hundred times. You would need more than eighty thousand Boeing 747s to transport them. Together, all those packages needed to travel more than 390 billion miles, the equivalent of over forty round-trips between Earth and Pluto. Indeed, the work of delivering that many packages might constitute the largest "migration" of consumer goods ever.

The hard work of fulfillment began immediately. Before 9:30 a.m., a hundred million packages had already shipped. Many consumers throughout the country received them that same day. A week after the extravaganza's conclusion, the vast majority of packages had reached their destinations. Because Alibaba is not a retailer that keeps its own stock, the packages came from around the country (and the world) and went to every corner of China, thanks to the technology of Alibaba's associated logistics platform, the Cainiao Network.

By day's end, Alibaba had processed 1.5 billion transactions, totaling 168.2 billion RMB (US$25 billion) (figure I-2). This is almost double what China's entire retail industry (including offline and high-ticket items such as automobiles and real estate) did on an average day in 2016. Indeed, 167 brands achieved over 100 million RMB (US$15 million) in sales. Consumers purchased everything under the

FIGURE I-2

Singles Day, 2009–2017, Alibaba's yearly gross merchandise volume (GMV)

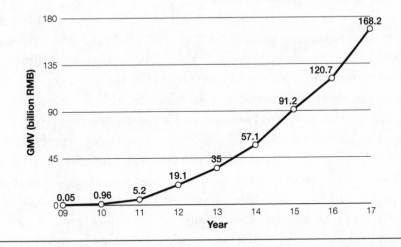

sun on the Tmall site: clothes, home goods, electronics, jewelry, and more—and in one case, a US$2.5 million limited-edition Aston Martin speedboat.

Singles Day is not merely a marketing miracle; it is a technological marvel. Everyone at Alibaba worked hard for months preparing for this day, conducting among other tasks dozens of pressure tests aimed at preventing any catastrophic failure across the system, from IT to the front-end website to payments to inventory and logistics. Powered by machine-learning technology, the entire network of Alibaba and all the independent merchants, payment providers, warehouses, and shippers Alibaba works with was activated to meet the enormous demand. Moreover, this powerful network is now expanding into new areas of the value chain and more areas of the world.

Alibaba Is Not China's Version of Amazon

Alibaba grabbed global attention with the biggest initial public offering (IPO) in history on September 19, 2014. Today, the company has a market cap on par with Amazon and Facebook. It has surpassed

Walmart in global sales and expanded into all the major regions in the world. Founder Jack Ma, once a young boy who grew up in a small Chinese city and who twice failed the college entrance exams, has become a global household name.

As a senior executive of Alibaba, I have met many people who think of the company as the world's largest retailer, or the Amazon of China. That impression is not only wrong but also obscures Alibaba's breakthrough business model and the window it provides on how the economic scene is evolving. Unlike Amazon, Alibaba is not even a retailer in the traditional sense—we don't source or keep stock, and logistics services are carried out by third-party service providers. Instead, Alibaba is what you get if you take every function associated with retail and coordinate them online into a sprawling, data-driven network of sellers, marketers, service providers, logistics companies, and manufacturers. In other words, Alibaba does what Amazon, eBay, PayPal, Google, FedEx, all the wholesalers, and a good portion of manufacturers in the United States do, with a healthy dash of the financial sector thrown in for garnish. But it doesn't accomplish all these functions by itself. Alibaba uses technology to harness and coordinate the efforts of thousands of Chinese businesses to create a very different and internet-native business ecosystem (one founded and primarily operated online) that is faster, smarter, and more efficient than traditional business infrastructures.

Alibaba's mandate is to apply cutting-edge technologies—from machine learning to the mobile internet and cloud computing—to revolutionize how business is done. China provided fertile ground for this model to unfold because the country's business infrastructure was weak and undeveloped. Taking advantage of new technologies, Alibaba transformed China's entire nascent retailing industry (nowhere nearly as sophisticated as physical and online retailing in the Western world) to the forefront of twenty-first-century business models. Alibaba's partner firms Ant Financial and Cainiao Network have done the same in payments and logistics.

The internet, especially e-commerce, has followed a very different evolutionary path in China than was followed in the United States. As Ma often says, "e-commerce is the main course in China but only dessert in the US." In a very short period, companies such as Alibaba have transformed the Chinese retailing industry and are making waves worldwide. In fact, the ratio of online-to-offline sales in China is more than double that of the United States. But Alibaba has done it in a way completely different from Amazon.

Why should all this concern Western readers? Think about it: if you were to restart almost any industry from scratch—food processing, furniture making, banking—with the internet and machine-learning capabilities available today but none of the legacy infrastructure existing from decades of business investment, what would you do differently? You would build a business that uses the incredibly powerful and relatively inexpensive capabilities of the internet and data technologies. Sure, Facebook and Google did this, too, but they created industries that had never existed before. In China, we are reconstructing industries with almost every business, be it traditional or brand-new.

In the United States, the large leading internet firms emerged when new technologies were applied to new problems, like online advertising, online auctions, or social networking. From my vantage point in China, I have seen what happens when new technologies are applied to old problems, like retailing, finance, and logistics. In writing this book, I hope to show what strategy in the latter case looks like. Inevitably, every industry will have to grapple with the application of new technology to old problems. So far, the United States has seen less penetration of new technology into traditional businesses because of the efficiency of established American industries, but change is coming. This is the value in glimpsing the "future" in China and understanding how firms use the newest technology to compete and create new value in traditional industries.

The Future Seen from China

A Chinese view of the future can give Western business leaders a fresh perspective. An unfamiliar observer may find it easy to imagine China as it was two decades ago: the world's factory, undeveloped and filled with copycat businesses. But this impression is a dangerous mistake in 2018. Especially in the internet industry, Chinese companies are creating world-class products and consumer experiences. Other industries are quickly learning by example, beginning to transform industry after industry through business model innovation.[3]

Indeed, China is already a virtually cashless and check-less society. Everything is paid for by a swipe of a smartphone. Where mobile internet technology exists, consumer banking and payments become smartphone based, especially when there are few ATMs, bank branches, or credit card companies. Meanwhile, in the United States, the traditional banking and payments industry is being upended by ferocious competition from the likes of Apple, Google, Amazon, PayPal, and a number of startups. Yet, Americans still need to carry around a wallet filled with cards, cash, and checks as well as their smartphone. When I am in the United States, as I am half of the time, it feels backward to deal with all the financial encumbrances.

This transformation happened in China earlier than in the United States, for exactly the reasons that economist Joseph Schumpeter explained. Revolution comes from the periphery, where dominant structures and logic are less embedded. China's lack of existing infrastructure and established players in many industries created an open field for experimentation and business building. That transformation was not burdened with legacies or switching costs. Such freedom is a vital part of Schumpeter's "gales of creative destruction."

In the United States, there is access to and comfort with the most advanced technologies. There are also mature consumer markets and efficiently optimized industries. Under these circumstances, it is hard to see the coming transformation. Although industry after industry is being disrupted, each has its own story and players, and changes seem incremental as many people and businesses progressively adapt. But in China, entrepreneurs are already using new tactics to reinvent traditional industries and create brand-new products and services as they experiment with new forms of large-scale coordination. China is not catching up; it is innovating in parallel and even leapfrogging Western companies in certain areas.

The success of Chinese entrepreneurs not only shows the way to transform old industries using new, successful strategies. More importantly, the Chinese experience hastens the transition for Western companies and pressures them to become smart businesses. The business model and strategies that I will describe in this book have too much power and momentum to stop at the borders of the Middle Kingdom. Already, Alibaba's e-commerce model is expanding rapidly in India. Our payment platform, Alipay, is rampaging across Asia, where it is rapidly becoming a new standard for mobile payments. It is even quietly making inroads into Europe and North America. In a recent survey, Alibaba beat out Amazon (number two) as the best of sixty-four top companies to invest in and hold for ten years.[4]

Gigantic numbers aside, Alibaba's key contribution to future business strategy is its use of cutting-edge technology at enormous scale to transform businesses and eliminate traditional economic inefficiencies. By providing the infrastructure and core mechanisms that incubate platforms in new markets or new parts of the value chain, we enable new businesses to operate and experiment.

Business strategists need to understand why Alibaba works the way it does because its strategy illustrates the changing dynamics of value creation and competitive advantage. Unpack Alibaba, and you get the CliffsNotes version of the future of strategy and competition. Divining this code and experiencing its emergence has been the intellectual adventure of my life.

My Leap

In 1998, after receiving my PhD in international business and strategy from the University of Illinois in the United States, I joined Europe's top business school, INSEAD, as an assistant professor. I was teaching a course on Asian business. With the internet frenzy running wild, I felt the need to teach a case about internet startups from China. At that time, most of these companies were just copycats of American models emulating Yahoo! (e.g., Sohu and Sina). But Alibaba caught my attention; this unusual company had no Western counterpart. With people hotly debating its future, Alibaba was a perfect case for MBAs. I contacted the company, and management agreed to let me study the firm.

I met Jack Ma for the first time in April 2000, when I interviewed Alibaba management for three days. Back then, the company was a small startup with around one hundred people. It had just moved from Ma's apartment to its first office. Ma had bought the domain name Alibaba with the precious little cash the company had in 1999, because it was intelligible around the world and implied hidden treasure. As risky as the venture seemed, its culture appealed to me. It reacted to the environment without relying on models of the past or from the West—in other words, it was innovating.

In the fall of 2002, I returned to China as one of seven founding professors at China's first private business school, the Cheung Kong Graduate School of Business, which had been founded by the Li Ka Shing Foundation of Hong Kong. I also began to consult on the side. At Alibaba, I gave talks on strategy and facilitated three strategy meetings each year. This was in the aftermath of the dot-com bust and during a tough time for Alibaba. But like Jack, I believed in the future of the internet. After all, I had earned my PhD at the University of Illinois, in the literal shadow of Marc Andreessen. The well-known alumnus had codeveloped the web browser Mosaic, which had popularized the web in the early 1990s.

In January 2006, I was in London finishing my first book in English, *Dragons at Your Door: How Chinese Cost Innovation Is Disrupting Global Competition* (Harvard Business Review Press), with my coauthor Peter Williamson, a professor of strategy at Cambridge's Judge Business School. The book summarized my research about emerging multinationals from China. On my way to the airport the night before Chinese New Year, I got a phone call from Jack asking me to join the company full time. I called him after landing in Beijing and accepted.

A Foot in Both Worlds

Since joining Alibaba, I have talked to hundreds of entrepreneurs and leaders from across the world—people trying to cope with the new realities of business. I can relate. At Alibaba, I quickly found that what worked there could not be explained by business and strategy theories that I learned in graduate school and then taught in academic institutions around the world.

Jack Ma brought me into Alibaba to help the firm navigate this new strategic landscape and bridge the gap between academic theory and industry practice. When I entered the company, Jack gave me a very unique title, *zong canmouzhang*, which is a widely known military title in China. This officer in a military unit is ranked number three and placed in charge of strategic planning. It is roughly similar to the position of chief strategy officer in a typical Western company.[5]

As strategic adviser to Jack, I have had to develop new conceptual frameworks as well as pragmatic approaches to fit Alibaba's unprecedented business model. Besides developing these strategies and assessing their effectiveness, I have also done so in close cooperation with the many businesses that use our platform. My day job has been a constant seesaw between high-level strategic theory and granular details of execution.

Another unique part of my perspective is the good fortune to be a researcher and practitioner on both sides of the Pacific. I was born in China, received my education in the United States, and taught at business schools around the world. In addition to my current responsibilities at Alibaba, for the past few years I have split my time between China and the Bay Area, keeping abreast of the most innovative practices in both countries. The strategies of Chinese firms arise when businesses apply the best and most current technologies to the newest of business problems. Consequently, China continues to leap past much of what is being done in the United States.

I do not want to increase Western apprehension about China, especially when so much anxiety is already unwarranted. Instead I want to shine a light on China's extremely relevant and enlightening experience. As the great Chinese military strategist Sun Tzu wrote in his classic *The Art of War*, "If you know the enemy and know yourself, you need not fear the result of a hundred battles."[6] My focus is not battle; it is sharing this knowledge. I can't escape my educator instincts—indeed, my team in China still calls me Professor.

Let me offer another glimpse of the future. This one is on a smaller scale than Singles Day but is no less significant or less important to understand. It, too, originates in China.

The Emergence of Web Celebs

Let's look back to April 20, 2015, and the experience of entrepreneur Zhang Linchao, then twenty-five years old and the head (and modeling face) of China's online clothing brand LIN Edition. Zhang got involved with apparel when she was an exchange student in the UK, selecting off-brand clothes from China to sell during her days off from school. Gradually, she realized that Taobao, Alibaba's Chinese e-commerce platform, could help her turn a hobby into an actual business. As of 2017, LIN is one of the strongest apparel brands on Taobao created by *web celebs* (in Chinese, *wang hong*), China's brand of social media influencers.[7] In the United States, influencers on social media post pictures and sometimes get sponsored by big brands, or they run small advertising-based video businesses. But in China, superb online business infrastructure means that entrepreneurs like Zhang Linchao create their own brands, sell their own goods, and lead very profitable businesses. There are now thousands of web-celeb businesses on Taobao.

On this spring day in 2015, Zhang is preparing for a batch of new apparel items to hit the online rack at LIN Edition. At 3:00 p.m., fifteen new pieces will debut on LIN's storefront. Tens of thousands of her fans are already waiting in front of their screens—they have seen previews of today's sale on social media and know what they want. LIN expects to sell several thousand items today, but it only has one thousand pieces of clothing in stock—not a thousand copies of each stock-keeping unit (SKU), but one thousand in total. Any regular offline brand manager would be shocked at LIN's lack of preparation.

At 2:58, the operating manager, Luo Kai, orders all the employees to turn the sound up on their computers. Two minutes later, the room is filled with a symphony of ding-dongs. Sixty thousand users are already visiting the store. Within one minute, every one of the fifteen clothing items sells out. LIN is ready: with a few clicks, the next batch of SKUs are posted, marked for preorder. Twenty minutes later, that preorder batch is sold out. The operating manager reconfigures the links for the third batch of clothing. As he types, he is calculating how much fabric will be needed and the time to completion. He factors in a return rate of 10 to 20 percent and metrics from customer interest on social media over the past two weeks to determine how much advance stock the store can feasibly offer.

Zhang has almost turned her apparel retailing business into an on-demand business—but at mass-production price points. An order placed on Taobao for LIN sets the entire value chain in motion. Buyers know that they are reserving clothing that will be made to order and that they will have to wait seven to nine days for manufacturing and shipping. LIN's partner factories have already begun working on the first batch of preorders.

At 3:17 p.m., Zhang posts a message to her social media account: "You guys are relentless." In minutes, more than five hundred comments come back at her, most complaining that they didn't manage to snag their favorites. By 3:45 of the release day, sales volume has surpassed the last sale a few weeks before and there are still fifteen hundred users waiting in line to ask questions. The factories are going to be overstretched completing this collection's customer orders. Once the dust settles, LIN has set a new record: more than ten thousand items sold, with each customer spending an average of 1,000 RMB (US$150).

Zhang is her brand's face, design inspiration, marketing department, and much more. She and other web celebs find their customers on social media. The companies that run the back end are small, often no more than one or two hundred people, supporting over a dozen brands like LIN's. They only sell online; they keep little to no inventory and own no factories. Yet they do a rousing business. In the first four months of 2015, LIN had 80 million RMB in sales (about US$11 million), keeping nearly 30 percent as pure profit.[8] LIN and other web-celeb companies have evolved quickly since 2015 and can show readers from traditional industries a new approach to operations, marketing, and data-driven strategy.

A New Paradigm

The stories of Singles Day and LIN Edition are examples of the revolutionary business models that are sweeping across China and that will soon replace less efficient and responsive ones everywhere. They show, at two vastly different scales, how interconnected players—buyer, sellers, and service providers—come together and coordinate through real-time data mediated by technology. Alibaba and companies like it have succeeded in connecting and coordinating all these players, relying heavily on machine-learning technology to achieve scale and manage complexity.

I call this strategy of embracing new technology to connect all your players and redesign industries *smart business*. Smart businesses like Alibaba use technology to coordinate business activity across a nearly unlimited number of interconnected parties. To enable such massive, complex interconnection, companies must automate many decisions and actions. To do so, machine learning, which will be described in more detail in chapter 3, uses algorithms to allow computers to "learn" from real-time data from customers and partners and coordinate with them automatically. The Singles Day bonanza is an example of smart business. Thousands of companies come together seamlessly and instantly to provide millions of customers with what they want. It seems there is no end in sight as to how big Singles Day can become, and this is ultimately the lesson of this book. Unimaginable scale is possible when businesses are smart.

Alibaba does not by any means have everything figured out. But its notions of strategy and organization have diverged drastically from traditional models and are producing previously unthinkable levels of growth. I have written this book to summarize the lessons we have learned at Alibaba and to guide businesses around the world through the new strategic landscape of smart business.

PART ONE

ALIBABA

The Emergence of a Smart Business

S ingles Day has grown from a tongue-in-cheek holiday for unattached young people to the biggest shopping day in human history. Taobao has grown from a small online forum for buyers and sellers to the largest e-commerce platform in the world. To understand Alibaba's phenomenal success, we need to analyze the forces behind its rise. By understanding Alibaba's story, we come to appreciate the innovative power of Chinese business. By understanding Chinese innovation, we can grasp a full vision of the future of strategy.

These first three chapters define the two core pillars of smart business, network coordination and data intelligence, and explain how to make them work. Network coordination enables large-scale business networks, while data intelligence ensures efficient operations and decisions across the network. Through examples from Alibaba's platforms, I will show how data and networks reinvent strategy. Every firm needs to know how these two new capabilities change the dynamics of value creation, and how these capabilities will affect their business.

CHAPTER 1

THE NEW FORCES OF VALUE CREATION

To get a handle on what smart business means in practice, we need to look closer at Alibaba. Every day, millions of business actors connect and coordinate through the Alibaba Group's vast consumer e-commerce networks, made up of Tmall, the website for larger brands, and Taobao, the wider online marketplace for small boutique brands, independent sellers, and innovators like the web celebs. (See the sidebar "Alibaba at a Glance" for a snapshot of all Alibaba Group's businesses and networks.) These networks present each customer with a personalized shopping experience, an individualized, virtual mall for every shopper. On the supply side, sellers have all the tools to run an online storefront, to partner with manufacturers, to coordinate with logistics players, and to arrange payments online on Alibaba's own platforms. And all of it is coordinated by data technology.

Alibaba exemplifies smart business, painting a vivid picture of the new, emerging business world. In this world, businesses use machine learning to gather data from their networks of participants to automatically respond to customer behavior and preferences. Smart business allows the entire value chain to be reconfigured to achieve both scale and customization, using the combination of two forces, network coordination and data intelligence (defined and discussed below). These twin forces engender smart business.

ALIBABA AT A GLANCE

Alibaba was founded in 1999 by Jack Ma and seventeen cofounders as a way for small Chinese companies to find each other and international customers.*

Today, Alibaba is the largest retail commerce company in the world. More than ten million active merchants run their businesses on Alibaba's China platforms, connecting to more than four hundred million active buyers. Alibaba's Chinese retail marketplaces generate a combined gross merchandise volume of more than US$0.5 trillion.

To fulfill our mission—"To make it easy to do business anywhere"—we enable enterprises to transform how they market, sell, and otherwise operate. We provide the fundamental technology infrastructure and marketing reach to help merchants, brands, and other businesses use the power of the internet to engage with their users and customers.

Our businesses comprise commerce, cloud computing, digital entertainment and other digital media, innovation initiatives, and other industries. Through investee affiliates, the Cainiao Network and Koubei, respectively, we participate in the logistics and local services sectors. In addition, we have a profit-sharing interest in Ant Financial, the financial services group that also operates Alipay, the leading third-party online payment platform in China.

In 2003, Alibaba introduced Taobao, a platform named after the Chinese term meaning "searching for treasure." Taobao was initially a forum with product listings. Over time, the website added pictures as well as other functionalities, eventually becoming the massive e-commerce platform that exists today. Sellers can list on Taobao for free, as the platform now works mostly on an advertising-based revenue model.

In the years that followed, Alibaba Group incubated several affiliate companies (see table 1-1):

- *Alipay:* In 2004, this escrow account system became an independent company. Alipay facilitated payments in a country without credit cards and/or remote-payment vehicles.

---

*For good historical background about Alibaba, including Taobao's early competition with eBay, see Porter Erisman, *Alibaba's World: How a Remarkable Chinese Company Is Changing the Face of Global Business* (New York: St. Martin's Press, 2015); and Duncan Clark, *Alibaba: The House That Jack Ma Built* (New York: Ecco, 2016).

TABLE 1-1

Alibaba at a glance

China retail marketplaces
- Taobao Marketplace
- Tmall.com
- Rural Taobao

Cross-border and global marketplaces
- AliExpress
- Tmall Global
- Lazada

Wholesale commerce
- 1688.com (China wholesale)
- Alibaba.com (global wholesale)

Digital media and entertainment*
- Youku Tudou (online video)
- Alibaba Pictures
- Alibaba Music
- Alibaba Sports
- UC Browser (mobile browser)

Local services*
- AutoNavi (mapping and navigation)
- Koubei (local services)
- Ele.me (food delivery)

Finance: Ant Financial, MYbank*

Logistics: Cainiao Network*

Cloud computing: Alibaba Cloud*

*Major investee companies and cooperative partners of Alibaba Group.

- *Tmall:* In 2008, Tmall was separated from the rest of Taobao as a site for the big brands and retailers. Its sellers pay a commission, normally ranging from 0.4 to 5.0 percent, for premium services.
- *AliExpress:* This international e-commerce site, launched in 2010, connects Chinese sellers with the rest of the world.

- *Cainiao Network:* Alibaba launched this smart logistics platform in 2012.
- *Ant Financial:* In 2014, Alibaba launched Ant Financial Services. This company now lends to consumers and small businesses across China.
- *Web-celeb companies:* 2014 saw the first wave of web celebrities starting their own companies.

For more background and history of Alibaba, see appendix A.

The Essence of Smart Business

The formula for smart businesses can be summarized in a single simple equation:

$$\text{Network Coordination} + \text{Data Intelligence} = \text{Smart Business}$$

That simple equation reveals what is behind Alibaba's success and captures everything you need to know about business in the future. As I'll explain, network coordination and data intelligence, two new capabilities enabled by technology, have powerful advantages over traditional business processes and structures.

In its broadest sense, *network coordination* is the breaking down of complicated business activity so that groups of people or firms can get it done more effectively.[1] Functions that were historically locked into vertically integrated structures or rigid supply chains are more easily coordinated through online connections. Nobel laureate Ronald Coase explained that businesses have been structured to manage prohibitive transaction costs.[2] But new technologies have driven down these costs, enabling new networked approaches. Using network coordination, business activities like sales, marketing, and all aspects of production are transformed into decentralized, flexible, scalable, and globally optimized processes.

Singles Day, with Tmall and Taobao behind it, is a perfect example of network coordination. Taobao holds no inventory and is instead a vast network of more than ten million sellers. These sellers coordinate with millions more partners, and all the parties work together to accomplish the complex work of online retail, transaction processing, and distribution all the way to the customer's doorstep. Impossible for humans, this level of interaction is the essence of network coordination: autonomous coordination with almost unlimited scale and a boundless number of partners over the internet.

As the network of business actors coordinates online, business activities are also getting smarter. That is, constantly flowing data, created from real-time interactions and processes online, creates a continuous feedback loop that automatically generates decisions that become increasingly "intelligent." For example, today, much of Taobao's routine work in finding and displaying products to customers is done by machines. Traditional retailers employ thousands of buyers, display artists, style editors, personal shoppers, and so forth, to accomplish something similar. Machine learning is the tool that enables this capability at Taobao. At peak on Singles Day 2017, Alibaba's databases made forty-two million calculations a second. This sheer volume means that machine-learning algorithms ran billions of iterations throughout the day to decide which items should be displayed on your smartphone screen after you had already bought a cell phone, tickets to Bali, and even those rainbow pajamas you'd been eyeing for the past month. *Data intelligence* is what I call this business capability of effectively iterating products and services according to consumer activity and response.[3] It is a radically different approach from how most firms today generate products and services.

By data intelligence, I refer to the capability of businesses to rapidly and automatically improve using machine-learning technology. You will recognize data intelligence in action if you have ever encountered recommendation engines. This most basic form of data intelligence is standard business practice for any company online, but the capability I'm describing is much more sophisticated. Companies can develop more highly evolved applications of data intelligence if they automate decision making and constantly run real-time data— say, suppliers' shipping times, fabricators' finishing notices, logistics tracking, or customer preferences. This automation is achieved through machine-learning algorithms that enhance coordination and optimize every link in the value chain. As more and more business activities go online, the decisions associated with all those activities can be automated and constantly refined. This is what I mean by data intelligence.

The advances in machine learning (a branch of computer science often understood as a subset of the larger field of artificial intelligence, or AI) have broadened the reach and effectiveness of what companies can do with data intelligence in a step function manner over the last decade. In the same way that machines have mastered the games Go and chess, algorithms can churn through extremely long chains of calculations or explore multiple scenarios to quickly arrive at optimum solutions. As new results occur, the algorithms recalibrate themselves to reflect this new information. Algorithms learn through continuous iterations, and their results improve as the volume and diversity of data increase. Through this machine learning, data intelligence increases. As more business processes go online and as business activities increasingly require the coordination of interconnected players, companies can transform themselves by ensuring that routine decisions are made automatically and with more computing power than is available to humans. This is the essence of smart business.

The Emergence of Smart Business and Its Implications

At Alibaba, link after link in the value chain is being modularized and reconfigured into technologically optimized networks, and much of business decision making is powered by algorithms. This heavy use of innovative technology changes everything. Data is the primary asset, a crucial factor of production. Strategy no longer means analysis and planning, but rather a process of real-time experimentation and customer engagement.

In smart businesses, as I will show in this book, the familiar forces of competition are falling away and giving rise to new forms of cooperation between businesses and myriad other players. When strategy is no longer predicated on competition but centers on coordination, the ways of creating value are completely transformed. And when companies apply machine learning not only to automate routine business processes and

consumer interactions but also to continually improve them, management's role in creating value is radically changed. Organizations are
no longer static, hierarchical structures that need managing and controlling, but rather are dynamic, fluid networks of interconnected players that must be engaged by mission and opportunity.

Don't fool yourself into thinking that network coordination and
data intelligence are only relevant to so-called internet companies or
digital natives. I have worked with and studied furniture manufacturers, apparel companies, and beauty salons in China. Even these
more traditional companies are reorganizing to exploit these new
forces. Indeed, it is precisely my global perspective that has led me to
arrive at this new strategic theory. Network coordination and data
intelligence exemplify what you get when you combine the cutting
edge of technology in the West with the dynamism of business model
innovation in the East.

Chinese companies are better positioned to take advantage of network coordination—combining business actors seamlessly across the
internet versus building up corporate organizations. Because most
Chinese industries have a relatively weak infrastructure and few
dominant players, there is more room to reconstruct whole industries
on the internet. Companies in the United States generally tend to
excel at data intelligence, using the most advanced incarnations of
machine learning to automate knowledge creation, applying technology to problems of image recognition, language translation, and DNA
sequencing. Years of research and business experience in both countries has convinced me that the forces of network coordination and
data intelligence—and their reinforcing power when the two forces
are combined—are acting on all businesses, old and new, everywhere.

Networks or data as I present them are not new concepts, but they
have not previously been integrated into a theoretical whole. They
are the twin helix that makes up the new business DNA. Looking at
business from both East and West reveals the whole picture. Only
when the yin and yang of West and East, of data and network, combine do we get a clear view of the future. Only then can we effectively
formulate strategy in the present.

Strategy as taught in business schools since the early 1990s has
focused on competitive advantages through either market position-

ing or core competences. But the sources of competitive advantages have shifted dramatically. Businesses need a new strategic approach that fits into an era when networks and data dominate. Under this approach, companies will use network coordination to achieve value, scope, and scale greater than that of their competitors and will deploy data intelligence to make their business smart enough to adjust nimbly to changes in the outside environment and the minds of consumers. The most successful internet companies in the United States and China are adept on both networks and data. This observation will hold for all winners in the future economy.

Various economists and business strategists have made valuable contributions to update for the internet age Porter's classic analysis of strategy—including Michael Porter himself. These contributions on digital and platform strategies have been deep and illuminating. This book tries to go a step further, creating a more overarching strategic framework that places both traditional and digital businesses in a unified landscape. (Appendix C discusses this in more detail.)

From Chinese Buddhism, there is an aphorism: "In the riotous confusion of blooming flowers manifests a solemn order." Similarly, the seemingly wild blossoming of new ideas and business models is not random; a new order is, in fact, emerging. In this book, I provide a structural framework for how to organize business, create value, and succeed in this new order.

How This Book Unfolds

My purpose in writing this book is twofold. First, I want to describe the new forces created by technological advances and explain a new "unified theory" of value creation. Second, I hope to reveal the strategic and organizational implications of these new forces.

Using Alibaba as the primary example in the book, I'll explain how our operations, our strategy development and implementation, and even how our conception of the organization diverge from traditional ideas. I'll use additional examples, such as web-celeb retailers on our platform, our partner company Ant Financial, and model internet success stories of Apple, Google, and Uber to illustrate these concepts too.

Having introduced myself, the new business environment, and my core strategic theory, I will provide a more detailed explanation of the core concepts of network coordination and data intelligence in chapters 2 and 3.

In part 2, "How Smart Businesses Compete: Strategic Principles," three chapters describe the new core strategic principles of creating live data, becoming consumer driven, and rethinking strategic positioning. Chapter 4 outlines the process for putting your business online and "softwaring" your workflows, so that you can automate decision making. Once you have automated decisions in place, machine learning using live data can create a virtuous circle of continually improving customer experience and business efficiency. In chapter 5, I discuss the strategic imperative to realign your business model around customers. I call this strategy the consumer-to-business model, and I give innovative examples from China. Finally, in chapter 6, I zoom out to explain how smart firms' positioning strategies have changed. Strategy and capabilities are interdependent; you must position yourself in a coordinated network to maximize your potential and create higher value for your clients and partners.

Part 3, "How Smart Businesses Run: Organizational Implications," outlines a new kind of strategy process in chapter 7 and a new vision of management in chapter 8. The spread of networks and digitally optimized operations recasts the function and mindset of the company. Smart business automates much of the exploitation to which firms are accustomed, but in return requires much more experimentation. Firms must consistently iterate between vision and action, taking an adaptive and even market-based approach to strategic objectives. This new approach is balanced with highly developed vision and culture to attract appropriate collaborators. Internally, as routine business activity becomes automated and as all parties are networked, management must go beyond managing or offering incentives. It must enable creativity by building infrastructure that supports frontline innovation and by creating mechanisms that foster collaboration across networks.

Today, business creates value through innovation, the product of human creativity. When creativity replaces muscle power and knowledge manipulation as key factors of economic production, we will witness a creativity revolution, moving one step beyond the knowledge revolution described by management guru Peter Drucker. Such a revolution is likely to change the nature of organizations and human experience. In chapter 9, I will summarize the concepts in this book to drive home how all these changes in the business landscape apply to you.

This book draws heavily on my experience as a senior executive driving strategy creation at Alibaba and years of original research on Alibaba's business models. Readers unfamiliar with Alibaba and its businesses are encouraged to refer to appendix A. Interspersed throughout this book are episodes and lessons from Taobao, Alibaba's main e-commerce platform, and appendix B presents a comprehensive history of the Taobao platform and its growth as an academic-style case study. Appendix C presents conceptual and theoretical material that underpins smart business that may be of interest to readers who want to go deeper into the material.

CHAPTER 2

NETWORK COORDINATION

How Interconnected Players Change the Game

October is a profoundly important month for consumers in China. For one thing, every October begins with the week-long National Day break, one of the longest holidays in the calendar. But when the holiday is over and the country goes back to work, an even more important holiday arrives just one month later: November 11, Singles Day. With the profusion of discounts and savings on offer during Singles Day, shopping at full price beforehand is imprudent. In October, you would do well not to make large purchases—Singles Day is coming. Also in October, you would be wise to make travel plans for the following year to catch all the best deals—Singles Day is coming. Not just travel plans, but even purchases surrounding important life events are worth the wait until Singles Day. Planning to buy a house, have a child, or get married? Draw up your shopping list early—Singles Day is coming.

But once early November arrives, another headache draws near. Don't plan to mail anything important during the second week of November. After all, the country's postal system very well might descend into paralysis the week after the sale. It certainly has in the past.

The entire country remembers November 11, 2012, the fourth time that Singles Day had been celebrated as a major shopping festival. In the retail industry, Alibaba's transaction volume of nearly 20 billion RMB (US$3 billion) in a twenty-four-hour span gave brands large and small, local and international, a rude awakening. In previous years, e-commerce hadn't seemed big enough to affect established players. Yet by the morning of the twelfth, the message was clear: e-commerce was here to stay. The waters of online business that had once lapped at the feet of established players were now rising, and everyone wanted a place on the lifeboat.

But consumers saw a different picture, namely, the complete and catastrophic failure of the logistics network around the country. Unable to cope with an unprecedented volume of seventy-two million packages, warehouses overflowed and roads clogged with delivery trucks. (For reference, Singles Day in 2010 and 2011 respectively produced one million and twenty-two million packages.) Planes, trains, and ships stalled. Postal workers and other delivery personnel were stretched to their limits, working around the clock just to keep up. Goods that had been ready for shipping on the eleventh and would only have taken three to five days to ship under regular conditions were stuck en route for more than two weeks. By the end of the month, some packages had still not reached their destinations.

Shocked by the fearsome force of China's consumers and terrified by the near-certain reality that the following year's volume of packages would increase by at least 50 percent, Alibaba and China's logistics companies sprang into action. They invested in infrastructure, but more importantly, they began the hard work on mechanisms and systems for coordination in the nascent logistics industry. On November 10, 2013, executives waited anxiously to see if the previous year's cataclysm would repeat itself. To everyone's surprise, it did not, and China was spared: in nine days, two-thirds of the 152 million packages created on November 11 by Alibaba's e-commerce platforms reached their destinations.

Efficiency only continued to improve. In 2014, 100 million of 278 million packages were fulfilled by the seventeenth, barely a week after Singles Day. By 2016, 100 million packages were fulfilled in a mere three and a half days. Today, Chinese consumer logistics is arguably the most efficient in the world. (It would have to be: between 2009 to 2017, the number of parcels issued as a result of Singles Day increased by a mind-blowing factor of 3,123.) Standard shipping for many packages from all corners of the country can be accomplished overnight or in two days, at minimal cost—a far cry from the disaster of 2012.

The full story of China's logistics transformation, and of Alibaba's affiliate Cainiao Network, could fill an entire book. (For an abbreviated version, see appendix B.) But the key to the industry's rapid evolution was doubtlessly network coordination. Various players, helped by internet platforms and data technology, learned to coordinate efficiently and at scale. In this chapter, I will explain what network coordination is, why it has been so powerful for Alibaba, and how it fits into the greater strategy of smart business.

From Line to Network

Network coordination is the nearly autonomous management of the simultaneous interactions of multiple parties to a business task. This type of coordination produces vastly different results than does a linear value chain, in which hierarchical orders are passed sequentially through players. Consider how the incredible online orchestration of Singles Day—sellers, buyers, producers, suppliers, and logistics players all coming together and processing volumes that no single firm possibly could—was facilitated by Alibaba without direct orders or executive directives. Network coordination allows many people or firms to cooperate online to solve a complicated business problem much more effectively and efficiently than could any party or parties structured through vertical integration. This new approach is what built Alibaba's e-commerce platforms and helped create niches for many innovative new players on the platforms, including the web celebs highlighted earlier.

Alibaba was initially forced to rely on network coordination since we lacked the time, skills, or investment resources to create some of the capabilities needed in-house. When sellers on Alibaba's platform wanted someone to ship a product without using China's very outdated postal system, Alibaba engineers could not just start a delivery company. But they could create some standard online tools and other mechanisms that would integrate the services into Alibaba's platform. Using those tools and mechanisms, the engineers could then work hard to encourage others to create the services that sellers wanted. In this manner, we at Alibaba brought more and more such complementary services to our platform, and Alibaba effectively became a network of coordination. Appendix B gives a detailed account of the evolution of this coordination network since the founding of Taobao in 2003.

Network coordination unbundles business activities from the traditional linear supply chain. A traditional retailer, online or physical, has a relatively simple task of coordinating a linear information flow from suppliers to customers, whereas Alibaba, an online market, coordinates expansive online networks of almost innumerable players. Inspired by Alibaba's success, other forward-thinking Chinese companies are using the internet to transform underdeveloped traditional industries from a linear structure to a network. These companies are reconstructing numerous industries, from furniture making to online education, and leapfrogging earlier business formations. Indeed, only a network coordinated through a decentralized structure can simultaneously handle all the core imperatives of today's business: scale, cost, speed, and customization.

More and more business functions will be reconfigured in this manner, not just in China but also across the world. Harnessing network coordination is one of the essential new drivers for value creation strategies in the coming decades. Let's see how it is being put into practice, using the newest breed of Taobao sellers: the web celebs.

I briefly told the story of these innovative sellers in this book's introduction. They have created brands completely online, do not have any offline sales channels, only keep 10 percent of sale volume in stock at any time, and manufacture and ship the rest out within twenty days after orders are placed. In part 2 of this book, I will explore exactly how the web celebs create their brands and manage flexible manufacturing. But first, we need to unearth the fundamental strength of their business model: network coordination.

Behind the Web Celebs: A Coordinated Network

Web celebrities emerged in late 2014 and surprised us at Taobao. With no offline presence or big advertising budgets, these somehow-magnetic people nevertheless displayed an impressive ability to bring in sales and drive conversions. Graphs of their sales volume looked particularly strange: on an average day, they would do little to no business, but their inactivity was punctuated by short and startlingly intense bursts of more than 1 million RMB (US$150 thousand) of sales at a pop. Because these sellers exhibited sales patterns starkly different from the average e-commerce store, Taobao's employees were originally concerned that the sellers might be engaging in some mysterious fraudulent behavior.

But they were instead something new. Web celebs appeared in the women's apparel category, selling casual fashion and light luxury items marketed at Taobao's youngest users, between fourteen and twenty-one. The web celebs would often plaster their Sina Weibo account information (the upgraded Chinese version of Twitter; see the sidebar "Weibo") in a conspicuous place on the front page of their Taobao storefronts. Most importantly, the face of these stores was, without exception, an attractive young woman. All the pictures for every item in the store would feature her as a model, but these pictures were most often shot in a nonprofessional manner (read: mostly selfies). These young women did not behave like typical models or celebrities; nor did their products and styles fit easily into the traditional categories of Taobao women's apparel, such as "Korean Urbanwear," "European Couture," or "Harajuku Street Style."

Every three to four weeks, these stores would post a group of new items. Unlike most Taobao apparel stores, which regularly "hang" dozens if not hundreds of SKUs on their virtual racks, web-celeb stores keep no more than twenty to thirty items in stock, mostly clothes but also the occasional shoe or accessory. A few days before new items hit the rack, the stores would announce their upcoming sales, which often begin at designated times like 2 p.m. or 8 p.m. Before every sale, hundreds of thousands of fans would wait before their computer or smartphone screens, ready for the frenzy to ensue. In Chinese, these flash

WEIBO

Sina Weibo was started in 2009 as the microblogging site attached to Sina, a major portal in China. (*Weibo* in Chinese means "microblog." There were originally many competing social platforms in China, but with the domination of Sina in the microblog space, *Weibo* gradually became synonymous with Sina Weibo. This book follows this common usage within China.) Though Weibo began as a clone of Twitter, it quickly evolved into a bustling social network that looks like a combination of Facebook, Reddit, and Twitter, with a little bit of YouTube and live streaming thrown into the mix. Because 140 characters in Chinese can contain much more content than the same Latin character limit would, the platform is inherently suited to substantive discussion and short articles, as compared with Twitter's focus on headlines. Topics trending on Weibo regularly start long and lively conversations between "netizens."

Most Westerners are unaware of just how pervasive social media is in China, indeed more so than it is for most Americans. Though Tencent's killer messaging app Weixin has eroded Weibo's dominance in recent years, Weibo is still a dominant player for social networks such as Twitter where activity is

sales are associated with a common term called *starvation marketing*, in which the impression of deprivation and scarcity drives frenetic consumption. (If you don't pounce, somebody else will.) Most clothes would be completely snapped up almost immediately.

Furthermore, as soon as the first batch of clothes sells out, the stores begin to offer the same SKUs through presale. In general, a popular SKU could go through two to three rounds of presale in a single sale, with each round specifying a shipping time—for example, the second round might be completed ten days after the sale. Some fans are even willing to wait a month for clothes sold by their favorite online icon, but a month is considered a long time. (Compare this schedule with common US retailers' backorder times, which easily go into several months.) Web-celeb stores and sales turn standard retail economics on its head. Unlike most retailers worldwide, most visible to all users. (Weixin's social functions look more like Facebook, where you can only see the activity of mutual friends.) In the United States, if your Twitter account is shut off, you have other ways to communicate, but in China, you have far fewer large-scale communication platforms. Weibo's content has blossomed like fields of colorful chrysanthemums, full of gossip, celebrities, individuality, genuine news, and advertising. For most Chinese people, Weibo is one of the best channels for up-to-the-minute coverage of breaking news events. Indeed, apart from businesses, organizations such as government offices, train stations, schools, and media outlets regularly use Weibo for regular communications and official notices.

In 2013, Alibaba bought an 18 percent stake of Sina Weibo. When the company went public in 2014, Alibaba exercised an option, bringing its stake to 32 percent. Since Alibaba's investment the two companies have deeply integrated e-commerce on Taobao and social media on Weibo, allowing merchants to advertise effectively and influencers to monetize their fan bases. In 2017, Weibo had nearly four hundred million active user accounts.

of the clothes sold in these stores have not yet been manufactured when they are purchased.

On Weibo, these web celebs also behave very differently from how the average large social media account behaves. There are two types of Weibo accounts: individual and enterprise. Enterprise accounts are often headed by organizations or firms, for example, Alibaba or Nike. Unsurprisingly, most of Weibo's ad revenue comes from enterprise accounts—they are the ones buying advertising and other services. Most individual users don't spend money to make friends. Yet the web celebs, while still using individual accounts, spent an enormous amount on advertising to find new fans. And the content of their accounts looks like those of any individual: pictures and stories of their lifestyle, aesthetics, or travel. But these accounts were clearly being used for business purposes, spending significant amounts of money to place ads targeting new fans. This counterintuitive behavior reflected a counterintuitive truth: the web celebs are businesses, albeit businesses operating brands with "individual" faces.

And these businesses do operate: a small web celeb needs to have at least several hundred thousand fans to even make a dent in the industry. Bigger players have millions if not tens of millions of followers. More importantly, these young women spend an inordinate amount of time interacting with their fans, responding to comments and questions, and posting content that their fans request. This interaction is in a sense a service for their followers: explaining how to pair a style with the rest of the fan's wardrobe, makeup tips, an in-depth description of the stitching or detailing on a particular SKU. At other times, web celebs and fans will talk about their feelings or worries, or how tiring and annoying their jobs or boyfriends are. Interacting with them feels genuine and natural.

By 2017, China's e-commerce industry had recognized that these young women were not a flash in the pan. Many web-celeb storefronts already place in the top ten within Taobao's apparel categories— whenever a web celeb runs a sale, it will definitely land a top spot for the day's sales. Currently, over four hundred web-celeb stores of significant size are operating on Taobao across different product categories, from apparel to cosmetics to sporting goods to food and fast-moving consumer goods. In women's apparel, several large stores bring in more than US$1 million per sale and close to US$100 million in yearly gross merchandise volume. That category hosts dozens of second-tier stores whose yearly sales hover around US$10 million to US$20 million, and many more up-and-coming competitors who are hot on the high heels of their predecessors.

How do young women like Zhang Linchao, the web celeb we met in the introduction, with a keen aesthetic sense and social influence but little concrete business experience, make this model work? In chapter 5, I will analyze the web celebs' business model in detail; for now, it is sufficient to observe that these brand-builders are supported by Taobao's vast network of business functions and services that empower entrepreneurs. Because all the players on the Taobao platform are technologically connected, calling on and bundling a group of services can happen in real time and with little human interaction. Such an infrastructure can enable a small player to scale quickly, taking advantage of these available services.

Fifteen Years of Coordination: Lessons from Taobao as Business Network

The history of Taobao is one of adding increasingly complex business functions to the network and hence supporting businesses of increasing sophistication to grow. As the network has expanded, more players have entered the marketplace, fostering deeper coordination and the recurrent emergence of innovative business models. A full case study of Taobao's growth could fill an entire book, and indeed, interested readers can consult appendix B for a highly abbreviated version of that story. In this chapter, I will sketch only the briefest outlines of the platform's evolution to give readers a better understanding of Chinese e-commerce, and how it relies on network coordination and data intelligence.

At its very beginning, in 2003, Taobao was little more than a forum for buyers and sellers to find each other. The Chinese government had encouraged rapid economic development, which gave birth to an enormous number of small sellers without access to large groups of consumers. Simultaneously, buyers wanted access to a vast universe of products from across China and beyond. Foreign companies like eBay were trying to get a foothold. The leadership of Taobao recognized the need for a marketplace for personal, consumer-to-consumer sales, but was unclear on how to jump-start it. Consequently, the platform's incubation proceeded in steps.[1]

Initially, Taobao employees did everything they could to populate the market with as many products as they could find—literally posting things from their apartments. The next year, the goal was to bring in as many independent sellers as they could. Finally, with a critical mass of sellers in 2005, Taobao started advertising to attract buyers to the website. It described itself as selling anything you could possibly imagine.

Surprisingly, the Taobao platform encouraged sellers to foster business connections and even formal organizations outside of the platform. Precisely because e-commerce in China emerged without models or precedents, Taobao's value as an online marketplace quickly began to spill over into the offline world—sellers formed informal networks encouraging more service providers onto the platform. Western readers may be used to companies like Alibaba making all the decisions relating to everything that happens to their business, but the opposite happened in the early days of Taobao. Sellers joined Taobao, saw the tools and mechanisms provided by the platform, and ran with them.[2]

Many sellers in Taobao's early days were individuals or very small teams learning on their feet. Although opening a store and doing business online was free, there were still significant hurdles involved in learning to use the growing array of tools provided by Taobao for managing one's storefront, connecting with customers, and processing transactions, as described below. There were also the perennial difficulties of ensuring product quality and availability in a country plagued by an underdeveloped retail and shipping infrastructure. Sellers often worked together, sometimes on official Taobao forums, but also in informal contexts off of the platform, learning from each other to overcome these hurdles to doing business.

Service with a "Dear"

To help with customer interactions, Taobao built an instant-messenger service in 2005. Every storefront on Taobao has its own account on the official messaging platform, called Wangwang. (The tool's Chinese name is a cute phonetic that evokes a feeling of brisk business.) Through Wangwang, consumers can ask sellers any question they like at any hour of the day. They can even haggle over prices or just shoot the breeze. The customer-service representatives manning a store's Wangwang account quickly took on an important new role in the network. In keeping with Taobao's early "cute" aesthetic, customer-service language even evolved its own suitably saccharine vernacular, popularized by the new idiomatic pronoun *qin* ("dear"), which was used in place of the Chinese word for "you." (In Chinese, *qin* is part of the word for "darling" and also means "kiss.") This affectionate form of address is quite unusual, given the cool and distant tenor typically associated with interactions with strangers on the internet. Thus, the person behind each Wangwang account is a source of warmth, ensuring a good consumer experience and creating a channel for understanding the customer.

For sellers, the customer-service representative is a highly specialized role, which in larger online stores is regularly handled by at least two groups of employees, one group handling presale inquiries and the other handling after-sale service. Both types of inquiries could come at any hour of the day from consumers used to immediate responses. In addition to training in standard techniques of professional service, Wangwang customer-service reps must know the store's products backward and forward, as well as how to handle disputes and other issues. These representatives were the first of many new specialized positions that Taobao created. Customer service in particular has provided employment opportunities for millions of people, including those barred from entering the traditional economy due to geographical barriers or physical impediment.

Supporting Independent Services Providers

By 2006, the marketplace was fully formed, and coordination between participants in the Taobao network began to grow deeper. Some sellers saw an opportunity to provide support services for growing merchants and started to change their role. Taobao entered a stage of rapid growth as the first independent service vendors (ISVs), a new and crucially important group of players, were born.

An early challenge for sellers was effectively displaying and describing their products to strangers from all corners of China. Most customers would at least require a picture of the product they were to receive, but in the mid-2000s, smartphones had yet to be invented. Sellers possessed of both professional photography equipment and expertise were rare, but they were willing to share their capabilities. At first, these sellers offered to help other nearby sellers take pictures of their goods, gratis. As time went on, the photography experts formalized the services on offer and gradually became full-time, professional service providers. Photographers, designers, and writers began to partner with sellers to decorate their virtual storefronts.

Taobao, in turn, began to introduce new tools, including Wangpu, a series of standard templates for storefronts, to enable sellers to better manage their online business. Wangpu (in Chinese, "a shop located in a bustling location perfect for business") quickly became a platform itself, as it opened up to and engendered additional independent software developers. Soon many developers were offering to design customized storefronts and create more features for sellers.

One notable group of ISVs consisted of young women from all over China who began to make an increasingly comfortable living modeling for the growing assortment of apparel merchants on the platform. Over time, both merchants and customers would know which of the large pool of models was best suited for their clothing line, and they would work with those models. Soon, Taobao developed a connecting platform to organize these ISVs, help them find merchant partners, and monetize their modeling services. These women would be henceforth known as Tao models, models whose careers were incubated on Taobao.

Company leadership was constantly talking with sellers about how to make business easier. It was not uncommon to have a half a dozen sellers in the small Taobao offices at Hangzhou a couple of afternoons a week discussing what new tools might be useful. For example, the earliest sellers on Taobao used to print out each order as it was received to begin fulfillment, as they did for their offline business. When you have ten or even dozens of orders a day, this is a workable solution. But sellers faced a farcical yet very real problem from getting hundreds or even thousands of orders a day: their office printers overheated, some of them even catching on fire. It became apparent that to streamline the fulfillment process, sellers had to move more of their offline activities online so that they could better coordinate and optimize—and avoid fires. Without this pressure to improve the entire fulfillment workflow, up to and including logistics, the Cainiao Network—the logistics platform catalyzed by the 2012 delivery debacle—might not have emerged.

Technological Support for Expanding Networks

In the early years, many Taobao sellers had offline businesses and sourcing channels, but by 2008, many new merchants joined the platform in a rush for online gold. They faced the challenge of building their businesses completely from scratch, online. Taobao then had to bring into the online network the many functions of brick-and-mortar retail so that every seller could access them. As time went on, the Taobao marketplace even began to incubate new functional roles unknown to brick-and-mortar retailing.

There was no way Taobao could provide all the services of offline retail by itself. Inspired by early successes such as the Wangpu store-front platform, which had led to the creation of many software service providers, Alibaba articulated a new strategy: fostering the development of an open, collaborative, and flourishing e-commerce ecosystem. The company positioned itself as a platform with the goal of developing the infrastructure to fully enable online commerce. With this step, Taobao entered a new stage of development, powered by the explosive growth of the collaborative business networks built on top of it. As the system grew in complexity, it had to develop data intelligence to improve coordination. Smart business on Taobao was taking shape.

Beginning around 2013, Taobao began to expand its services higher up the value chain into areas such as marketing and financing. Since then, the main challenge has been to connect the Taobao platform with outside platforms like Weibo, Ant Financial Services, logistic companies, and the supply chain. Taobao does not offer the services these networks do, but the e-commerce platform does need to let them interact reliably and safely from a technical perspective. For example, web celebs, who manage their fans aggressively on the Weibo platform, have driven integration between Taobao and Weibo. Data intelligence can coordinate the interactions between platforms and can improve the services each party can apply for the benefit of customers.

Given the complexity of Taobao's ecosystem, I will examine only a few important business functions that it provides for its users. These examples illustrate the core lessons that we have learned and used to guide Taobao's development. (For further details, see appendix B.)

ISVs, TPs, and the All-Important API

As the Taobao network evolved, we experienced some real aha moments that informed our strategy going forward.[3] Once the online market was up and running, but when straightforward merchants were still the only businesses on the platform, a new and crucial role on the platform emerged: the Taobao partner. This individual or company takes on the job of storefront operations and marketing for individuals and brands.

These TPs, as they are now known, assumed a key role in the ecosystem. Their specialized expertise enabled the largest sellers to expand further and paved the way for offline sellers and brands from the major stores in Beijing and Shanghai as well as luxury-goods importers from abroad to make their way onto the platform. If you are an offline brand with no experience with online selling, you will use a TP to manage the day-to-day operations of your store. (Chapter 6 will tell the story of one of Taobao's most successful TPs, Baozun.) Beyond TPs, a vast array of third-party service providers sprouted through Taobao. To run an effective business, you need to use all sorts of software, from customer-relationship management to order management, to marketing and search engine optimization. Within a single firm or among partner firms, all this software must work together.

The key thread that connects ISVs to sellers and buyers in the ecosystem is data. For a Taobao seller, it is of the utmost importance to keep the data encoded in incoming orders flowing to those who need it, including customer-service representatives, sourcing, marketing, and logistics. A third-party developer that provides order management software must to be able to access a client's transaction data. In turn, sellers should be able to share the data created on Taobao with whomever they need to, to effectively do business. As the value of doing business on Taobao grew, the platform attracted a multitude of external entities interested in working with users of the site and using that data to do business.

In 2010, Taobao implemented a technology called application programming interface (API), a set of tools that any programmer can use to create software that interacts smoothly with other software in the system.[4] APIs are the technical basis for network coordination, and make it easy for ISVs to provide sellers with comprehensive services. API technology had far-reaching consequences for the whole ecosystem—I will discuss it in detail in chapter 4.

The future, not only for Taobao but also for most other businesses, is to bring higher and higher reaches of the value chain into the network.

Advertising and retailing have successfully moved online to platforms such as Google and Taobao. Web celebs, in essence, have moved brand building online. I will explain in part 2 how online interactions through social media build brands more effectively than do traditional approaches, and how business can digitalize core functions across the firm.

Once the network is coordinated in this new way, all sorts of new business models and forms of value creation emerge from ever-new coalitions of players. Each time a new level of network coordination develops on Taobao, the addition expands the reaches of the network and enriches the breadth of the entire online economy.

The Building Blocks of Network Coordination: How to Get Started

We have now seen a multitude of new business roles and functions that have gradually been integrated into the network of Taobao's market. But how exactly does network coordination operate and how should we facilitate it? Business networks are goal oriented: various players come together to solve a complex commercial problem for a client base. Only those actors who share the vision and are able to contribute to the solution will come online and work together toward that goal. From our experience at Taobao, we can share four operating maxims to foster effective network coordination (table 2-1).

To support a network structure, encourage direct connections and interactions.

Networked business is superior to rigid linear organization because collaboration can find the most efficient path through the network. The organizational structure must allow actors to connect directly to and work with whoever is available and most qualified, regardless of how roles are defined.

Wangwang is the earliest example of Taobao's explicit encouragement of direct communication between buyers and sellers on their own accounts. eBay, by contrast, hid sellers' information; sellers could only

TABLE 2-1

The building blocks of a coordinated network

Step	Examples from Taobao
Direct connection and interaction	Taobao created the Wangwang instant messenger to connect buyers and sellers and created the Taobaoke affiliate marketing platform to connect sellers and small websites.
Role evolution	Experienced sellers became Taobao University lecturers; Taobao partners (TPs) emerged as offline brands joined the network.
Investment in infrastructure	Alipay lowered barriers to trust; the Taobao application programming interface (API) allowed independent service vendors (ISVs) to work with merchants.
Putting business activities online	Taobao's product database (see chapter 4) allowed for any SKU imaginable to be bought or sold; the web celebs coordinated marketing and manufacturing online.

contact buyers through eBay. This closed arrangement discouraged off-platform transactions and allowed eBay to efficiently collect commissions. Taobao believed that direct connection would increase engagement and result in better business. To encourage parties to complete their transactions on the platform, Taobao offered transaction protection and guarantee services, adding value without resorting to artificial barriers to connection. There are many touching stories about the interactions between Taobao buyers and sellers online, and to many people, buying from a small Taobao shop whose customer representatives the buyers know well is almost like buying from an old mom-and-pop store in the neighborhood. This encouragement of direct communication between parties was an important factor in Taobao's beating out the much larger eBay, which abandoned the China market in 2007.

From then on, each new actor that has entered the Taobao network has been able to directly interact with its collaborators to the greatest extent possible. Direct connection's chief virtue is its flexibility. But to avoid significant transaction costs, solutions and mechanisms must allow for global coordination, not simply local collaboration. Taobao ensures that all data and software are technically integrated and can be used across the network. The site's sellers can work with third party software developers to enhance their storefronts or improve marketing campaigns, or connect with their desired logistics provider or providers and share order tracking and shipping order information.

Another mechanism for direct connection is Taobaoke, a marketing affiliate program set up by Taobao's advertising department Alimama. Taobaoke directly links millions of Taobao sellers with millions of small websites in China to help sellers attract new customers. When a website places an advertising link for a Taobao seller, the website gets a fixed commission if people click and buy, and the seller reaches a new prospective customer. Over time, more of the links are suggested by Taobao's advertising engine, letting data intelligence make the whole process smarter. (For more information on Alimama and Taobaoke, see appendixes A and B.)

Let players' roles evolve, and do not rush their codification.

To achieve flexibility, you cannot plan any network meticulously. It must develop according to the actors that enter and the consumers it serves. In practice, this means that participants' roles initially need to remain fuzzily defined. This unformed state might sacrifice some efficiency, but it allows for emergent forms of collaboration with new functions and capabilities. When roles do solidify, the platform can "recognize" them by giving them official support and a status within the network. In practice, a player's role is recognized when official avenues allow it to generate income.

The first truly emergent role within the network was the Tao University lecturers. Because so many sellers were inexperienced, knowledgeable sellers were constantly on call with company leadership or platform newbies. Taobao's leadership realized that it needed a new business to properly train and thus support the development of Taobao University. Under this program, Taobao created a framework for experienced sellers to give teaching seminars to users, who would pay to attend in facilities provided by Taobao or through Taobao's online education platform created for the lecturers.

Another important early role was the third-party software developers. With Taobao's rapid growth, the simple standard storefront provided by Taobao soon became a burden for sellers. Taobao initially planned to upgrade its storefront services including the templates offered on Wangpu, but realized that the platform simply couldn't cope with the diverse needs of so many sellers. So Taobao decided to open this service to third-party software developers, with Taobao itself building software interface tools and creating the rules for mediating relationships and fees. The arrangement worked—third-party developers created a multitude of customization solutions for sellers to use. Consumers enjoy the diverse stores on Taobao, with styles ranging from the most froufrou to the most austere aesthetic. More significantly, Taobao's choice to promote collaboration and openness set the tone for later growth. This new role on the platform—and the infrastructure that supported it—was the precedent for the development of many new roles.

These adaptable roles filled gaps in the network, stepping in to offer functionalities that sellers lacked. Yet, we found that once gaps were plugged, new gaps—and, hence, new roles—continually emerged.[5] Besides TPs and ISVs, which are online versions of offline functions, even more interesting are the new opportunities or new solutions for old problems. These opportunities often appear at the confluence of different networks and create great value. Web celebs are an example, which I will analyze in much detail in chapter 5.

More recently, new examples are developing at the intersection of the PC-based online world and the mobile world; these two areas have only distantly related offline counterparts. The new roles developing at this intersection are product recommenders (*daogou*), expert buyers who share Taobao products across the internet to consumers and earn commission; live-streamers, who advertise products in real time from around the world; and content creators, who write promotional articles describing sellers and products. Many of these people make substantial income on commission. Appendix B discusses these new roles while chapter 6 illustrates their function within the ecosystem.

From a business perspective, it may seem logical to clearly define roles and responsibilities to facilitate cost-effective collaboration, but in an online setting, such strong definition often hamstrings the network's growth. As consumers and their needs evolve, so too do businesses. Individual contributors should be able to determine their best contribution and function, and all actors in the network need to be able to experiment to find the best solutions. Once the new opportunities have been effectively filled, the roles can be gradually codified.

Invest in infrastructure to drive network effects.

As newcomers to the online retailing game, traditional players didn't believe in Taobao's potential, and Taobao had to go the extra mile to attract sellers. Taobao didn't charge sellers to open a store and run its daily operation. Especially in the earliest days of the network, this free admission greatly reduced the entry barriers for trying out the new platform. At its core, Taobao created the infrastructure for the marketplace as a whole, and that infrastructure fostered powerful network effects. *Infrastructure* refers to the tools and mechanisms that undergird a business network, such as reputation systems, search functionality, virtual computing resources, or APIs. As such, infrastructure comprises the basic services needed by every participant in the platform's work environment. Because infrastructure often requires significant investment, it is akin to a public good in the terminology of economics, whose supply and maintenance exceeds the responsibilities of any single player. It is incumbent on the platform to create infrastructure for the marketplace that will enhance coordination, engendering network effects.

Taobao continually introduced important features to solve major barriers to doing business. One of the most important early innovations was Alipay, whose escrow service significantly reduced trust barriers in the early days of e-commerce. Over the next few years, Taobao began to work with newly formed logistics companies to provide crucial shipping support for sellers. Coupled with strong promotion of the website and the new buyers it brought, virtuous cycles quickly emerged, driving the growth of the marketplace. By the middle of 2006, daily merchandise volume reached 100 million RMB (over US$15 million), and the network started to gain the momentum to grow on its own without constant assistance from the platform. Only then did the team at Taobao feel that the platform had passed the first critical test of survival.

In every stage of Taobao's development, the platform has intentionally focused on investing in the basic infrastructure of doing business, from marketing (advertising, search, and recommendation engines) to collaboration (APIs) to IT operations (Alibaba Cloud's cloud-computing platforms). Many of these tools rely on data intelligence. In the current mobile landscape, our company has continued to develop tools and resources for seller success, as I will describe in chapter 4. By deliberately lowering barriers to entering and operating within the network, network effects multiply, and the business grows rapidly.

Encourage parties to put as much information and business activity as possible online in digital form.

I will discuss so-called business "softwaring"—retooling a business and its decisions using digital software, so that it can best achieve network coordination and data intelligence—in the next two chapters, but briefly, network coordination only works when as many business activities as possible are operating online. Taobao has found that our most innovative platform users do the hard work of turning every facet of their business operations into digital form and putting it online. The factories that produce top web celebs' apparel use sophisticated patterning, fabric layout, and cutting software. This approach allows the manufacture to be seamlessly coordinated across several manufacturers and production steps. When this information and instruction can be transmitted digitally with clarity and immediacy, the network can act on it with confidence.

Our discussion here foreshadows the data-intelligence capability described in chapter 3. Rapid progress in datafication (the encoding of an activity or a phenomenon into a form understandable by computers) has better enabled network coordination. More network coordination generates more data, which leads naturally to data intelligence. In fact, the two poles of my equation for smart business—network coordination and data intelligence—represent the entwined and mutually reinforcing double helix of the business DNA of the future. Although each of these forces has arisen somewhat independently and may be familiar to readers, the business world is now at a tipping point because of the synergy of these forces. The many technological and business advances that enabled both of these forces to emerge, and the amplifying effects of their interdependence, is creating a new economic reality. I will unpack the more complex details of this observation in the following chapters.

Coordinated Networks in the United States

Though this chapter has focused on developments in China, network coordination has played an increasingly important role in the US economy as well. Wikipedia, the news media, and other media are clear examples. While the revenue model of the Wikipedia system may not be transferable, the ability of a coordinated but very loosely controlled network to produce a significantly more comprehensive and accurate catalog of the world's information testifies to the power of a network structure.

Network coordination could not happen without the development of open-source cooperation as the dominant form of software development. The initial release of the Linux kernel—a kernel is the most fundamental code of an operating system—by Linus Torvalds in 1991 jump-started what is called the open-source movement. At the time, the only operating systems available for computer users were proprietary and costly. They also often had bugs, needed regular updates, and were extremely difficult to customize. All these problems were resolved with the introduction of Linux, now the most commonly used operating system in the world. Like Wikipedia, Linux is constantly updated and improved by individual programmers around the globe, and because the source code is open to all, the operating system is easy to customize. Torvalds's initial motivation was ethical; he thought that software, as the language of computers, should be free. But his innovation was not an either-or proposition—besides encouraging an ethical standard, it produced better software.

Linux's resilience and versatility is unsurpassed and has served as a model for many other software development projects. Every time the code is modified, it is labeled and stored so that its progression can be tracked. This process has resulted in software that is more reliable and versatile. When many minds work on a problem, they find better solutions than just one person would; multiplicities of users find more bugs and correct them. Additionally, developers can use and reuse a well-tested base code and simply modify it, making software development much more efficient—the wheel does not need to be reinvented.

Linux initiated the open-source movement, but it was quickly followed by others, including the Apache Software Foundation, which developed Spark, Hadoop, Databricks, and MySQL. (The firm that released MySQL is now owned by Oracle.) These programs are vital for today's internet and cloud-computing companies. Starting with Netscape, which released its browser source code in 1998, internet companies have pushed the boundaries of the open-source movement much further. Most companies formerly in the business of exclusively proprietary software have been forced to adapt and adopt some parts of the open-source mantra, such as releasing source code but selling proprietary products built on top of them. The introduction of open APIs is a part of this development.[6]

Fueling the Coordinated Network: Data Intelligence

Although the principle of network coordination has played out mostly in internet-centric sectors in the United States, it has already had far-reaching effects in transforming China. Chinese entrepreneurs are better positioned than their US counterparts to transform traditional industries such as manufacturing and services and to create new types of net-native businesses. In a business context, the network is precisely the dynamic organizational form that can offer consumers the immediate, customized service that they demand.

But to coordinate networks, businesses need more than just a networked structure. They also need the technological solution to coordinate activity across the network. That solution is data intelligence: the data, algorithms, and machine learning needed to ensure efficient, effective coordination. Data intelligence is the yin to the network's yang, the invisible forces stewarding the network's growth and dynamics. This is the topic of the next chapter.

CHAPTER 3

DATA INTELLIGENCE

How Machine Learning Uses Data to Make Business Smart

Every month, more than half a trillion users browse the Taobao app. They wander through the world's largest virtual shopping mall, flitting from store to store and peeking at the world's most exciting products at unbeatable prices. But the end user only sees the tip of the iceberg of Alibaba's marketplaces. Little does the average consumer know that he or she is selecting from a carefully chosen subset of Alibaba's more than 1.5 billion product listings (compared with Walmart's 17 million or Amazon's 350 million in 2017) offered by millions of sellers.[1]

The experience for sellers is similar. The average seller only needs to know that Alibaba's tools and dashboards work well enough to find necessary services and optimize the seller's business. During Singles Day 2017, merchants accessed data in Tmall's online data analytics dashboards over eleven *billion* times to monitor their business in real time. (In those twenty-four crucial hours, merchants on average spent ninety-three minutes and fifteen seconds browsing and analyzing traffic and sales data.) Little do the merchants know that to ensure a healthy marketplace, Alibaba's security algorithms work around the clock, combing the platform for spam and fraud. The algorithms execute thirty billion protective scans per day, engaging in minute-level detection of invasive events and prevention on trillions of data points.

The surface of this sprawling retail network obscures the second half of our strategic equation, data intelligence—the combination of data, algorithms, and adaptable services. Combining all our buyer and seller services, Alibaba's platforms process the equivalent of twenty million high-definition movies a day. Our technical stack—the set of software that handles the computer or platform infrastructure—can handle over 8 billion internal data access calls at peak. Making sure this internal data flows smoothly is the engineering feat that explains why retail companies like Alibaba and Amazon have become the world's leading providers of cloud-computing services.

I use the term *data intelligence* to emphasize how the constant stream of data created by interactions with users can be used by machine-learning algorithms to make businesses smart. Google's web search, Taobao's recommendation engines, and Uber's ride matching are all examples of data intelligence in action. These companies run the data they collect through algorithms to deliver constantly revised and highly relevant results to customers in real time. Most of these companies' operations and interactions with customers require little to no human action. No one assigns an Uber car to a rider, and no Taobao associate recommends a dress; the algorithms do it. Although there is an enormous amount of human effort and creativity involved in creating these services, once that effort is done, the business practically runs itself.

Thus, the model enjoys amazing leverage and scale. By automating the retail process, some thirty thousand employees at Alibaba can achieve comparable sales to that which Walmart pulls in with its two million employees. (Alibaba has over fifty thousand employees around the world, but not all are involved with our core e-commerce business.) Looking at maps and churning through possibilities is something a computer can do much faster and more accurately than a human dispatcher can—hence, Uber's advantage in minimizing wait times. Data intelligence is becoming the most important source of competitive advantage.

Nevertheless, few businesspeople have appreciated how this capability can be generalized to almost all economic activity, despite the attention paid to machine-learning technologies in today's media. For good reason, the confluence of cloud and mobile computing, advances in datafication (the encoding of an activity or a phenomenon into a form understandable by computers), and especially progress in artificial intelligence, are creating truly new capabilities that will change how companies operate and compete. This chapter describes the business implications of using machine-learning technologies to integrate data intelligence into a business and to make it smart.

Machine Learning: The Intelligence in Data Intelligence

Technically, machine learning is one technology within the larger umbrella of AI, but the rapid progress of machine learning has practically buried many other approaches to creating AI. Machine learning uses algorithms that describe the parameters to be optimized or the goal achieved, but does not lay down a series of rules to follow precisely. This lack of preset rules differs from many other approaches from computer science that were top-down, rule-based instructions telling computers exactly how to do what they were supposed to do. Machine-learning programs operate more like natural selection. What works becomes amplified, and what doesn't dies out. For a simplified example, imagine that the problem you are solving had a mechanistic device like the one an optometrist uses to determine the prescription that most improves your vision. The eye doctor spins a lens to the next degree and asks you if the letters on the far wall are clearer or fuzzier. Then the doctor repeats the procedure several times until the process converges on a specific prescription. The algorithm works similarly. It takes every piece of new data it gets and asks, does this produce a better result or not?

Machine-learning algorithms train and refine themselves by churning through loads of data. In 2017, there was an enormous amount of excitement, especially in China, about the success of a machine-learning program called AlphaGo. The program beat the masters of the Chinese game of Go—a game that has hundreds of millions more move combinations than chess has. Programmers "trained" AlphaGo by having it play millions of digital Go games against itself so that it had already simulated countless moves and countermoves. The program "knew" how the game would play out across a multitude of scenarios. In actuality, however, the computer knew nothing about the game. AlphaGo was not programmed to put its piece here when its opponent's piece is there. Instead, it notes the piece position, then, using its millions of experiences, calculates the probabilities of the outcomes of any next step on the board, and picks the best one.

Data scientists are continually uncovering new ways to model problems and to program machine-learning algorithms to make the algorithms more powerful. They also layer algorithms and engineer them to work together. Uber's basic algorithmic engine connected riders and cars as quickly as possible. The rideshare company then went on to develop algorithms that do dynamically differentiated pricing so that even though you may have to pay more, you can get a car in a downpour. Google clears billions of dollars of advertising through an auction model built into its algorithms that use performance—the number of sales or click-throughs—to automatically set prices. Taobao's recommendation engine maximizes whatever appeals to each consumer individually, using both individual and collective knowledge.[2]

The Contribution of Big Data

The expanding capability of machine-learning algorithms is made possible with the increasing power of computing and the plethora of data—both large data sets and the continual stream of data created by interactions online. AlphaGo could learn by playing itself, but most machine-learning algorithms need to learn by processing huge amounts of data, usually before they are unveiled to the public. The iterative process that machine learning uses churns through large data sets and refines the internal calibrations the algorithm does to achieve more-accurate results. Once it does a good job, a company can put the algorithm into operation in real time with real customers. The algorithms continue to improve as they use the data stream gushing from something like the 2017 Singles Day, when our platform handled 325,000 transactions per second at peak, the near equivalent of 20 million transactions per minute.

The Impact of the Cloud

Numbers like these require great computing power, which would not be possible without the development of cloud computing. In the United States, Amazon pioneered cloud computing and has since become a giant in an industry otherwise populated by traditional IT players like IBM and Microsoft. Amazon originally developed cloud computing to handle the immense server loads created by its warehousing and logistics services.

Cloud computing allows a company to access a large bank of cheap servers for calculation power, speed, reliability, and cost savings. Deployed as a commercial service, cloud computing allows companies to buy small chunks of computing power, thus turning the fixed cost of in-house servers into a variable cost. Amazon's cloud division accounts for over 10 percent of the company's total sales.[3] Alibaba's recent investments in cloud computing do not come from a desire to ape Amazon. They came from company leadership's realization in 2008 that IT expenses paid to companies like Cisco and Oracle would soon outstrip the company's entire revenue stream, not just its e-commerce businesses. To avoid being crippled by IT expenses, Alibaba decided to invest in its own cloud-computing capability. But there was bitter internal resistance to this massive undertaking. Engineering talent was worked to exhaustion, and some engineers decided to leave the company. Meanwhile, operating teams complained of bugs and system failures.

Cloud computing is complicated and extremely expensive to develop. Without acute internal demand, neither Amazon nor Alibaba could have risen to the top of an IT industry only peripherally related to their core businesses. Today, Alibaba Cloud is China's largest provider of cloud computing and is the official cloud services partner of the International Olympic Committee. Alibaba Cloud has also incubated the development of richer data and algorithm-driven services for users and nurtured a community of developers and apps that crisscross China. Most importantly, the commercialization of cloud computing has made large-scale computational power accessible to anyone, much like a public utility. The cost of storing and computing large quantities of data has dropped dramatically since the turn of the century. For business, this means that far-reaching, real-time applications of machine learning are now possible and affordable.

The Role of Mobile Computing

On another front, mobile computing, which records data from a device anywhere in the physical world and sends it across the network using wifi or other means, is creating reams of data and making it accessible for use. For instance, the combination of so many activities accomplished by the smart phone—interactive maps, calls, texts, photos, searches, video—uploads enormous amounts of data onto the web. The emerging internet of things (IoT) promises even more; it is "datafying" our physical world in innovative ways. More and more technologies emerging to quantify thorny problems and slippery phenomena present an opportunity for companies to use data to produce new insight and even create new businesses.

As a small but evocative example, Augury, a startup based in New York and Israel, developed a proprietary stethoscope-like device that can listen to sounds produced by all kinds of commercial machines. Using algorithms running in the cloud, Augury can conduct a digital "physical exam" and then deliver the results via an app on a technician's phone. If the machine is "unhealthy," Augury will diagnose its problems and suggest solutions. If everything is working smoothly, Augury will record the exam for future reference. Augury can continuously compile trends and statistics on herds of machines, helping to inform manufacturers or providing better services to customers. The industrial IoT market is growing rapidly, estimated to reach US$320 billion by 2020. With data intelligence, a mundane business like mechanical maintenance has become a lucrative smart business. In June 2017, Augury closed its Series B round of funding, securing US$17 million to continue commercializing its technology.[4]

When all these tools are brought together, they create data intelligence. Data that is collected when it is produced in the course of business, processed through machine-learning algorithms, and fed back into the business setting thus creates a smart feedback loop that powers business decisions. This virtuous, digital cycle is the essence of data intelligence. The business learns in real time, and the product evolves as the needs of its clients develop and are incorporated into an ever-new and more satisfactory result.

Google Maps was originally a mapping application accessed through a web browser on a personal computer. When Google Maps launched on the Apple iPhone, it became one of the very first successful mobile services. The combination was truly a smart business. Before Google Maps, the experience with the old GPS was pretty bad—static maps with regularized directions that were never current with traffic delays or construction detours. Google Maps made navigation a simple online exercise. The service is constantly improving as the data engine churns through user after user's path and makes more-complete maps and finds more-efficient routes. Google Maps works with you. If you miss the turn, no problem—it reroutes you. The Waze navigation app added the capability for individual users to contribute in real time data such as the location of a pothole or the traffic police.

Let's examine in detail how a spin-off of Alibaba, Ant Financial Services, developed the data intelligence that has resulted in a company valued in 2017 at more than US$60 billion.

Data Intelligence at Ant Financial and MYbank

China has not had a sophisticated financial system. Banking has historically been a government function designed for large state-owned businesses and individual savers. Lending to small and medium-sized enterprises (SMEs), a substantial and standard part of the US business finance market, has been beyond the scope of most

Chinese banks. SME lending, however, is evolving in China as more privately owned banks have gained a foothold. But "small-business lending" still typically means loans of more than US$1 million and is hence beyond the reach of tens of millions of actual small businesses.

With no official history of small-business lending in China, there are no useful credit scores or the like. Many small businesses have relied on informal or personal avenues for obtaining capital. To make matters worse, the average small business in China does not adequately—or even accurately—document their business activities, rendering a loan application nearly impossible, even to the most accommodating of institutions. The result is a dismal lending landscape for small businesses, which are often forced to take refuge in the solicitude of local loan sharks and accept small loans from nonprofessional institutions at exorbitant interest rates. Most businesses on Alibaba platforms are very small and have real difficulties in getting loans to grow their operations.[5]

In 2012, we at Alibaba saw this need on the part of our customers, and we realized that we could create a valuable and complementary business service. Along with developments in machine learning and access to huge amounts of relevant data, we had all the necessary ingredients for creating a high-functioning, scalable, and profitable SME lending business. This business was originally called Alibaba Microloans and was part of Alipay, which later became Ant Financial Services. Today, that microfinance business is located under MYbank, the online lender established in 2014 as one of five of China's first completely privately owned banks. MYbank is a completely virtual bank, with no offline locations. (MYbank is 30 percent controlled by Ant Financial. And to answer your likely question, the name *Ant* was, in fact, chosen for its bug imagery. We wanted to capture the idea that we were empowering all the small, ant-like businesses. Besides appealing to small businesses, we hoped that the name would also communicate our strategy: since each ant only eats a little, we were not threatening the traditional big lending businesses.)

Our microlending business began by serving the millions of sellers on Taobao and Tmall, offering loans no larger than 1 million RMB (approximately US$160,000) and as small as several hundred RMB (around US$50), to be repaid in up to three months. As of December 2016, MYbank (and its loan business's earlier incarnation Alibaba Microloans) has made more than 87 billion RMB (US$13.4 billion) in loans to nearly three million small- and micro-sized businesses and entrepreneurs across more than thirty-two provinces and administrative areas across China. MYbank alone has made over 40 billion RMB (US$6.15 billion) of loans to 1.17 million rural Chinese users, with nearly four billion of those loans going to 1.86 million business owners from counties suffering from extreme poverty.[6] Over half of the online bank's loans go to businesses and individuals in third-, fourth- and fifth-tier cities in China. (Fifty-one percent of the owners of these small- and micro-sized enterprises are under thirty years of age.) A user can apply for a loan as small as 1 RMB (US$0.15), and the average size of a single loan application is about 8000 RMB (US$1231).[7] For reference, the average minimum loan size from Chinese banks was about 6 million RMB (just under US$1 million) when Alibaba's microloan business started.

Many of MYbank's clients are individuals with minimal education and resources. They cannot procure collateral and often cannot produce a respectable balance sheet. Yet when sellers apply for a loan, they do not have to submit any paperwork. They are approved or rejected in seconds. Their loan could be deposited into their Alipay online account in as little as three minutes. Most importantly, even at such a large scale, MYbank's loan business is sustainable: the default rate on loans consistently hovers around one percentage point. MYbank's success is due to the data intelligence it built into its business, a machine-learning-based lending engine.

At a most basic level, lending institutions need only answer three questions when faced with a potential borrower: Do we lend to them, how much should we lend, and at what interest rate? As any person who has applied for a loan knows, the answers to these questions depend on the borrower's credit history—his or her creditworthiness. The standard method for this assessment is to collect and process mountains of paperwork, with the hope of obtaining useful information.

In contrast, MYbank is placed to easily access information about its potential borrowers because they do business on Alibaba's platforms or use Alipay and Ant Financial's products. When authorized, the lender can look at transaction data to get the answers to many kinds of relevant questions. How well is a seller's business doing? Has he or she engaged in any untrustworthy behavior? MYbank can even ask questions that a traditional bank would be hard-pressed to investigate: Do the seller's friends have high credit ratings? How much time does the seller spend working online on the business? Are the seller's offerings competitive in the market? The data is much richer and more accurate than what a bank could hope to obtain from paper documentation or a traditional credit score.

Machine Learning, Ant-Style

The key to the success of Alibaba's microloan business is not simply its mountains of data about Taobao sellers, but also the intelligence it builds into its business model to use such data to best advantage. Data scientists at MYbank compare groups of good borrowers (those who return money on time) with bad (those who do not) to isolate common traits from both groups to calculate a credit score for all its clients. This data-driven credit-score approach may sound simple or even old-fashioned. But what is revolutionary is that such comparisons are done by computer routines or algorithms automatically on all borrowers, not a sample, and on all their behavioral data—at least thousands and sometimes hundreds of thousands of traits—in real time. Every transaction, every time sellers communicate with a buyer, all the items in their store, their connections with all the other services available on Taobao—indeed, every action that is recorded on the platform—affects their credit.

At the same time, the algorithms that calculate credit scores are themselves evolving in real time, thus improving the quality of decision making. MYbank's model is built on probabilistic reasoning. Rather than an exact theory of why certain traits will differentiate between good and bad borrowers. Algorithms improve their own predictive power through continuous iteration. If a seller with terrible credit pays back a loan right on time, or a seller with stellar credit catastrophically defaults, the algorithm clearly needs tweaking. The algorithms are built so that it is easy to digitally check their assumptions and make small but important changes. Which parameters should be added or removed? Which parameters connected to which kinds of user behavior should be given more weight? Most banks would take at least half a year to recalibrate their models.

MYbank uses similar methods to determine how much to lend and how much interest to charge. To calculate an exact credit limit, MYbank's data scientists must analyze many more types of data: gross profit margins; inventory turnover; and more difficult, less mathematically precise information like product life cycles and the quality of a seller's social and business relationships. For product life cycle, the scientists might ask, Is a particular item a new product that is building market share? Is a product on sale? Is it nearing obsolescence and dropping in price? For relationship quality, they might look at frequency, length, and type of communication (instant messaging, email, or other types more common in the Chinese internet setting than in the American environment). The data scientists study and test which data points provide the insights they seek, and they design algorithms to do this process for them. More data and better data models mean more-accurate understanding of how much to lend and how much interest to charge. Through this sort of machine learning, MYbank can steadily decrease risk and cost. As a result, the borrower's experience gets better—they get the money they need, when they need it, and at an interest rate they can afford.

The Three Cornerstones of Smart Business

MYbank's business model requires three fundamental steps for data intelligence to operate: adaptable products, datafication, and machine learning (iterating algorithms). First, MYbank's dynamic process has an adaptable product—loans of varying amounts with varying terms, depending on customer needs. Second, MYbank datafies all aspects of the borrowers' business by putting this information online. And finally, the data recorded is used by the carefully engineered machine-learning algorithms that the company's data scientists created.[8]

Adaptable Products

Algorithms cannot iterate without the *products*—the online consumer interface that delivers customer experience directly while gathering consumer feedback to adjust algorithm models. Google's famous search bar has become a classic example of product design (figure 3-1). Customers enter keywords into a simple bar and then immediately see the product, the search result page. Google puts tremendous resources into designing this product so that customers can find what they want in less time and with less effort.

When Alibaba first created our online loan business, we started essentially the same way. The lending product was embedded in the online operations desktop of Taobao sellers. All the customer needs to do is click, and the funds will be provided almost immediately. The smart design of the consumer interfaces is crucial to the success of internet companies: the feeds and alerts of Facebook, the few hundred characters of a Twitter message, the "delete after you read" feature of Snapchat—are all inviting and easy interfaces for customers. Even more importantly, they work in tandem with the data-intelligence engine in the cloud (the back-end calculation consumers don't see). They are designed to provide the right kind of feedback loops to work

FIGURE 3-1

Data intelligence feedback loop

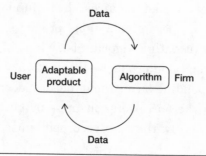

with the machine-learning algorithms. The ensuing insight is then looped back into the product itself to improve user experience. In this sense, the products of the future are capable of adapting to the user and environment by themselves, and hence become "smart."

These products share a common design philosophy. For businesses, online products are the crucial interface between machine-learning technology and business problems. On the business side, the product interface connects the customer to the firm, so the firm can observe customer behavior and preferences, zeroing in on the key problem that the company wishes to solve for the client. The data created from this interaction then becomes the raw material for algorithms to process. Thus the design of the interface determines the volume, features, and quality of the data collected on the customer. On the technology side, products are the medium through which the results of machine learning are delivered to the customer. How much machine-learning technology can actually affect the customer experience is circumscribed by product design and implementation. A well-designed product offers ample opportunity for machine learning to create tangible value, such as MYbank's adaptive loans.

For many traditional industries, creating an adaptable product is a real challenge. For smart businesses, it is their lifeblood. Every business of the future will likely have an internet-product component to allow for direct interactions with their customers, no matter what physical products the business produces and sells. If it does not sell to the final consumer, the business can still be gaining information and interacting with its customers. The data intelligence working throughout the value chain will facilitate greater network coordination.

Datafication and Live Data

The starting point for the smart system that underlies MYbank's microloans is encoding business problems into digital form. How should offline business activities be rendered into data? Beyond simple operations and sales metrics, which present numbers easily digitalized, other valuable questions can be answered through the use of more indirect data points. For example, to gauge how committed and active a seller is, our earliest loan product looked at how many seconds a seller takes to respond to customer queries and to customer comments on products and service. The use of such data would be unimaginable if the cost of recording it online hadn't become negligible. Gradually, Ant and MYbank ventured into more complicated data, using it to construct the social networks of sellers or estimating the gross margins of their businesses.

Datafication, which as defined encodes an activity or a phenomenon into a form understandable by computers, is rarely easy or cheap, but it is the most important step in data intelligence. I use the word *datafication* instead of the more common *digitalization*, which is associated with the translation of words and numbers into binary code, to emphasize the breadth of types of data being recorded and the intention of using it for applications and knowledge creation. Datafication requires both human ingenuity and hard work. Google has converted an endless sea of web pages into data through its web crawlers (simple, repetitive programs that look for certain information on the web). Facebook has brought social relationships online; Fitbit and exercise apps have begun to datafy the workings of our bodies. Indeed, Shigeomi Koshimizu of Japan's Advanced Institute of Industrial Technology has developed the digital coordinates for a human backside. Humor aside, this technology can recognize if a car is being driven by an unauthorized user or if a known user is sitting in a way that suggests sleep or unconsciousness.[9]

Acquiring the data that a business needs can be a difficult challenge. The countryside still needs to be electrified, metaphorically. I will discuss the steps toward datafication that allow business to tackle such a challenge in chapter 4. It might not have been possible to get Alibaba's microloans operation off the ground if Ant had needed to collect all the necessary data for its models by itself. Even the most basic layer of data, on storefront operations, is the result of more than ten years of Taobao's growth. Similarly, Google's advertising engine works so well because it had already run countless searches through its search function. It is very difficult to bootstrap a smart business, because even knowing what data to collect is difficult. Datafication is a creative and expensive trial-and-error process. However, the difficulty of datafication is dropping precipitously as more and more data goes online, for example, with the expansion of IoT technology and devices. As more and more data sources surrounding the business emerge and are pooled together, a company can create new value with little additional investment.

Machine Learning: Iterating Algorithms

Data can only create value when it is processed through a machine-learning engine. For a business, algorithms must make explicit the underlying product logic or market dynamics that the business is trying to optimize. Besides constantly refining themselves, algorithmic engines can also test various scenarios to improve business performance. For example, MYbank's data scientists embed an experiment into the lending interface, giving different groups of sellers different interest rates and measuring real-time response rates. Each time the model gave a seller a particular interest rate, the platform records the seller's reactions in real time, from acceptance of the loan to the time to repayment. This data in turn is used as input for the lending model to adjust its parameters, in a constant stream of minute calibration.

These practices, in which researchers compare two variants (A and B) to see which variant gives better results, are often called A/B tests and are common in internet companies. Through real-time online experiments, algorithms can get direct feedback from consumers about their performance and hence can self-adjust constantly. A digital response then triggers the next adjustment, which produces another consumer response, which triggers another adjustment, and so on, in a perpetual-motion machine for improving product and user experience.

When all of a business's operations are online, data floods in from all parts and processes of the business. Firms must struggle to assimilate, interpret, and use it to their advantage. Business leaders around the world already see that many decisions can no longer be based purely on human judgment but must utilize data intelligence. Network coordination will increasingly need this intelligence. In the future, automated auctions might assign production quantities to competing facilities or arrange procurement of necessary inputs. This development is still in its infancy but has great potential.

Data Intelligence in Action

The best criterion for judging whether data intelligence works in your business is whether a particular business decision is made directly by machines or still has to be made by a human, with the support of data analysis.

Alibaba introduced an AI-powered chat bot to help field customer queries in 2016. This chat bot, called "AliMe," is different from the robotic service providers familiar to most people—those robotic responses are simply programmed to match the answers in their repertoire to your query. AliMe, on the other hand, relies on training from experienced representatives of Taobao merchants. With the help of these "robot trainers," the chat bots in each merchant's store learn all about the products in their categories. At the same time, they are well versed in the mechanics of Alibaba's platforms— return policies, delivery costs, how to change an order or its delivery destination— anything a customer might ask. Using a variety of machine-learning technologies like semantic comprehension, context dialogues, knowledge graphs, data mining, and deep learning, the chat bot is rapidly improving its ability to diagnose and fix consumer issues automatically, not simply return static responses that prompt the consumer to take further action. AliMe confirms with the customer that the presented solution is acceptable, then executes it. Minimal human action by Alibaba or the merchant occurs. The chat bot can even make significant contribution to a seller's top line. Apparel brand Senma started using a chat bot a year ago and found that the bot made 200 million RMB (US$30.8 million) in sales, twenty-six times as much as the merchant's top human sales associate.

There will still be the need for Wangwang customer representatives to deal with more complicated or personal discussions. Yet the capability to handle routine queries is most useful on days of very high volume, such as sales. For big events, most large sellers need to hire temp workers to handle consumer inquiries anyway. How useful is the chat bot? On Singles Day 2017 alone, AliMe shouldered more than 95 percent of customer questions, addressing the questions and concerns of 3.5 million-plus consumers. (Note that while we are very proud of our chat bot, it is not intended to be the all-purpose digital assistant that Apple, Google, or Facebook have been working on for years.)

The Future Is Now

As Taobao continues to apply data intelligence to more business problems, its competitive advantage becomes hard to surpass. Take image-recognition technology, which already operates in many areas of the platform. Optical character recognition software identifies malicious ads hidden in otherwise innocuous product photos. The Taobao app offers users the opportunity to search for products by taking a picture with their phone, after which algorithms get to work identifying the product "seen" with those available on the platform. The visual search product is getting more accurate and is quite popular, boasting over ten million unique user visits per day.

Data intelligence has huge first-mover advantages as it grows off positive feedback loops. Getting relevant data in quantity is difficult and expensive, but the more data that is used, the more valuable the business becomes. For example, when AutoNavi (Alibaba's mapping business) or Google Maps become more accurate, more people use the products, the underlying algorithms have more data to work with, and the apps becomes even more accurate. This virtuous cycle is fundamentally different from physical products. With such a cycle, there are no diminishing returns. It is very hard to compete against a smart business with a strong head start.

PART TWO

HOW SMART BUSINESSES COMPETE

Strategic Principles

P art 1 of the book has described the transformation of the business landscape through the dual forces of network coordination and data intelligence. Familiar strategies are being turned upside down. But what does all this mean for any individual firm? What should you do differently in this new environment?

In the world of smart business, not everyone needs to become Taobao, Google, or Facebook. Firms large and small, from legacy companies to internet startups, can all win in the new competitive arena. However, you have to grasp the essential logic of smart business and understand the strategic implications of the new business world. The chapters in part 2 lay out the principles and practices companies need to become smart businesses.

CHAPTER 4

AUTOMATING DECISIONS

How to Strategically Leverage Machine Learning

Coordinated networks and data intelligence upend traditional strategic thinking at every level, but nowhere is this shift more dramatic than in how business decisions are made. Smart businesses automate every decision possible. Data intelligence makes such decisions continually smarter—both in terms of responding to consumers and to efficiently coordinate the network. With data intelligence and coordinated networks, businesses can simultaneously scale and customize. This is the ultimate business advantage brought on by the internet and AI.

The Five Steps for Automating Decisions

At the most fundamental level, to transform any business into a smart one, business decisions must be made directly by machines (fueled by live data), not by humans supported by data analysis, the traditional business-intelligence approach. This, then, is the first strategic principle: You cannot compete as a smart business without

TABLE 4-1

The five steps for automating decisions

Step	Key action
Datafy the physical world	Put capabilities and assets online
Software the business	Encode decision-making chains
Get data flowing	Institute application programming interfaces (APIs) to allow data connections
Record data in full	Record "live data" in its entirety
Apply machine-learning algorithms	Coordinate and optimize

first automating almost all your business decisions through machine learning. Five steps are required to achieve this level of automation (table 4-1).

Automation Step 1: Datafy the Physical World

I have discussed datafication in the previous chapter. The convergence of cheap and widespread computing power with the explosion of technologies and opportunities for encoding data has meant that businesses have more data at their disposal. However, the data any company needs will be particular to its own situation. Businesses can access public data or lease data owned by another entity, but the most valuable digital information is the live data naturally created through the business processes.

Translating the physical environment into a digital setting is daunting, but new technologies such as the IoT are emerging to make it easier. Only after a company can complete this digital translation can it effectively datafy its business activities as they take place in the physical world. This datafication is what I mean, in part, by a business's *going online*. It creates a digital counterpart for the physical business and is a precondition for leveraging the power of data intelligence.

When the business is online, it can connect through the internet and create a live-data feedback loop, which is the basis of machine learning. In this way algorithms link up to real time user response. The smart internet companies today are built on the fact that consumer behavior online can be recorded at low cost and in real time. Even today, broadcasting companies have been unable to record the behavior of someone watching TV, and that is why these companies have yet to become smart. If what consumers see can be digitalized directly, for example, through an augmented-reality glass, the results would be revolutionary.

Important aspects of many businesses are not currently recorded online and will require innovative datafication of physical objects or environments. Let's look at the simple example of the booming bike-rental business in China.

The datafication of shared-bike services in China

By mid-2016, the streets of major cities in China played host to a new and colorful addition to the country's raucous streetscapes. Teeming masses of bright, shiny shared bicycles—color-coded by company in shades of orange, blue, green, and yellow—created a veritable rainbow of new mobility solutions in urban China. With hopes of mobilizing pedestrians and unclogging transportation bottlenecks, a dozen-plus companies got their bikes on the pavement almost overnight. Valuations for firms like Mobike, Ofo, HelloBike, and BlueGogo skyrocketed; the largest firms are now valued at more than US$2 billion and expanding worldwide.[1]

Indeed, it can seem like a plague of colorful bicycles on streets, as well as the small armies of laborers and trucks tasked with transporting the transport—moving swaths of idle bicycles to other areas of the city where demand is higher. Low entry barriers, exemplary manufacturing capabilities, ample venture capital, and rapidly expanding cities struggling to offer affordable transportation solutions have all contributed to China's bike-sharing craze. Yet a less apparent but more critical cause of China's bike-sharing mania is the innovation and creative datafication involved in making these bikes a pervasive reality. Live data has been baked into the operating model of these bike-sharing companies.

China's bike-sharing services work from a mobile phone, similar to Uber's solution for cars. By opening the bike-sharing app, a rider can see available bicycles and reserve one nearby. Once the rider arrives at the bicycle, he or she uses the application to scan a QR code on the bicycle. Assuming that the person has money in his or her account and meets the rental criteria, the QR code unlocks the bicycle's electronic lock, after which the rider can pedal off into the sunset or to whatever the day has in store. Parking the bike and closing the lock concludes the service, and the rental charge is automatically debited from the rider's account. The process is simple, intuitive, and often only takes several seconds.

In this fairly straightforward process, datafication has already occurred at several junctures:

1. First, the GPS systems embedded in mobile phones and the bikes themselves allow complete tracking of the bikes in real time. Much like Uber, this real-time tracking could only occur if it was supported by mapping technology, which has already creatively datafied the physical landscape of Chinese cities.

2. Second, the application itself relies on a datafied version of the registration process for rentals and especially for screening users. Besides the regular authentication requirements such as an uploaded copy of the rider's ID and a deposit, more and more bike-sharing companies are integrating with Alipay and Sesame Credit, Ant Financial's online product for consumer credit ratings. If a user's Sesame Credit score is high enough, he or she can rent bicycles without submitting any separate ID. Sesame Credit itself is a complex business that attempts to datafy trustworthiness. It uses financial data from Ant Financial's Alipay mobile wallet and payment services, as well as associated buying data from Taobao.

3. Third, the combination of QR codes and electronic locks has cleverly automated the checkout process. Whereas stationary bike-rental services would require physical authentication, often accomplished by swiping a public transportation card, new bike-sharing models have digitalized the check-in and checkout processes to make them automatic. This level of

automation requires sophisticated mobile communications technology: a signal from the app can instantaneously unlock the bike, as well as lock it again when the bike is returned.

Innovation in this third area, more datafication of a particular physical activity (bike check-in and checkout), is a new innovation in the bike-sharing scene and an important driver of its growth. The other two examples utilize existing datafication and smart-business infrastructures that have been created for other applications. Live data enables the company to identify the person, track every bike, and, most importantly, record every interaction between the bike and rider. Renting a bike is as quick as a swipe on your phone. By incorporating the datafication done by others with their own innovation, these bike-share companies have become efficient, smart businesses. As demonstrated here, the datafication of any given area often opens up many new avenues for smart-business creation. Smart businesses are only growing in number, as data-recording and data-storage technologies are increasingly cheap and as new technologies for collecting and encoding phenomena in the physical world develop.

Creative datafication in the early days of Taobao

Another good example of datafication is the enormous amount of creative encoding of retail activities that occurred during the early years of Taobao's growth. The platform gradually expanded from a forum to an e-commerce marketplace that would sell anything under the sun, thanks to a database that could encode product information across industries for hundreds of millions of SKUs in a searchable form. However, this evolution was neither quick nor easy. Every seller had his or her own way of describing products. And the challenge became worse with unstandardized or unconventional products. A Taobao seller once became headline news when he sold a batch of dead mosquitoes at almost US$1 apiece. How do you put these products into your database and help consumers find them? Not a simple task. So datafication of products has always been at the core of Taobao, and it has evolved through many iterations. The most recent attempts build knowledge graphs of products using the cutting-edge technology of machine intelligence.

Taobao had to datafy the retail industry in many ways, some of them hidden from most users. For example, Taobao has become one of the largest repositories for physical addresses in the world, thanks to its enormous number of transactions. How to store and manage these many addresses across my enormous country has been challenging for the platform. It also creates headaches for logistics partners. For example, "The Forbidden City," "The Palace Museum," "4 Jingshan Front Street," and "Across the Street from Tiananmen Square" all refer to the same place in Beijing.

The consumer logistics industry in China, in fact, did not really exist before Alibaba. Previously, the country's only large-scale logistics service was state run and far from efficient. The Taobao e-commerce platform helped jump-start the growth of a dozen logistics companies operating across China, many of whom now partner with Alibaba's affiliated delivery platform, the Cainiao Network. Every standard within the logistics industry had to be created from scratch to fit the complex geography of China. (For more information on Taobao's contribution to China's consumer logistics industry, see appendix B.) Now, the Cainiao Network's challenge is to apply data intelligence to the rapidly datafying logistics industry in China and create a globally optimized, coordinated network of shipping across the country and even across the world.

Automation Step 2: "Software" Every Activity of Your Business

Next, every decision step has to be *softwared*, that is, configured into software and operated online. In 2011, Netscape founder Marc Andreessen penned a famous essay titled "Why Software Is Eating the World."[2] His observation was premature but not wrong. For smart business to run, every activity of the business must be softwared. Firms must capture every business activity, not just knowledge management and customer relations, in digital form so that decisions affecting the activities can be automated.[3]

The point of softwaring business is to exploit certain characteristics of software that are highly beneficial to businesses in all industries. Businesses in nondigital industries operate very differently from those working with software. Traditional—or hardware—businesses have strong inertia, high transaction costs, and can rarely be monitored cheaply or adjusted on the fly. Decisions take time, especially when manufacturing is involved, and firm operations are inelastic. Software is the opposite: engineers can implement changes quickly and cheaply, adjust dynamically, and optimize globally. Though these advantages are not perfectly transferrable to the hardware world, the goal in softwaring business is to implant these qualities to the greatest degree possible. In practice, this means that computers need to understand and be able to operate the business as a human would.

Softwaring is not a straightforward process. Because machines lack innate intelligence, we have to software every step in the decision-making chain. In essence, we need to understand how humans make decisions in all these settings. Then, smart businesses have to find ways to automate human decision making. Automating such a complex activity is a formidable task, as many human decisions are built on common sense or even subconscious neurological activity that is seldom completely understood. For this reason, some professions or industries such as health and education may be slower to automate. In many arenas, human input will always be indispensable.

Softwaring does not mean that a firm needs to buy or build software to manage its business (e.g., enterprise resource planning [ERP] software). Indeed, it is often the complete opposite. Traditional software is designed to optimize the efficiency of a restricted and finite functional area within a business. But because it solidifies processes and decision flows, traditional software often becomes a straitjacket. In contrast, a smart business's main prerogatives are to act on demand, to react in real time to changes in the market, and to coordinate effectively with partners and clients across many functional areas. These prerogatives are all required if a business wants to scale exponentially. Softwaring a business, then, is the process of retooling a business, its people, and its resources using software, so that it can best achieve network coordination and data intelligence. Such an achievement ultimately requires coordinating business activity end-to-end, and often between the firm and other partners or platforms.

Softwaring is an essential step in making sure that resources within the business can be allocated elastically. Once assets or capabilities in the physical world have gone online through datafication, the processes that utilize them must be engaged through software. Using software is a precondition for globally coordinating and maximizing business operations, as I will describe in the remaining three steps.

The new bike-sharing business just discussed is an example of softwaring. Bike rentals are operated completely by software online, with no human intervention. The efficiency gain is tremendous: Chinese users can now rent a bike for an hour for just a few pennies.

Automation Step 3: Get Data Flowing, and Introduce Application Programming Interfaces (APIs)

In smart businesses, machines have to be able to "talk" to each other. Business decisions are rarely simple actions occurring in isolation, especially when network coordination is important. Practically, this communication requires having data flow between everyone connected to the work and having machines coordinate with each other online.

This coordination is achieved through communication standards, such as TCP/IP (the rules that enable communication between different machines all across the internet), and through the relatively recent innovation of application programming interfaces (APIs). APIs are a set of tools, protocols, and routines that any programmer can use to create a software tool that interacts smoothly with other software in the system. APIs, in effect, allow applications (the output of which is usually a certain kind of decision) to communicate with one another. When applications can communicate automatically, a complicated business decision that involves many parties can finally be processed effectively by machines. Only after a firm can automate its decision making online can it implement data intelligence and reap the benefits of the continual improvement of this core capability.

As Taobao grew from a buyers' and sellers' forum to China's dominant e-commerce website, not only did merchants grow—so did their requests for aid. The only solution was to create more infrastructure.

Essential to this infrastructure was the ability to translate language from other machines so they could all interact smoothly on the platform. Hence, beginning in 2009, Taobao began to develop its APIs. On Taobao, the average seller might subscribe to more than a hundred software modules offered through the platform. But since the software was developed by third-party providers, the API and the live data services it enables drastically decrease the cost of doing business.

A similarly important move in Amazon's history was Jeff Bezos's 2002 ultimatum to completely institute internal APIs within the company. Every time a department shared data or code with another department, the interaction had to be recorded, forcing every department to define its data in a way that could be understood and used by other teams and their machines. Ultimately, these APIs ensured that Amazon's business could be managed and optimized in a globally efficient fashion.[4]

Automation Step 4: Record Data in Full (Live Data)

Once every step of the business process has been datafied, put online, and intelligibly connected, a company can start applying machine learning to business problems. However, machine learning is meaningless without data to work on. That's why step 4 is recording live data, which I define as data collected and used in real time in the course of doing business.

The concept behind live data is not difficult, but translating that understanding into correct action upends many conventionalities that businesspeople are accustomed to using to solve problems. They have learned to be data driven, to support proposals and solutions with carefully selected data and metrics. Unfortunately, this approach is the exact opposite of how live data works. Smart businesses use live data to "copy" the entire workings of a business setting into the language of data, not picking and choosing. Since machines do not have a theory of cause and effect and only note what produces better results, the goal is to create as complete a digital copy of the business as possible, so that data intelligence can begin to optimize operations. Thus, companies must record data in full as the business operates; they cannot limit the data collection to what seems relevant to only one decision.

In the current operating environment, live data is a crucial competitive advantage, not merely a nice thing to have. The opposite of live data is static data stored for analysis at a later date. Though this kind of data remains useful, data that is old loses value very quickly in a fast-moving environment. (Imagine if Google Maps gave you directions based on where you were standing ten days ago or what the traffic was doing hours ago during rush hour.) Without access to fresh and plentiful data, even the most cutting-edge algorithms are of little value for companies. Both strategically and tactically, I cannot overstate the importance of harnessing live data to improve the functioning of your business.

Working with live data involves a lot of hard and complex work. I have described challenges associated with datafication above, but mostly ignored the complicated technical challenge to use data organically. Live data also requires metrics and infrastructure that can interpret and evaluate the data, and smart businesses must develop these metrics and this infrastructure in the algorithms they use and their data-intelligence engines. The conclusions drawn from live data ideally emerge from the data itself through a dynamic process of testing and adjustment, for example, through A/B testing presented in the previous chapter.

Automation Step 5: Apply Machine-Learning Algorithms

Live data is constantly churning and updating. As machine-learning algorithms process live data, they improve and the business grows more and more efficient. Clearly, then, machine-learning algorithms are critical to automating business decisions.

At the heart of a smart business are algorithms. Uber's algorithm matches car and driver, minimizing wait times and making mapping calculations in a way that would challenge any human dispatcher. The company has hired thousands of data scientists to make its algorithms more effective. If your business is not powered by an algorithm, you simply don't have a smart business.

One of the most important milestones in Taobao's transformation to become a smart business was the replacement of its indexing engine to a search engine. Buyers initially browsed categories on Taobao to find the products they wanted. However, with product listings multiplying almost daily, more and more people started to use the search bar to find products. It was clear that upgrading the search experience was a crucial way to create value for both buyers and sellers.

The key question for search is how to rank. Initially, Taobao search rankings were primarily based on SKU lifespan. When sellers upload a product, they could set how many days a particular product would remain on the website, for example, seven or fourteen days. Thus, ranking by lifespan meant that products that were about to expire from the website would be displayed at the top of the search results. Such a rule was simple and straightforward in the early days, when most sellers worked part-time and rarely competed directly. Unfortunately, this format only incentivized sellers to repeatedly post products over again, providing little helpful information to buyers.

In 2006, Taobao changed its method of search rankings to one based on popularity. Products were displayed according to core metrics like transaction volume and reputation scores. The logic behind popularity search is that products that sold well and were highly rated by users were good-quality products and should be rewarded with higher placement. In turn, this method should help buyers find good products and would separate the wheat from the chaff. Indeed, popularity search ushered in a wave of immense growth among Taobao's early sellers.

But ranking by popularity had serious philosophical problems. Though such a search method seems logical at first blush, in practice it was far too simplistic for the already-complex marketplace. Under such rules, products that sold well became even more successful, while new sellers found it difficult to gain exposure. As a method for ensuring the healthy, balanced development of an ecosystem, where large and small sellers could simultaneously grow, popularity search was seriously inadequate. So starting in 2008, Taobao began to continuously upgrade its rules for popularity search. Sellers worked hard to accumulate a reputation in the specific manner that improved search rankings, and many sellers quickly grew by using search traffic to their advantage.

The popularity search was not driven by machine learning, however. It simply worked by aggregating seller statistics, equivalent to large-scale counting. Consequently, large sellers that had the resources to build scale quickly grew even faster, thanks to optimal placement. Meanwhile, small and medium-sized sellers starved for volume. The heart of this problem is that pure counting is not sufficiently intelligent. It is simply a more efficient method of human tactics to solve problems. Real data intelligence needs machine methods, not a faster version of the human brain.

Using machine learning, Taobao launched its first truly large-scale search product, called Archimedes, in 2010. From a technical perspective, Archimedes was an enormous improvement on popularity search. In addition to traditional benchmarks such as conversion rates, average customer spend, and transaction value, Archimedes added a slew of metrics connected to seller service levels. Taobao collects an enormous amount of data besides the purely transactional. For example, it looks at whether products are returned by the buyer, when buyers and sellers enter disputes that need to be resolved by the platform, when buyers have complaints about sellers, and whether a seller has a good credit rating. When buyers look for products, they are also searching for trustworthy sellers and good service. It was logical to consider these previously ignored metrics, but how to unravel which metrics improve the search results, and to what degree?

Over years of improving search functionality and technology, Alibaba began to implement a new form of machine learning. In *reinforcement learning*, the machine starts with an end goal ("find the products that lead to buyers making the most transactions") and then does its best to connect the dots in a way that leads to that goal. Data engineers program search algorithms to work by conducting innumerable online experiments—the A/B tests discussed before—using simultaneous tests of different variables and monitoring the feedback to tease out consumer preferences. If the engine shows these products at the customers' query, do the customers click? Do they buy? Do they end up returning the product? The result is a very complicated but powerful online apparatus of algorithms continually churning in the background, returning results that are more and more tailored to the system as a whole.

In the years after the introduction of Archimedes, search volume began to be distributed in a healthier way, accruing not only to the largest sellers, but also to many smaller sellers with quality products and good service. Volume started being siphoned away from sellers with less than desirable service or business behaviors. Overall, buyers found it easier to find better products, and business improved. As the years passed, search results accounted for more and more traffic to merchants, gradually surpassing the traffic created from regular category browsing. The search engine greatly improved the entire structure and dynamics of the marketplace through its algorithms. However, the long process of change also illustrates the challenges in implementing automated decision making.

Taobao's Mobile Recommendations: The Five Automation Steps in Action

Singles Day 2016 was the "year of genesis" for Alibaba's mobile recommendation engine. In twenty-four hours, the platform made trillions of smart matches between consumers and items, using machine learning to generate nearly a hundred billion customized product displays. Personalized recommendations were updated every hour as users browsed sales and special offers. The recommendation engine drove sales, ensured a variety of offerings for users, and increased conversions. Most of all, it operated with minimal management from employees. It was a triumph of smart business, repeated in 2017.

Taobao has prided itself on creating individualized stores, even individualized malls for its diverse users. But when your entire mall is the size of a smartphone screen, you have to get creative. The story behind Taobao's implementation of a mobile recommendation engine demonstrates how employing data intelligence requires clear, holistic, and nonconformist thinking about your business.

In the internet industry, we talk about all facets of the user experience through a product lens. Every one of the Taobao apps's hundreds of millions of users access the same application on their phones, but each user browses a completely different selection of services and content. From the banner ads at the top of the app to the articles on industries and services in Taobao Headlines, to user product reviews or live-stream channels and algorithm-curated product recommendations, the Taobao app is personalized down to the user.

Numerous sections of the Taobao app now use recommendation technology, but this was not always the case. In late 2013, Alibaba completely retooled its entire e-commerce marketplaces for the smartphone. Initially, the content and structure were copied from the web-based marketplace. The main gateways for the average consumer into Taobao had been the category lists (e.g., men's apparel, food and beverage, or mother and baby); the search bar (e.g., "Longjing green tea harvested before the spring rains" or "black leggings"); or specialized events and sales curated by category teams at Taobao or Tmall. The ample real estate of a browser window gave consumers the latitude to explore. For many young people in China, wandering (in Chinese, *guang*) through the vast panoply of rarities on Taobao became a common way to while away an afternoon.

Yet this approach no longer worked in a mobile world. Users rarely had long stretches of time to shop. Screens were smaller and had less room to display information. Users began to rely more on the search bar, but even when they searched for uncommon keywords, only a few listings could fit on the small screen. This limited space for sellers to reach consumers meant possibly negative outcomes for smaller and niche merchants. The mobile environment, if designed ineffectively, might starve both consumers and merchants alike. We needed a new approach to discovery.

The answer was not intuitive. In the Taobao organizational universe, product recommendations were managed by different engineering teams, depending on their location within the app. A recommendation on the front page of the app—Alibaba's most expensive online real estate, for which changes needed approval by upper management—was managed by a different team than were the recommendations at the bottom of individual product pages or the recommendations that appeared after a transaction had completed, for example. Consumers who viewed these different recommendations might see quite dissimilar products. And their feedback on these products delivered through browsing data, such as buying or ignoring, was largely irrelevant to recommendation products managed by different teams. Different teams managing separate products made sense in a desktop setting, where each of these separate business settings required supporting different groups of sellers and consumers. But in a mobile world, even objectively discrete business problems needed coordination for an effective solution.

People outside the industry are accustomed to thinking of mobile as an app on the phone. But, in actuality, *mobile* refers to a whole series of organizational and technological structures, including ways to collect, use, and evaluate data. Without a mindset of smart business and the five automation steps enumerated above, you can't make all these pieces work together to unlock the power of data intelligence.

At Taobao, we moved quickly to consolidate the various recommendation teams under the search department, because it had the best technical tools and infrastructure for ensuring synergies across disparate recommendation products. We had recently acquired new international technical talent, so we assigned several people to develop the algorithms and knit together the complex engineering needed to make large-scale, real-time calculations. All the data flows and their interfaces and metrics had to be coordinated with the new algorithms. Our product and industry teams had to reconceptualize the many rules and mechanisms affected by the expanded recommendation activity across the marketplace. Recommendations after a customer ordered a book communicated with the algorithms that made recommendations after a customer loaded a new app or after a customer searched for and did not buy a piece of clothing. The results were noticeable. Sales and transaction volume began to steadily increase for users that used the recommendation products.

The key message is that applying data intelligence is not merely a question of expanding the budgets of engineering teams. It requires clear and comprehensive thinking across the business using these five steps. Our changes to mobile recommendations illustrate each of these steps. To reconsider where recommendation solutions should be applied, we needed (1) new forms of datafication and (2) softwaring. The recommendations had to influence each other so the engines could (3) "talk" among themselves. Finally, we needed (4) a live-data mindset so that all the behavior of all the consumers was recorded in the same place and fed into the same (5) machine-learning algorithms.

Smart Business Enabled

In part 1 of the book, I introduced the concept of a smart business. From this chapter, you should now recognize that the complex coordination of smart business requires thinking about data in a new way. Your understanding of business-process activity determines how it becomes data, which in turn determines the products and services that can be created to solve the business problem. To automate these decisions about products and services, a smart business follows the five steps outlined in this chapter. First, creative datafication enriches the pool of relevant data on which the business can become smarter. Next, softwaring the business puts workflows and essential actors online. Third, APIs enable real-time coordination. Fourth, recording data in full and, fifth, applying machine learning to the resulting rich live-data feed, finally arrives at data intelligence.

The past two chapters have focused on data intelligence, its applications to business, and the proper strategy for implementing this new capability. Readers should also understand that besides enabling data intelligence, the five steps illustrated in this chapter are also the foundations of network coordination. By now, you should see clearly why I call network coordination and data intelligence the double helix of the DNA of smart business. They work in tandem. In keeping with my framework of the double helix, it is now time to turn to the strategic implications of network coordination, exploring how firms must relate to consumers and to their partners.

CHAPTER 5

THE CUSTOMER-TO-BUSINESS MODEL

How to Build a Feedback Loop

To use data intelligence and operate as a smart business, you need a tight digital feedback loop between your firm and the customer. However, as pioneering firms have realized and I have witnessed up close with many Chinese entrepreneurs, centering your business around direct interaction with your customers sets into motion a striking reorientation of all business activities. I call this change the customer-to-business (C2B) model. The C2B mindset turns the traditional business-to-consumer (B2C) concept of business on its head in profound ways.[1]

When business decisions are driven by machine learning through feedback loops, the firm's actions can finally be dictated by the customer. "Customer first" is no longer just a slogan, but the starting point of the business operation. The entire customer experience should operate on demand. But for the experience, including the products and services themselves, to be truly dictated by the customer, the company and the network in which it operates must be agile and responsive. In practice, every function in the business must work on demand.

Making any one function of the business operate on demand is difficult. How do you economically prepare for the potential span of demand? But when a firm starts retooling any given activity, it has to subsequently retool every aspect of its operations, from branding to product design to manufacturing. Only once processes are functionally independent but smoothly and automatically integrated, firms can then create products and services in concert with users, with key production and design decisions informed by this interaction. In doing so, the entire firm's operating model runs on network coordination and data intelligence.

Completely retooling one's entire business and making all functions coordinate dynamically is a daunting prospect for any company. Nevertheless, a C2B company has immense competitive advantage. Those who manage to start down this difficult path will find that their efficiency and responsiveness begin to increase exponentially, while cost does not.

I cannot give readers an action plan for how to reorganize each of their firms, as the process differs greatly from industry to industry and even from firm to firm. But in using an extended example from the apparel industry, I hope to give readers an idea of what they need to do and what the correct C2B mindset looks like. I'll use as an example Big-E, China's most successful web celebrity, who employs platform capabilities to execute C2B strategies. Big-E is the nickname for Zhang Dayi, a former model with no previous retail experience. Her online-only clothing brand did an amazing 1 billion RMB (over US$150 million) in 2017.

The Power of Brands Built Online

Think about social media influencers. In the United States, an example might be Kim Kardashian or Chiara Ferragni. Do such influencers represent the future of brand building and entrepreneurship? In China, I think they do.

Some people conceive of web celebs as canny but opportunistic entrepreneurs—China's latest flash in the pan. But this notion misses the surprisingly robust business model that gives web celebs unprecedented agility within the apparel industry. Big-E did US$35 million in sales on Singles Day 2017. Ruhan, the company that runs her brand as well as dozens of other web-celeb brands, employs only eight hundred people and has only been working with web celebs since mid-2014. How does such a small company manage so many colossal brands? The answer is C2B. Big-E's business model comprises on-demand marketing, on-demand operations, and on-demand production, coordinated by Ruhan's software stack, dubbed Layercake. (See the sidebar "Ruhan and Big-E (Who's Who).")

To her social media fans, Big-E is the young woman who everyone wants to be. She spends her time flying around the world, taking pictures, and buying clothes. She appears to live and breathe on Weibo. Big-E shares updates from her life, posts new clothes, and replies to fans at a nearly constant stream. Like Zhang Linchao from this book's introduction, she makes millions of dollars a year taking selfies and chatting online. But Big-E has taken it further than Zhang and just about every other competitor, making every aspect of her business reflect a C2B mindset. That innovation is why she is China's most successful web celeb.

Big-E's social media account is not just for fun, although she and her fans clearly have a lot of that. It is an integral part of a very serious business whose core value proposition is consumer interaction with the celeb. Big-E showcases a dozen new designs every two or three weeks on her Weibo account. They are then snatched up by her rabid fan base in flash sales on Taobao. These flash sales always oversell. Immediately before and during these sales, Ruhan gives notice of sales volume to its manufacturing partners, which begin producing the amount of clothes demanded by the consumers. These clothes ship within days, and because they are produced on demand, there is rarely significant spare inventory. Big-E's C2B brand is agile, powerful, and immensely profitable.

The first step of her on-demand model is on-demand marketing, which Big-E mostly accomplishes through social media previews and associated flash sales. This activity on Weibo constitutes an interactive experience for the consumer. As fans interact with the celeb, their actions jump-start a feedback loop that informs the web celeb's decisions on design and production.

RUHAN AND BIG-E (WHO'S WHO)

Ruhan is one of China's largest web-celeb incubators and the first web-celeb-related company that Alibaba invested in. The company has been valued at over 3 billion RMB (almost US$500 million). Ruhan has operated in China's e-commerce space for a decade and has successfully incubated more than a hundred key opinion leaders from China and across the rest of Asia. Ruhan's signed opinion leaders together reach two hundred million social media fans, 90 percent of whom are young women between eighteen and twenty-eight, the vast majority hailing from first- and second-tier cities in China. The company's incubation services include social media marketing, content production, e-commerce operations (including analytics and advertising), and end-to-end manufacturing management.

Because of her status as the undisputed queen of Chinese social commerce, Big-E's success on Taobao and Weibo heralded the rise of the web celebs across the country. I call the model turned web-celeb pioneer Zhang Dayi "Big-E," as that is the easiest version of her many nicknames to translate into English. She and her fans never use the actual English equivalent of her name, which is Eve. Instead, she and her community use funny names based on the word *da*, big, and the sound *yi* taken from her first name such as

Brands Constructed by Fans

A web celeb's brand is not a static message pushed to customers. Such an approach would reflect a more traditional B2C mindset, where social media is merely a megaphone for broadcasting marketing copy. Instead, the brand is constructed together with the celebs' die-hard group of fans; it is created for and by the consumer.

Big-E's marketing presence is a curated set of images on social media with exactly the right human touch. What to write, which pictures to post, what filters to put on their selfies . . . everything needs to reek of a genuine human behind the screen. In practice, the most successful celebs are immersed in the curation themselves. What makes a celeb a celeb is her ability to express herself distinctively *dayima*, which phonetically sounds like "Big Momma E" and literally means "oldest aunt," a common Chinese euphemism for menstruation. In fact, her fans refer to themselves as "E-cups," clearly an exaggeration and an in-group joke that, like the funny pet names, illuminates the tight connection Big-E and her community have among themselves. Big-E had studied fashion in college and began her career as a model at *Ray Li*, one of China's top fashion magazines. But she had bigger dreams, and she opened an online apparel store on Taobao in 2014, when Ruhan began working with her. At the time, Big-E had two hundred thousand fans on Weibo; now, thanks to Ruhan's involvement, she boasts five million-plus.

On May 20, 2015, the first anniversary of her store's opening, she sold more than 10 million RMB (US$1.5 million) worth of product. During Singles Day 2017, she sold 100 million RMB ($US15 million) *in the first half hour of the sale.* According to BBC, Big-E reportedly earned 300 million RMB (US$46 million) in 2015, a number that compares favorably to the yearly take of China's top actress Fan Bingbing, US$21 million.*

*Grace Tsoi, "Wang Hong: China's Online Stars Making Real Cash," *BBC News*, July 31, 2016, www.bbc.com/news/world-asia-china-36802769.

and originally—from the style of her selfies to the clothing she wears in offhand pictures to her jokes about herself. This style cannot be imitated: even the largest web celebs often still edit their selfies themselves.

In the words of Nicole Shen, the brand manager for Big-E, "when you look up at a celebrity, your head is inclined sixty degrees. Web celebs are fifteen degrees up, you can see and even touch them. They will get on social media and argue with you about whether an outfit looks good or not. She's somebody you see in your friends list."[2] Social media for web celebs is not a grandstand. It is an open-ended venue for interaction. Anybody can enter, listen in, and take part in the chatter. They can ask whatever they want of the celeb.

In a web celeb's Weibo account, you will see a ceaseless stream of life updates, travelogues, snapshots of clothing, and embarrassing selfies. Under most posts lie hundreds if not thousands of replies that range from adoration to complaints to personal questions. The celeb will reply to comments as she sees fit. Though marketing teams sometimes write copy for social media posts, top celebs never let others compose replies. It is through this back-and-forth that the brand emerges—not through discussions in the meeting rooms of advertising agencies.

The gradual aggregation of comments and discussion, of information about consumer beliefs and preferences, becomes the brand. This valuable content was previously only indirectly accessible to brands through market research; now it is created constantly in real time and recorded online in social platforms. This is branding in a C2B world, a process of cocreation and coevolution—a process that consumers enjoy.

Products Chosen by Consumers: On-Demand Product Development and On-Demand Manufacturing

Big-E the entrepreneur is not nearly as fancy-free as her pictures might suggest. Every pose in every outfit on every street corner the world over requires that the outfit in question be ready for shipping within one or two weeks of said photo appearing online. Especially given the fierce competition in the web-celeb space, there is simply not enough time to engage in month-long cycles of product development, as is common practice in the apparel industry. How do web celebs get the right clothes to market just in time?

Consumer interaction is the lifeblood of not only the web-celeb brand but also product development. In the world of social commerce, consumer interaction creates content, which creates the brand, which drives sales. The genius of the web-celeb model is that consumers' voices are heard long before the sale occurs. From the first moment that clothes appear online, days or weeks before they go on sale, consumer reactions already begin to inform production decisions. Even during the brand's flash sales, consumer action is recorded and visible in the form of purchases measurable through Taobao's data dashboards. These actions are crucial inputs for the web celeb's manufacturing processes. Thus, through the flash sale, the web celeb's on-demand marketing coordinates with on-demand product development and manufacturing.

The flash-sale marketing tactics that web celebs use to great success have a special place in the Chinese retail world and are often paired with starvation marketing (*ji'e yingxiao*, described in chapter 2). Using this common practice in Chinese e-commerce, companies will intentionally restrict inventory numbers to artificially stir up the consumer's sense of urgency to buy. In a country not too far removed from real consumer deprivation, starvation marketing is very effective. It also comes with the added bonus of testing the market's reaction to a particular product and, consequently, avoiding excess inventory.

Using Taobao's flash-sale services, an online infrastructure that enables a seller to easily schedule a sale at a specified time, a merchant can announce an upcoming sale and the time when products go live. Often, merchants preview the products that will be on offer, as well as the prices and quantities available. These sales are normally first come, first served, and feature extremely limited quantities to maximize the starvation effect.

Web celebs innovated on this basic model by expanding the preview process. They regularly use previews as an exploratory tactic to determine merchandising choices and price points. A week or two before a sale, the web celeb will begin to post previews of an upcoming sale on her Weibo account. In some cases, these previews look like regular content, such as a shot of a celeb at dinner wearing a new sweater. In other cases, the celebrity will explicitly release a set of pictures depicting several new items. The purpose of these images is to gauge interest. As soon as these images go live, fans will immediately start to discuss the items on display, debating between different styles, colors, and cuts.

All the interaction generated by fans is meticulously scrutinized by Ruhan's product, procurement, and sales teams. The metrics the team looks at (primarily the volume of sharing and comments across the social media platform) directly influence product selection, the manufacturing schedule, and even future design processes. For example, if a certain color of a certain SKU is discussed more than expected, the celeb will often decide to produce a larger first batch of the product in that color or secure access to a larger volume of similar fabric. If fans ignore or dismiss an SKU, it may be dropped from the sale, and similar designs eliminated from future development.

By skillfully executing flash sales every few weeks, web celebs increase engagement and loyalty, gather precious insight about customers, and dynamically tweak manufacturing schedules. Even once the sale begins, interaction continues. The lucky fans who managed to snag their favorite items will boast of their pickings, while their unlucky friends will gripe. The content from both crowing and complaining customers provides essential information for which SKUs to replenish and in what quantities. Celebs can even conduct private presales to select VIP groups. These sales bolster customer loyalty and provide valuable information about product popularity. Once the clothes arrive at each fan's doorstep, the person will start posting selfies in the new outfits, experimenting with clothing pairings and showing off in front of onlookers. On Taobao, these pictures are called *maijia xiu*, or "buyer shows." Some web celebs will reward buyers who post the best pictures by reposting them to their own Weibo pages. Seizing any opportunity to promote interaction is good business.

How On-Demand Marketing Makes On-Demand Firms

Keen-eyed readers will notice that the function of the web celeb's marketing channel has expanded from that of traditional apparel businesses. The channel is not just a one-way conduit to customers; it fosters interaction and obtains key information about how to make effective business decisions across the value chain. On-demand marketing necessitates an on-demand supply chain. Otherwise, the results could be disastrous. Consumers would wait considerably longer for their items and complain vociferously on social media, destroying trust and the brand image. To avoid such a downward spiral, the supply chain must cope with the stringent requirements of web-celeb flash sales: clothes made in three to seven days, in small quantities, at low marginal cost, and with exemplary quality.

Smart businesses intelligently and flexibly integrate the supply chain with all other constituents of the value network, including marketing and design functions. Network coordination and data intelligence provide such smart integration. As a recent report by the consultancy KPMG explains, "operating in today's omni business environment requires a supply chain fit for purpose. The optimal structure is fully integrated with the front end of the business and possesses the flexibility and agility to react to constant change in customer needs."[3] China's web celebs have fashioned a business model where front-end and back-end operations are deeply interwoven.

The web-celeb production schedule is clearly distinct from most fashion and retail companies that plan months in advance. Even fast-fashion global heavyweights take at least two or three months to fully produce one lot of clothes. But web celebs are mercurial by nature. They might see an inspiring motif or silhouette while wandering through Parisian boutiques or the streets of Tokyo, and with a tap on a touch screen, they snap a picture and post it to social media. The design team might only have weeks or even days to produce a finished product before the item is meant to go on sale. The sheer time pressure, to say nothing of the quality or workmanship, would strain a traditional supply chain to its limits.

For context, traditional clothing manufacturing can be split into four stages: patterning, cutting, sewing, and finishing. For items of regular complexity, the average Chinese factory can accomplish all four tasks in twenty days at the low end or sixty business days at the higher end. Of this total time, two weeks is spent on patterning alone. If the manufacturer's client accepts the sample based on that pattern, production at scale can begin (cutting and sewing), followed by quality inspections, ironing, and packaging (finishing). This timeline assumes a ready stock of fabric, but purchasing or even producing customized fabric can add weeks if not months to these times. These industry-standard time frames have largely determined how the large brands worldwide structure their business cycles.

Big-E's Fast Restocking Model: The Value of C2B

Big-E's brand image and profitability depend on Ruhan's fast restocking practices. Two counteracting forces have long created huge headaches for traditional industries, especially apparel. Produce too much, and you run the risk of bearing huge inventory costs. Produce too little, and you lose the opportunity to make sales when you have a hit product.

It is precisely here that Ruhan's C2B model has a huge advantage. Most production for web celebs starts when orders are placed. After the first batch sells out (this could occur in seconds or minutes during a flash sale), fast restocking begins. Comparing consumer response with expected sales (estimated from social media activity during the preview period), Ruhan immediately places the order for the second batch. If demand is high, Ruhan could restock several times. Quite often, the restocked order is larger than the initial order. This practice reduces the burden and risk of prediction. Although fast restocking was originally conceived as a way to keep up with volatile demand, not as a forecasting tactic, the research and constant interaction with customers have given sellers a much more precise pulse on underlying consumer demand than that used by traditional models.[4]

Obviously, for fast restocking to work, turnaround times have to be fast and reliable, usually five to seven days, including shipping and delivery. The speedy turnaround requires tight communication with factories and a healthy dose of network coordination.

Ruhan's Networked Production Model

As a full-service brand incubator, Ruhan covers back-end and certain front-end operations for brands like Big-E. But rapid client growth (to the tune of 100 percent a year) and a diversifying celeb portfolio stretched Ruhan's capacity, forcing the firm to look for nearby factories with excess capacity.

Fortunately, the company is located in northern Zhejiang Province, where, in the industrial corridor between Hangzhou and Shanghai, a substantial portion of China's clothing production occurs. The factories here run the gamut of sizes and capabilities, from the largest and most experienced, which handle manufacturing for world-class brands such as Burberry and Louis Vuitton, to the smallest of workshops that are nothing more than several sewing machines in a small room off an alleyway. It is easy to find excess capacity, but distinguishing the better facilities from the not-so-useful ones is no small matter. If worst comes to worst, a factory can meet tight time schedules in a piecemeal way, albeit with a lot of running back and forth and discarding of finished pieces that don't make the cut. But that haphazard approach to production is neither economical nor scalable.

To solve its capacity problems, Ruhan established a basic model for partnership. The firm intended to form a network of partner factories that could cope with the sharp peaks and valleys of demand inherent in the web-celeb business model. First, Ruhan modularized the standard process for clothing manufacturing by delegating different stages to different factories. Its largest partners handle the work of patterning, which can be done in several days if integrated centrally and often with high-end automation machines. Once Ruhan's design team confirms the style and workmanship of the sample, Ruhan's manufacturing software splits the pattern into a checklist of different procedures, which are sent electronically across the network of partners. Partners, as well as clients, can monitor the production process anytime. By refashioning collaboration and the division of labor, Ruhan drastically reduced production time and even cost.

In experimenting with networked production, Ruhan worked with a hundred-plus external factories, assessing their capabilities and beginning to select the best partners. All these partners operate on Ruhan's SaaS platform—i.e., software as a service, a type of software delivery in which Ruhan directly allows partners over the internet to use and access software remotely. SaaS solutions allow for direct communication and coordination at minimal cost to users. With four factories distinguishing themselves for their scale and quality, Ruhan started delegating the centralized work of patterning to them. In turn, those factories gradually began to directly coordinate the work of smaller factories and workshops, centralizing fabric cutting and leaving the sewing to the smaller partners. Fully sewn garments are now sent back to the larger factories for finishing, after which they are shipped from Ruhan's storage facilities. By the end of 2015, Ruhan had essentially perfected its model, successfully spinning off all its own productive capability into external, separate entities. Its former manufacturing department evolved into facilitators of the entire production process, not the actual labor force that makes clothes.

Coordinating the Network

Although Ruhan no longer does the actual work of cutting and sewing clothes, the facilitation of such a complex network is nothing to be sneezed at. First, Ruhan must decide how much initial stock to produce. Even before a large sale, Ruhan may keep only 10 percent of its estimated sales volume in stock. (Not every web celeb on Taobao is lucky enough to work with a partner with Ruhan's facility for production. For web celebs unable to access first-rate manufacturing capabilities, the amount of an initial batch of product and its time frame can vary depending on the celeb's tolerance for risk. Nevertheless, a web celeb rarely produces more than 50 percent of total sale volume before the flash sale begins.)

The general manufacturing process proceeds as follows. The teams in charge of a celeb's manufacturing decide on the initial batch sizes, using past sales metrics. A week before the sale, marketing previews of social media begin, and data from fan interaction leads the team to decide on the size and timing of the second batch. Three days before the sale, presales go live on Taobao, and a new set of sales and cart metrics determines the size and timing of the third and often last batch of clothes. In extreme cases of very popular items, one last production round can occur three to four days after the sale. Because of the brevity and frequency of the flash-sale model, nearly 80 percent of sales volume for most SKUs occurs on sale day. The whole process is usually completed in less than a month.

Putting All the Platforms Together: Ruhan's Layercake Software

To facilitate this complex process, Ruhan has developed its own software back end. For each order the company places, it knows exactly which production line is being used in which factory and how many workers are involved. It knows when the constituent parts need to be delivered, where they need to go, and when and where the finished products are stocked. Every step in the production process is now controlled by a software program and visible to everyone in the network.

As I pointed out in the previous chapter, softwaring a business (i.e., configuring the business's activities with software and operating them online) is an important step toward building a smart business. Ruhan has invested heavily to software the Chinese apparel industry. Its in-house Layercake software solution coordinates all the work of building a web-celeb model, from back-end manufacturing to social media to retail and sales, ensuring that web celebs get the services they need, at the right time. Finally, it makes sure that the customers get their purchases. The Layercake software, though still relatively early in its development, is a key innovation in Big-E's ability to implement C2B.

All the work that moves through the Layercake system is visible from desktop or mobile interfaces. Thus, when design teams create clothing, factories immediately know—down to the person-hour—what they must do to produce these SKUs. And when marketing teams need to supervise social media content, they know exactly how much stock is available and how long it would take to produce a new lot of clothes and ship them. Factory managers can see their related workflows, and designers can see the procurement and manufacturing associated with their designs. As long as the data is online, it is automatically transparent and accessible to every party in the business. Simultaneous information access by multiple parties is an essential feature of network coordination. Layercake is still far from real-time coordination, as people need to track the process and make sure that their task is completed, but the software system is updated in real time and can support the basic feedback loops inherent in the web-celeb business model. Even this degree of improvement is already a significant upgrade from the initial state of the apparel industry: Big-E's sales figures testify to that.

Big-E knows her business at an exceptionally microscopic level. On the mobile interface developed by Ruhan, she can see how many designs are in the pipeline; the stage of the designs; at which factory or warehouse the products are located; and at what price they will sell. Her marketing plans are available too: when the next campaign will start and what products it will feature. In essence, the whole value network is visible to her, in real time and at a granular level. The network is at her fingertips, and she can act on it on the go, from anywhere in the world.

The Layers of Layercake

Efficient on-demand operations on the front end of the firm require a big overhaul of the whole back end. Ruhan started as an apparel maker intending to do small batches with quick turnaround. But it found that it had to first become a software company and transform a very traditional industry. Currently, Layercake connects and coordinates data from four areas of Ruhan's business: social networks, trade, warehousing, and manufacturing. These four areas roughly correspond to the Weibo and Taobao platforms, and the combination of workflow management software and supply-chain management (SCM) software.

Ruhan gets social media data from Weibo, either from Weibo's own API or by crawling the social network. To support Big-E's interactions with her fans, Ruhan runs extensive data analysis. Ruhan's workflow management software tracks order information and status, which come from e-commerce platforms such as Taobao. Warehousing, too, is straightforward and integrated with Taobao's logistic platform service.

More importantly, once this trade data enters the Layercake infrastructure, it can be mapped onto social network and manufacturing data. Ruhan's SCM architecture is complicated enough that it deserves more explanation. Layercake's processes begin with design in the SCM module and, from there, proceed to procurement and manufacturing before finally creating an order. The key benefit of this coordination is that if the designers know ahead of time the impact of their designs on the fabric, patterning, and processing, they can make better decisions about their designs. For example, if they choose a fabric not on their inventory list, they know that their choice will extend the production cycle time. They will also know how long and how much a particular pattern will cost in the manufacturing stage. Having all this information available at the design stage is essential to effectively coordinate with manufacturing. It is especially helpful in controlling cost and total cycle time.

Manufacturing software continues to improve the system's efficiency by organizing information about production. This information includes standard documentation and process design, both of which are used by factories to manufacture clothes. Ruhan also adds its own information: routing, work scheduling, production capacity, and order of material usage (which materials are crucial and will affect production schedules, and which can be outsourced without creating bottlenecks). The company is working on efficiently connecting and standardizing its workflows and data so that production can proceed quickly and easily across multiple partners large and small.

The key virtue of Layercake is not simply to manage the production process in a more efficient way. Every ERP or WPS system has worked to improve operational efficiency for decades; this advantage in itself is not groundbreaking and certainly does not constitute C2B. What is new is that all of the data involved in the design and manufacturing processes are coordinated with real-time demand from consumers. As I mentioned in the previous chapter, while ERP software focuses on improving the efficiency of a narrow swath of the business, the point of softwaring and live data is to make sure that the entire business process, including (I cannot stress this enough) the consumer's activity, all flows freely across the entire coordinated network. With Layercake, and the five steps to automated decision making described in the previous section, all of Ruhan's online functions can be accessed and deployed on-demand, in response to the needs of consumers.

Ruhan is also expanding the value network it coordinates. It is developing a B2B fabric supply platform that will be directly connected to its SCM software. Such a platform requires complex datafication that could precisely identify colors, weaves, textures, and thicknesses and eventually automate fabric selection and ordering.

Thus, within the firm's entire software system, Layercake constitutes a first and broadest layer, onto which SCM works to optimize the entire process. As Ruhan's softwaring of the fabric selection process continues, the level of network coordination in their business model will increase, bringing efficiency gains across the board. If Ruhan can get this B2B fabric platform off the ground, its Layercake system will knit all stages of the apparel business into an end-to-end solution, pulling even procurement into this coordination network.

Ruhan is one of China's pioneers in reimagining ancient industries as smart business. However, the company believes that it has only just begun to encode the complicated task of design. Ruhan is developing its own software platform for fashion designers, called Deep Fashion, which will crawl the web and analyze fashion trends on platforms like Instagram. (The company already collates Instagram pictures that are tagged and organized by its design team.) Company leaders hope that by applying machine-learning techniques to the images in Deep Fashion, designers will be able to gather inspirations quickly and produce new patterns easily in China's fast-paced, competitive market. In the future, if Ruhan can integrate an automated understanding of fashion trends from Deep Fashion into its design and production modules, the firm's entire manufacturing process will work even smoother. The clothes that its web celebs design and produce will get to market faster, and fit better with consumer tastes.

Previous software solutions just focused on efficiency of an isolated segment of the business, i.e., the factory or procurement. Spurred by escalating consumer demand, more and more firms in China are starting to use online technologies to piece their entire business together, connecting consumer activity to back-end operations and decisions. The future is C2B, business that is more and more coordinated, and ever-smarter. Smart business is just beginning.

Other C2B Models in China

In more and more industries, the C2B model enjoys competitive advantage over the traditional approach, especially as most traditional Chinese industries are less mature than are their US counterparts and thus less efficient, and entry barriers for innovators are lower.

The whole business landscape in China is shifting toward supporting more C2B companies like Ruhan. Let's take a look at two more businesses, Red Collar and Shangpin.

Red Collar's Mass-Customization Model

Red Collar, which produces custom men's suits, has developed its own flexible, on-demand manufacturing system for customization.[5] After working as a typical OEM for leading foreign brands for nearly two decades, Red Collar's founder, Zhang Daili, was determined to transform his company to produce tailor-made suits. After five years of hard work and more than US$50 million in investment, Zhang softwared the suit manufacturing process into over four hundred standardized steps and designed a new production line that is very much like the cell production pioneered by Dell. A very experienced tailor, he even invented a new way to measure a customer; the technique represents a 90 percent cost saving over the old method.

Red Collar has found that fit is also a matter of personal opinion, rather than just an objective function that can be optimized. Thus, the firm's current approach to the customer relationship is different from that of a web celeb. Instead of having an online store, which would be unable to take individualized measurements, Red Collar has enabled tens of thousands of small merchants in countries across the world to do the selling. The merchants talk to the customers about their preferences, take measurements, and then send the orders to Red Collar through a B2B platform. This arrangement helps sellers around the world to better use direct customer feedback—crucial to C2B and the smart business model—and provides a custom suit fit to the buyer's taste for about the same cost as a mass-produced one, a feat made possible by a reinvented manufacturing line completely run by online software.

Shangpin's Customized Furniture Model

Another pioneering company that runs on a complete C2B model appeared in a rather surprising industry: furniture. As a Chinese company making its offerings both customer driven and scalable through network coordination, Shangpin Home Collection is one of the fastest-growing companies in this sector. Using his background as an instructor at the South China University of Technology, Li Lianzhu founded Yuanfang Software in 1994. The company provided design software to furniture makers.

With China's rapid urbanization and the construction of millions of new apartments, furniture became a fast-growing big business. Given the high price of real estate, space utilization was at a premium and many apartments across the country with different layouts used radically different designs and brands of furniture. With the fragmentation in the market, Li saw an opportunity for furniture customized for the whole apartment, but he couldn't convince any of his customers to venture into this business. After much thought, he decided to start his own furniture making business. He opened stores near new apartment complexes, sent customer reps to measure entire apartments, and then designed the furniture with his own software. After customers approved the design, the CAD-supported design would be directly translated into manufacturing orders, with all the patterning information encoded. It took him several years of experimentation to find a way to fully digitalize furniture making. Decreasing barcode costs, for example, significantly helped the company keep track of every piece of wood needed for manufacturing. A set of furniture is just a different combination of hundreds or even thousands of pieces of wooden boards in the company database.

Now called Shangpin Home Collection, the company collects data on homes from thousands of real estate developments to create a "room library" supplemented by the firm's product library. Consumers can choose, compare, or tweak furniture designs according to real floor plans. After all, when tens of millions of apartments were built in a few years, they weren't exactly Frank Gehry designs; many followed fairly standard configurations. Using these two databases, customers can combine all kinds of products into various household spaces.

Shangpin invested heavily in both software and hardware, including new electric precision saws. While for the customer, all the furniture is tailor-made, for the firm, every order is based on a package of wooden boards in different shapes and sizes. Thus, the company is able to achieve great productivity gains in manufacturing by aggregating the orders. Since 2007, Shangpin's daily capacity has increased tenfold as material utilization increased from 8 to 90 percent and its manufacturing error rate dropped from 30 to 3 percent. Since production does not begin until after the order is placed, Shangpin carries little to no inventory and has a rate of capital turnover three times the industry norm.[6]

The beauty of data intelligence started to kick in later for Shangpin Home Collection. As the company served more and more customers, it found that despite the huge geographic differences across China, there were just about fifty thousand types of house designs, and Shangpin had data on almost all of them. In addition, most people tend to have similar tastes in furniture. As the company has accumulated enough designs for each apartment, the design stage has become much easier because most customers just click on existing designs in Shangpin's database. The company has found that people with minimum design training can still do a good job.

Today, Shangpin is still thriving, having gone public on the Shenzhen stock exchange to much fanfare in March of 2017. In the first half of 2017, the firm did over 2 billion RMB of sales (over US$300 million), representing over 30 percent growth from the first half of 2016; and made 65.9 million RMB (about US$10.5 million), an increase of over 127 percent during the same period in 2016. Shangpin places ads featuring famous celebrities in some of China's largest train stations, and has over one thousand franchised stores across the country. By 2020, its market cap is expected to double to over 23 billion RMB (US$3.6 billion).[7]

Principles behind C2B

C2B already defines the operational mindset of most internet companies, which focus laser-like on users and their experience. Yet we may forget that the simplest and oldest version of the C2B model is "made to order." Dell did it with computers more than thirty years ago. Moving this model to more industries was insurmountable until the internet provided the right infrastructure. C2B presages a future where an increasing number of products and services can be produced on demand at acceptable cost. Network coordination and data intelligence allow information and decisions to flow throughout the network simultaneously, coordinating every aspect of the business in real time and dramatically reducing the cost of coordination and transactions.

Although the companies described in this chapter focus on apparel and apartment-sized furniture, the C2B model means much more than selling customized products. It overhauls the very concept of business itself. Despite traditional companies' slogans and sincere intentions of *customer first*, most such businesses are *company first* by design. Through various means of customer and market research, a company tries to guess what its customers need. It next comes up with a product and convinces customers, through advertising and marketing, that the product is what they want, and then pushes the merchandise through distribution channels. In this model, customers are passive. Now, businesses can and do truly respond to the customer.

I have watched emerging companies in rather traditional industries in China configuring themselves into C2B models over the past decade. Every industry and firm's approach to C2B will differ, because every firm needs to ply different capabilities to cater to different customers. However, from my research on companies such as Ruhan, Red Collar, and Shangpin, and by observing how Alibaba operates under a C2B mindset, I can offer four general principles for implementing C2B-aligned operations.

Develop a Smart Network

Big-E produces only the clothes that her fans want, when they want them. To this end, Big-E and Ruhan have reworked all aspects of her business, from sales to product design to manufacturing, to operate online and coordinate in real time. C2B firms consistently use two familiar strategies: network coordination and data intelligence. For this reason, the C2B model is almost synonymous with smart business.

In my strategic work at Alibaba, I often return to a paradoxical but profound insight. If you want to fulfill the needs of any one consumer, you need the capabilities to fulfill the needs of every consumer. Today's consumers demand cost, speed, quality, and personalization— all at the same time. In previous formulations of business strategy, these goals were opposing and often mutually exclusive. Now, they are reconcilable and indispensable.

Only a network can dynamically adjust the supply and quality of service offerings by balancing load capacity globally. Linear supply chains cannot respond effectively to peaks and troughs of demand, much less to changing and complex consumer needs. To create a globally optimized network of productive capabilities that can adapt to any consumer requires network coordination, data intelligence, and no small measure of live data. Everyone in the network is a partner providing an on-demand service, linked by SaaS solutions delivered online and informed by data flowing through frictionless APIs. Your service is being requested when it is needed; it is not being managed through a prearranged order.

Instead of long-range planning, smart business reacts immediately to consumer needs in real time. As a result, previous questions of local tactics, such as branding, marketing, and design, now concern the entire supply chain. Indeed, the entire network's design constitutes a global strategy. Only such a comprehensive strategic mindset will be sufficient for competition in the future.

Design the Right Internet Interface

C2B follows a pull logic rather than a push one. Because business operations and decisions grow out of interactions with customers, C2B firms must have an interface where customers can articulate their needs and responses. Internet-native companies intuitively understand this point and often design their products to reflect a C2B mindset. Google doesn't push its service to you; it responds to your query in its minimalistic box. Adaptable products are ideal, because they also generate the feedback loops necessary for creating data intelligence, as discussed earlier.

Building an internet interface does not necessarily entail making your own customer-facing mobile application; businesses should choose the right online interface based on the touchpoints of interaction with their clients, and the devices they use. As described earlier, Big-E intentionally structured her marketing to solicit consumer feedback at several key junctures. From social media previews to flash sales to comments and pictures posted on Taobao after a customer buys an item, consumers are constantly giving the brand their feedback. The value in establishing an effective medium for direct interaction with customers cannot be underestimated, even for companies in industries traditionally far from tech. Using the internet's huge business advantage of simultaneously interacting with masses of people and getting their real-time feedback at very low cost is almost a no-brainer.

The internet interface provides often-overlooked but important benefits to firms in the upper reaches of the value chain. Manufacturing firms don't have to bend over backward to establish contact with end users. Rather, they need to design interfaces with their partners so that feedback flows to those who need it, ideally in an automated fashion. These interfaces must be embedded in all the parties' workflows to ensure effective coordination, as Ruhan has done with its manufacturing partners. It aims to move further up the value chain to sourcing with its online quality-control platform for fabric.

Build a C2B Beachhead

Most C2B businesses evolve over time. The good news is that once you build the first module and create a beachhead, its competitive advantage will create momentum to pull in all of the related functions. The firm will experience enormous pressure to reconfigure step after step of its value chain.

Big-E started with her online community at Weibo and then discovered that the flash-sale model on Taobao meshed well. Over the years, she and Ruhan were able to deploy their restocking model by developing a flexible network of manufacturing partners. In a relatively short time in business development terms, the network grew to simultaneously coordinate marketing, product design, manufacturing, and sales.

The C2B model is a complicated coordination network. Building an entire network may seem overwhelming, but as soon as you begin directly interacting with customers online, the snowball will start rolling downhill, picking up more and more functions of the value network on its course. Go with the flow, or don't start at all.

Utilize the Capabilities of Platforms

The web celebs we have examined use three platforms to stay agile and resource-light: the social media marketing arena of Weibo, the e-commerce infrastructure of Taobao, and the growing networks of flexible apparel manufacturers. As detailed earlier, Ruhan's operations depend on these platforms whose use represents a new model for apparel entrepreneurship. The same strategy portends how other companies that create products or services will operate and structure themselves in the future. (As I will discuss in the next chapter, platforms and individual operators follow different strategies in the world of smart business.)

Without these platforms, Big-E would have had to find her millions of fans on her own. She would have had to create a mobile app that could handle the excruciatingly steep peaks of demand that occur during flash sales, as well as mechanisms for transactions, payment, and dispute resolution. And she would have needed to manage an enormous factory in-house. Without these platforms, Big-E could not have delivered affordable, high-quality products nimbly and adaptably. I will explain this strategy further in the next chapter.

Implications of the New Landscape

Early C2B movers such as Big-E and Ruhan face considerable challenges, and how far they can go is a hot topic in China. However, the trends they embody are likely to stay, if not become stronger. As smart business develops, more and more functions will be made to order—yet with less waste and little or no additional cost. When all firm functions and consumer activity are integrated into a tightly coordinated network, businesses of the future will deliver customized service on demand at any time.

The C2B model has two important implications. First is the ability to customize your offerings for the customer. In C2B, every activity with the customer happens in real time and is dynamic, fluid, and responsive. In modern developed societies, there is an oversupply of almost any standardized product, and customers want products and services customized to their own circumstances. To continuously improve the total customer experience, you need to focus on much more than just your physical product. You tailor everything, from marketing messages and product design to sales and service. The experience coevolves with the customer in real time.

Second is the automation of decision making. With C2B, the traditional division of marketing, product design, and manufacturing no longer applies. In a static, linear mindset of business functions, these three functions operated independently, often across silos. Cycling through them took a long time. In the new C2B world, these functions are happening more simultaneously through similar interfaces across the network. Hence, service cycles for new product development, marketing campaigns, or sales are all reduced dramatically. Many traditional organizational divisions, such as channel and product design or marketing and manufacturing, are no longer tenable. Firms need to ply an all-in-one C2B operational model.

Fundamental to C2B business models is the rise of large, online business networks, or platforms. Google has datafied advertising, moving offline advertising into smart online markets. Amazon and Taobao have brought the traditional retailing industry online. Facebook, Tencent, Weibo, and other social media are working to move offline functions of marketing and branding online. The business model for Big-E and other web celebs rests on the infrastructure created by Taobao and Weibo. The spread of platforms is only gaining in speed: many firms in countless industries in China are trying to move different supply chains online. When more and more supply chains go online, it will be easier than ever for companies to string together intelligent business models that respond quickly to consumer demand. The infrastructure supporting innovative C2B models is getting better every day.

We have now looked at two of the most important strategic implications of the new forces creating smart businesses: how decision making can be automated and how coordinated business models build services focused on the consumer. Another deeper takeaway is that no part of the business can be considered in isolation. In smart business, all functions must operate seamlessly, coordinated by technology. Online operations change the strategic relationships between firms. Hence, we need to reexamine one more traditional cornerstone of strategy—positioning. As I'll elaborate on in the next chapter, positioning is critical for a smart business.

CHAPTER 6

POSITIONING

How to Create Value in a Network

Companies like Big-E, Ruhan, Red Collar, and Shangpin don't just emerge haphazardly or in isolation. They leverage platform capabilities painstakingly built on Taobao and the vital resources gathered there, namely, the many independent service providers detailed in chapter 2. At the same time, these firms enable the growth of platforms like Taobao. New players always grow together with the platforms and with the platform partners the players rely on for various support functions. In essence, brands, support functions, and the platform all grow together as an ecosystem.

In the technology industry, *ecosystem* is one of those overused buzzwords that make eyes roll. However, at Alibaba, the term *ecosystem* is critical within the organization for aligning strategic objectives and diagnosing whether a business is on the right track. A core idea of the ecosystem is that, unlike traditional notions of positioning, in which the firm determines strategy mostly independently, each party in the ecosystem relies on the other parties for success. They are interdependent.

In this book, we can define *business ecosystem* more precisely as a smart network that evolves to solve complicated customer problems. ("Smart network" is just another way to express network coordination + data intelligence. Without both capabilities, you do not have an "ecosystem," in other words, a smart network.) The business ecosystem attracts resources and has the infrastructure and mechanisms that permit players to flourish and evolve robustly. I further separate an ecosystem into three distinct roles: point, line, and plane. The power of the ecosystem is to enable innovative new firms like Big-E to serve customers better. These ecosystems challenge the old business world by helping companies provide superior customer value and enjoy competitive advantages.

A New Framework: Points, Lines, and Planes

I often ask leaders or entrepreneurs where they envision themselves in the growing ecosystems of their industries. Without fail, the vast majority have a platform dream. They want to create expansive platforms with highly profitable and scalable business models. They want to make the decisions, call the shots, and rake in the profits.

Then I ask them a different question. Would you rather be Alibaba, whose US$500 billion market cap rests on a sprawling and mind-numbingly complex global organization of tens of thousands of people, who in turn manage tens of millions of sellers and third-party service providers, to say nothing of rapidly growing subplatforms for logistics, finance, and cloud computing? Or would you rather be Big-E, who owns no factories, collects nearly half her brand's profits, and makes millions by flying around the world and posting pictures of her new outfits to social media? Alternatively, perhaps you would be satisfied to be a writer or designer, or a talent shop like Toptal, supporting other firms or aspiring web celebs by putting your writing in all kinds of social media and enjoying exemplary exposure, immediate payment, and flexibility. Suddenly, the platform dream doesn't seem quite as attractive.

I then reframe the question in a different way: what role do you want to play in the ecosystem or network?

Who Are You?

At the core of traditional strategic theory is positioning, which asks three fundamental questions: Who are your customers? What are your value propositions? How is your positioning different from that of your competitors? In response to those questions, the classical strategy as defined by Michael Porter proposes three positioning strategies: cost leadership, differentiation, and niche.[1] This simple positioning framework has been very powerful in helping firms shape their strategies.

However, as more and more economic activity occurs within some kind of smart network, today's firms must know their strategic position within that network or web of interconnected networks. In internal strategy discussions here at Alibaba, we refer to the three basic strategic positions in the ecosystem using geometric metaphors: point, line, and plane.

Points are the individuals, or firms, that possess specialized skills but often cannot survive by themselves. Ruhan's factory partners from chapter 5 are examples. *Points* provide functional services. *Lines*, such as Big-E and Ruhan, are the firms that combine productive functions and capabilities to create products and services, often utilizing the services provided by the points and planes. And *planes* like Taobao and Weibo are the platforms that help new lines form and grow by providing infrastructural services and jump-starting point growth.

Each player's key value proposition, competitive advantage, and organizational capabilities are distinctive. The strategy of each strategic position is unique. Table 6-1 summarizes the most important differences between the three core positions within a business network.

Would you rather create a product or service within a network, as Big-E does? In that case, you are a line. Your strategy is to take advantage of the resources of platform partners and effectively align them to create your products. Though your primary concern is serving your target customers, one of the most difficult strategic question is which platforms to join. In China, for example, whether a company chooses Taobao, JD.com (another online Chinese retailer), or Tencent as its main operating platform has huge implications on what the company can do in the future.

Are you a specialized actor within the network, such as the Tao models, or a designer or factory that makes apparel for a web celeb or any other apparel retailer? If so, you are a point. Your flexibility comes precisely from the simplicity of your business goal: to align your skills with developing networks and to join up with the platforms and

TABLE 6-1

The three strategic positions in a business ecosystem

Feature	STRATEGIC POSITION		
	Point	Line	Plane
Value proposition	Selling a function or capability	Creating a product or service	Connecting related parties
Competitive advantage	Expertise	Value, cost, and efficiency	Matching efficiency
Organizational capabilities	Simple; no complex operations	Streamlining and optimizing workflows	Designing systems and institutions to mediate relationships
Core strategy	Advance into the next rising plane and find one's niche in a fast-growing line	Use the resources of robust planes to incorporate strong points	Enable the growth of points and lines
Web-celeb analogy	Factories, clothing designers	Ruhan	Taobao, Weibo

products that can best utilize your expertise. Find your niche, and you can make money without fretting over the complexities of business operations in their entirety. These niche positions are emerging every day. You just have to be ready to seize the opportunity when it emerges.

Or do you aim to run the whole network as a platform like Taobao? If your answer is yes, then you are a plane. Your goal is to create markets that connect disparate parties, facilitating their business models. You will be making the rules and systems of interactions so that every individual company within your marketplace experiences the potential for growth. If you survive the long and harrowing incubation period, you can build up an impressive market cap. However, your life will be a constant struggle between control and laissez-faire and between your own interests and those of the actors on your platform.

When assessing these three positions, firms must understand both the core logic of each approach and how the different positions relate to each other.[2] Firms must also realize that each position represents a completely different arrangement of capabilities, which you must possess in order to compete. Although there are examples of points and lines that "progress" into higher dimensions, such a huge endeavor requires a fundamental transformation of the firms' positioning and corresponding capabilities. In many cases, a strategic alignment at such a basic level can be more difficult than moving into a different vertical or industry.

There is no normative difference between these three positions and no a priori reason to choose one position over another. Firms in different strategic positions do not directly compete with each other, although they may fight on relative shares of the value each position captures. I counsel managers and entrepreneurs to base their positioning not only on the valuation to which they aspire, but also on their mission, vision, and capabilities.

Of the three core positions within a coordinated network, the strategies for points and planes are relatively straightforward. It is the brand, the line firm, whose strategy is significantly different in a world of smart business. Moreover, most of the companies that readers are used to creating and analyzing are line firms. Thus, I will first explain that position's strategy and tactics.

Line Players: New Brands

As described earlier, the core function of web-celeb incubator Ruhan's Layercake software system is to integrate and coordinate operations across several internet platforms and manufacturing facilities. Ruhan's value proposition (through web celebs like Big-E) is to quickly and affordably create products and services, such as women's apparel or Big-E's new line of makeup. The firm produces this value by connecting different functionalities to the business, stringing them together into a coherent workflow. This operating model is the essence of the strategy of line firms.

The line position constitutes the majority of companies that scholars are accustomed to analyzing in the traditional business literature and which entrepreneurs are accustomed to creating. Line firms provide direct services to clients, much like traditional B2C companies. Intuitively, we can imagine a line player as an integrator of different points, forming an efficient and scalable business model. The core capability of the line as an organization is to coordinate different functions to create a tangible product or service.

The new line player is different from a traditional player because the new version relies heavily on the platform for all kinds of services required to run its business. For example, the web celebs are lines that rely on platforms like Taobao and Weibo for many crucial capabilities to their business model. Lines take advantage of platform infrastructure and other resources to access and coordinate the points that build their own business. The new line player can do so much more efficiently than can a traditional B2C model, with a fixed supply chain of locked-in partners. Within a coordination network, line firms can call on the services of any functional areas through open APIs, without the need to negotiate between businesspeople. Switching service providers is hence very simple. In addition, since such outside service partners often serve many customers, they can provide excellent service at a lower cost than in-house departments of a traditional company can. A typical Taobao seller, even a small one, often connects to hundreds of functional partners, or points.

The line player must decide to partner with the right platform, or plane. The planes that make the best partners offer the resources you need in the present and bring the best growth opportunities in the future. In other words, access to, rather than owning, the right resources is what the new line companies seek. Open networks offer a rich and diverse supply of resources for building business models. Thus, like the web celebs, line companies can grow quickly, unencumbered by the resource constraints of a vertically integrated company. They don't need to spend time or money to build these capabilities in-house.

Many Western observers of Chinese e-commerce make the cardinal mistake of understanding Taobao as a line firm. They compare us to Amazon and the websites of online brands, such as Burberry, Apple, or GNC. All these firms are, in fact, lines in our framework. Taobao, on the contrary, is a plane. It doesn't create or design goods itself; millions of Taobao sellers do.

The merchants at Taobao are the owners of their brands and sell directly to customers, just as traditional offline brands do. They are integrated product owners responsible for the customer experience. Yet Taobao sellers rely heavily on the services available through the platform. For example, very few of these sellers run their own logistic operations or have large in-house software departments. For all but the largest of storefronts, these services are too expensive and complicated. Instead, the platform connects these points to the lines that need them. Using the resources made possible by the platforms, merchants on Alibaba's e-commerce platforms have become one of the fastest-growing business sectors in China since the mid-2000s. Combined with direct access to millions of customers, cheap marketing resources (especially in the early days), and increasingly strong data analytic capabilities, these new brands have enjoyed a strong competitive advantage.

As Taobao evolved, a strong group of new brands emerged online around 2010. These sellers appeared seemingly out of nowhere. They first arrived in apparel, the largest and strongest category on Taobao, exemplified by brands such as Inman, and HSTYLE.[3] Then came sellers in other categories. Impressed by the emergence of these online-only brands, we dubbed them Tao brands and began to create specialized submarkets and services for them. (The Taobao Mall, later Tmall, got started in large part because of these Tao brands.)

These brands have achieved striking results: dozens reached 1 billion RMB (some US$150 million) in annual sales in the years between 2010 and 2018, and many are filing IPOs now. In the same period, many established offline brands have had a very tough time surviving the onslaught of online retail, much less breaking into the online retail world. Around 2011, encouraged by their early success and pushed by venture capitalists, the first group of successful Taobao sellers began to *chu tao*, or "leave Taobao." As the *chu tao* wave spread across the industry, brand after brand started independent B2C sites to avoid their dependence on traffic provided by the platform. In the end, almost all failed, and the majority returned to Alibaba's platforms. The Tao brands realized that the advantages offered by a plane are impossible for a small B2C company to replicate. In practice, to create a fully independent brand portal online, a firm needs to build everything from scratch, in addition to doing the difficult work of building consumer trust and mindshare. Far better to take advantage of existing resources.

The gales of creative destruction are powerful in the Chinese market. New line firms are emerging constantly, such as the web celebs who effectively use different platforms. Big-E and Ruhan use Weibo for marketing, Taobao for e-commerce, and a growing set of distributed networks of flexible manufacturing. In our terminology, each of these platforms (Weibo, Taobao, and manufacturing networks) is a plane that contributes resources and capabilities to the web celebs' businesses. By building their business on these planes, web celebs can remain flexible, asset-light, highly scalable, and very profitable. Though most web-celeb brands are still not strong enough to directly compete with offline fast-fashion brands like Zara, generations of new line models, from the earliest Taobao sellers to the Tao brands to today's web celebs, are swiftly growing in power.

Let's compare the success of Big-E's web-celeb brand with her earlier work as a model. Before starting her own brand, she was a leading model in the industry, employed at one of China's top fashion magazines. As one of the top models in the field, in a good year she could take in nearly one million RMB in income (US$150,000). By Chinese standards, this is equivalent to at least a midlevel managerial salary.

Now, Big-E is in a completely different league. As the creative force behind a line position, running her own brand, she can make millions of dollars a year. Yet the organizational capabilities necessary to become that line are completely different from those of a model (in my framework, the point position). It is a significant challenge for point players to orchestrate such a change—other models have died trying.

The key virtue of the line position is the ability to leverage network effects provided by plane companies. A line must secure access to essential resources within the network, but needn't actually own or control them. This approach lies counter to textbook business theory that suggests the most efficient way to achieve economies of scale is through resource integration and building internal capabilities. These theories overlook the importance and value of network effects and will quickly become outmoded.

The most important strategic decision for a line is which plane or planes to partner with. Choose correctly, and you will have excellent future growth, almost independent of your own competitive advantage. Choose incorrectly, and no amount of competitive advantage will bring prosperity, because the entire sector is on the decline. The cold, hard truth of competition is that individual fortunes only partly depend on individual effort. The line strategy implicitly acknowledges the very loose connection between individual effort and business results. It encourages you to think rigorously and strategically about your relationship partners in different dimensions as they compete as a system.

Due to deep mutual dependence, you need to understand how planes operate and how the plane strategy also relies on the success of its line partners.

Plane Players: The Marketplace

Since around 2010, the most valuable companies in the world, such as Alibaba, Facebook, and Google, have all based their core products and services on platforms. Today, most entrepreneurs aspire to this strategic position. As I have implied throughout this book, the platform is largely responsible for facilitating network coordination and data intelligence. Thus, platform firms are key to the ecosystem's direction. Moreover, platform businesses can be highly lucrative; the plane position can realize some very attractive numbers in a quarterly report.

But the plane strategy comes with substantial risk, suffers from long and costly incubation periods, and mandates a constant balancing act between the interests of all the players on the platform. The underlying economic logic and the strategic dynamics of the plane are complex and often misunderstood. Put most succinctly, the plane company focuses on connecting related parties to a business activity. But what plane firms actually do is to enable the success of lines. This accomplishment requires the coordination of large groups of individual points to every player's mutual advantage.

Since the late 1980s, the business world gradually began to conceive of group after group of companies as platforms: from Intel and Microsoft, to Yahoo! and Google, to Alibaba and eBay, and further on to Facebook, LinkedIn, Tencent, and more. *Platform* has now become a catchall term, and in the strategic context here, I will refer to these businesses by the more specific term *plane*. Intuitively, a plane is a two-dimensional network, where business actors across the value chain can connect to each other.[4]

What plane companies' core businesses have in common is that they do not sell products and services in the traditional sense. Their core value proposition is the matching of buyers and sellers (Alibaba), search users and advertisements (Google), social network users and information (Facebook), to name a few. These companies derive their competitive advantage from their matching efficiency, often measured by the accuracy and return of their advertising products. Such matching efficiency speeds the growth of the lines that grow on the platform, whether those lines are sellers on Alibaba or advertisers on Google or Facebook.

Planes like Taobao generally provide highly effective and scalable customer acquisition because of their powerful network effects—more sellers attract more buyers, and vice versa—and advanced tools powered by data intelligence. Especially in the early days, web celebs were able to attract lots of fans from Weibo and Taobao, thanks to a comprehensive infrastructure for matching. Better consumer targeting for line firms results in better customer satisfaction, recommendations, and retention. Plane income thus comes from monetizing the matching process. In practice, matching is monetized through advertising or recommendation engines (how efficiently you can connect people or information) or commissions (how efficiently you can bring about a certain result).

Another concept very closely connected with the plane business model is that of the marketplace. Planes are marketplaces that connect disparate actors that would be hard-pressed to connect on their own; the marketplaces help actors transact, whether the transaction is the sale of actual products, as on Taobao, or of information, in the case of the Googles and Facebooks of the world. The marketplace nature of the plane firm explains why the core product of these firms is not a product in and of itself. The "product" of a plane is a market, which requires the development of institutions and systems that create the marketplace and keep it running healthily. Thus, the day-to-day work of the plane firm is governing the market. This work includes managing different groups of users, optimizing systems, and creating rules and institutions, often through techno-logical design.

Consider the relationship of a web celeb to a plane firm. In the case of Weibo, the social media plane or platform connects the celebrities to her fans, Taobao connects the web celeb to e-commerce service providers, and emerging supply-chain planes or platforms connect fashion icons and designers to factories. (Web celebs often use Tao-bao advertising tools to find more customers, too.) In all cases, the business of the plane is connection. New line businesses like web celebs can leave much of the heavy lifting to the planes and simply focus on connecting the dots across planes. Considerable help from plane partners makes for a powerful and nimble business model.

Well-constructed planes often provide richer benefits by exploiting economies of scale for infrastructure services and network effects for distribution. In Taobao's case, the various functions provided by the platform—such as cloud computing, SaaS software solutions, pay-ments and finance, and logistics—compete not only on cost, but also on the quality of the service. A typical in-house IT department of a midsize company can hardly juggle enough engineering tasks to go toe-to-toe with the comprehensive and high-quality software services now available on cloud-based marketplaces.

From our experience running many marketplaces at Alibaba, my colleagues and I know that the plane's main challenge is to attract as many relevant players to the network as possible and then to enable them to grow and connect to others by providing them with services and institutional support. In addition to supporting the basic goal of matching, Taobao also provides the technical capacity to withstand a torrential volume of simultaneous transactions, to say nothing of other marketplace services such as escrow, dispute resolution, and reputation systems, to name a few. The core task of the plane is facil-itating cooperation and coordination within markets. That task is often neither simple nor foreseeable. Operating an online market-place requires much trial and error and even a good measure of luck.

An in-depth discussion of how to build a network or ecosystem lies outside the scope of this book. I have, however, encapsulated as much insight as possible into the Taobao case described in chapter 2, in appendix B, and in the principles at the end of this chapter.

For Taobao, the inevitable result of the plane business model is the emergence of new point players. This result makes economic sense: planes lower transaction costs and entry barriers, allowing small players to emerge where previously only established companies could exist. However, the unpredictability of the genesis of new points makes the plane strategy both exciting and difficult. Plane businesses must stay vigilant for new point opportunities and quickly develop services and infrastructure that can fold new points into the network, allowing them to coordinate intelligently with other players.

Point Players: Service Providers

Taobao is a plane, but many observers don't appreciate why it is such a powerful platform. Taobao's value goes much further than the mere connection of buyer and seller. Especially for nimble firms like the web celebs, Taobao connects merchants with many of the partners in their business, from third-party software vendors such as ERP to advertising optimization, allowing them to coordinate online through technologies like the API and other tools. In the terminology of this chapter, these partners are points inside the plane. Taobao helps line businesses like web celebs access these points, reducing entry barriers to almost zero and encouraging the participation of newcomers—often people with little retailing experience—to the plane. The way that new points enter the marketplace and work with line players is exactly the process of network coordination I have detailed in previous chapters.

The core value proposition of a point is to offer a very specific function or capability and to provide that function exceptionally well. Points thus compete on quality. For example, in the apparel industry, they might be designers, models, pattern makers, or even a small factory. In most cases, points do not offer complete products or services to consumers or clients. In our strategic discussions, we generally ask two simple questions to determine whether a firm constitutes a point in our positioning framework: Are they responsible for more than one function within a supply chain? Can they develop a complete product or service for their clientele? If the answer to both these questions is no, the firm in question is most likely a point. We call these companies points because they are the most basic node in a business network.

Traditionally, the functions of points have been subsumed into larger organizational structures to minimize transaction costs. But the rise of the internet has dramatically reduced transaction costs and built up markets for the easy exchange of point skills. Accordingly, points have seen explosive growth in China since around 2010, liberating individuals to engage in all manner of new forms of work. Taobao encouraged all kinds of software service providers to provide SaaS to sellers, greatly enhancing seller productivity. Each of Alibaba's associated platforms, such as Ant Financial, the Cainiao Network, and Alibaba Cloud, caters to a different group of point companies, from the Tao models discussed earlier to financial institutions, logistics companies, and software developers.

The story of Taobao illustrates how many new roles or points are created over time when new markets are introduced on the platform. As I described in chapter 2, most sellers were unfamiliar with the internet in the early days of Taobao, and lecturers teaching how to run online stores became very popular. They made good money and were even welcomed like heroes when they visited different cities. Around 2007, as internet speed ramped up, appealing photos became an important selling factor on Taobao. Suddenly, models, photographers, and studios all saw a huge spike in demand and revenues. In no time, an online market was rolled out on Taobao matching models of different body types and looks to hundreds of thousands of stores.

But the promise of the internet is not only to release points from their subservient, rigid roles as a cog in a larger mechanical apparatus. Smart business also creates new points. Whenever a new plane emerges, so too emerge many new varieties of points, as Taobao's story demonstrates. In the United States, similar examples abound, from Airbnb's home-sharers to TaskRabbit's handy people to Instacart's grocery shoppers.

Because points' value propositions are very simple, many point opportunities have little in the way of entry barriers. Point positions are thus very suitable for individual players or small firms. But for the same reason, competition can quickly become fierce. For example, although Taobao's platform for models was introduced in 2007, supply remained tight and the money made by the top Tao models peaked in 2010. By 2012, their rates had dropped substantially because of new entrants and strong competition. This speedy rise and fall can be common for micro to small business. Markets usually stabilize over time; unique or exceptional qualities will distinguish competitors, or skills and requirements will change, catalyzing a new realignment. Inevitably, some points evolve into lines. Big-E started out as a Taobao model but has become a very successful brand builder.

In the decades before business was conducted on the internet, point players could theoretically make a profit, but in practice, such opportunities were difficult to organize. Now, point players like Tao models, designers, or software engineers can exploit business opportunities without having to take on many of the costs and challenges of operating a business. These players can scale up and become profitable very quickly.

When I have brought up the concept of points in lectures and strategy discussions, most businesspeople are skeptical or dismissive of the potential of the point. In a world composed of sprawling platforms, who wants to be a minor player in a huge marketplace, jostling for elbow room amid white-hot competition? This is a serious misconception. For the players who know how to creatively apply the flexibility and agility of the point position, the opportunities for individual points are significant. In fact, in a fast-growing ecosystem, new opportunities come up all the time, and many can be very lucrative. The core strategy for a point player is to enter the right plane at the right time and to capture as much of the value created as possible, even from its partners, for as long as possible.

Certain point opportunities can be big and sustainable, especially the new demand for essential services that are emerging on a platform. Capable point players, such as the ISVs described in chapter 2, can take advantage of huge market opportunities. Points provide important complementary services and can grow very quickly when the marketplace expands. For example, China's Baozun, the one-stop e-commerce service provider, offers a suite of e-commerce-related services such as online store development, sales promotion, IT, and logistical management. Its founder Qiu Wenbin was a distributor for Philips Electronics in Shanghai in 2007 when he opened a Taobao store online. Around 2010, he saw that big brands were rapidly migrating online but were lacking any online operating experience. Qiu transformed his company to focus on serving big brands opening Tmall stores, a fast-growing market. The company now serves more than 150 big brands, such as Microsoft, Samsung, and Nike, and has expanded its services to a full range of online business solutions. Baozun went public on the NASDAQ stock exchange in 2015 and now has market capitalization exceeding US$700 million.[5]

Interdependencies: How Competitive Advantage Is Redefined

No matter which position in the network your firm occupies, you must remember that each positioning strategy relies on the other positions for success. The strategy for any one firm is defined in terms of the activity of other firms. None of the three positional strategies exists in a vacuum. All three positions rely on the importance of networks in today's economy and are ultimately built on different aspects of the same network effects.

Consider again Ruhan and the web celebs who initially exploited the e-commerce infrastructure and resources of Taobao. On the simplest level, they chose Taobao because this platform (as opposed to Tmall or other e-commerce platforms) does not charge for transactions, a boon for rapidly growing online brands. But the deeper reason reflects a deliberate strategic choice on the part of the web celebs. Big-E relies deeply on Weibo for social media marketing; Alibaba is an investor in Sina, Weibo's parent company. When the web-celeb phenomenon was just beginning in 2014, the e-commerce infrastructure of Taobao and the social media infrastructure of Weibo mostly operated independently. However, Alibaba's investment in the social media company gave sellers reasons to expect further synergies between the platforms.

Sure enough, by 2016, Taobao and Weibo had fully integrated their technological platforms, allowing for easy linkage, data sharing, and transactions for sellers. This complicated engineering work especially benefited the web celebs, who could execute flash sales more effectively, as well as better analyze data and metrics across different platforms. The bet on Taobao's future growth had paid off.

For a seller, the choice of whether to sell on Taobao/Tmall or competitors JD.com and Amazon is not only a question of which platform offers better consumer coverage. Sellers also must consider which plane can offer cheaper access to point players, whether those points are suppliers, technology providers, or service partners. To this day, sellers on Taobao have access to more data analytics and third-party software solutions than any other e-commerce platform in China. (Many of those solutions are provided by point players, accessing data through Taobao's API.) As a line, Ruhan understands that Taobao is making significant effort to expand its services and solutions for merchants. Taobao also understands that its job is to enable brand builders like Big-E to grow quickly.

Points, lines, and planes are interdependent; they coevolve. Planes work by supporting more and more lines with increasing efficacy. Lines work by finding the best points and combining them into services that minimize transaction costs while achieving quality and economies of scale. Points work by finding the best plane, which in turn helps them find the best line. This coevolution represents business thinking in higher dimensions.

Strategic Principles: New Sources of Competitive Advantage

In a world increasingly dominated by smart networks, putting network effects to work is the first strategic priority for all three types of players. The story of WhatsApp highlights the importance of network effects. It took only some fifty people with few physical or financial resources to build this mobile messaging company, which was valued at US$16 billion when it was purchased by Facebook in 2014. WhatsApp, Instagram (photo sharing), and Zynga (social gaming) grew so fast because they mobilized resources on networks such as Amazon Web Services' cloud computing, Facebook's API, and Google's search and advertising. With these planes available to them, these three social network startups could scale up, despite very limited internal resources. On the other hand, Facebook acquired

WhatsApp and Instagram because these two companies could have become competing planes.[6]

In a world of smart business, entrepreneurs and strategists need to assess the entire network when deciding how to position themselves and create value. Just like the previous chapters on live data and C2B, the strategies for points, lines, and planes will differ from industry to industry and even from market to market. Here I will offer four general principles for strategic positioning.

Core Strategic Positions Are Interdependent

At the risk of overemphasis, I want to stress that strategy, and competitive advantage, is no longer the sole provenance of your own firm and its own decisions. In a world of smart business, firms cannot construct competitive business models on their own: they will be outcompeted by competitors that exploit network resources more effectively.

When considering your own position, in addition to your capabilities as an organization, you must consider which players can bring you opportunity in the short term and growth potential in the long term. This consideration is important for line firms, but especially so for point players, which often only need to connect to the right plane. The platform will help them do the rest.

As described earlier, the ecosystem is a smart network composed of points, lines, and planes. Each of these three players has a unique and indispensable role. Be clear-eyed about diagnosing the present and future positions within your industry, and from there, determine the opportunities and risks of different strategic choices in the present.

Be Very Clear on Who Is and Isn't Your Competition

One of the biggest strategic mistakes made by firms, and especially non-internet firms, is misdiagnosing their competitive relationship with other firms in the network. In this chapter's framework, firms located in different dimensions (either point, line, or plane) do not directly compete with each other. Of course, interests do diverge and frictions do arise, especially between lines and planes. But strictly speaking, a firm only competes with the same type of players.

Alibaba competes with other e-commerce platforms, not with brands like Big-E, much less with point players like Baozun or any individual factory. Brands on Taobao compete among themselves for the hearts and minds of consumers, not with Taobao, which does not create products and services.

Although this point seems simple, in practice it is easy to experience "dimensional slip," especially for lines with platform aspirations. There are many examples of brands or content companies that try to create their own online marketplaces or media portals. It is not impossible to compete with players of a different dimension, but to do so, a firm needs to completely acquire the capabilities of the new dimension in which it wants to operate (see table 6-1). In practice, obtaining these capabilities often requires significant investment, hiring, organizational surgery, and time commitment.

Be Creative in Building New Lines

Although platform businesses are complicated, the strategies for incubating them are becoming relatively clear. Similarly, point players rarely need to rely on complicated strategy per se. It is enough to seize timely opportunities for growth. However, both the strategy and the organizational forms for line firms still very much remain open for discussion and definition, especially in the next two decades of continued business disruption.

Two principles are becoming clear, though. First, lines have the core advantages of being customer driven; they are exemplars of C2B. Second, being customer driven, C2B businesses are likely to be embedded in a plane; they can access the vast supply of very different yet efficient point players and build a flexible coordination network. We are witnessing huge transformations as new brands emerge. With these great changes, line firms must stay open-minded and creative to survive.

Planes Must Steward an Ecosystem of Superior Value

Many details of the strategies for platform firms, or planes, are beyond the scope of this book, but one core takeaway bears noting.

The key strategic question for whether a plane possesses true competitive advantage is whether the entire ecosystem provides much better customer value than do existing solutions. This is a crucial question because many planes are not merely compete with other platforms. Often, they directly compete with mature industries.

Without compelling, revolutionary, and highly focused customer value, a plane will not survive the long and difficult period of incubation. As appendix B details, Taobao spent a full five years before truly getting its footing in the industry. (Many employees did not believe that Taobao would survive as a business until 2008.) Extraordinary customer value may sound like an extremely high bar to reach for a new plane, but I have found that this is the main predictor of long-term platform success.

Planes create value by incubating line firms that are much more efficient than their traditional counterparts. The average plane (or, strictly speaking, an ecosystem composed of points, lines, and a plane) gets off the ground slowly because it needs to ensure smooth coordination between multiple players in the ecosystem. All of the parties to the plane's business model need to learn to work together, which takes patience and lots of adjustment. It takes time for new, profitable lines to form, and time for new points to enter the network. This is to say nothing of the time needed to create technology and mechanisms that underlie the marketplace. A viable, coherent ecosystem requires network coordination and data intelligence, as well as an effective C2B mindset. If you are determined to stick it out through your plane business's long period of incubation, stay laser focused on building the core capabilities of smart business.

Implications of New Positioning

A new positioning framework mandates a completely different mindset toward strategy. The new strategy of mobilizing resources available on the network, instead of owning them, is immensely powerful, but you cannot employ this strategy without analyzing the ecosystem and your position and leverage within it. All companies, even entirely offline businesses, are now playing in a world defined by networks, data, machine learning, and algorithms. Whether or not you already operate in an ecosystem, you will in time, and quite likely much quicker than you expect.

Up to this point in the book, I have discussed the many changes to strategy brought by smart business. But firms don't only need to reorient their strategies. Organizations themselves need to transform and become smart as well. I turn to the implications for organizations next.

PART THREE

HOW SMART BUSINESSES RUN

Organizational Implications

I n the first two parts of the book, I discussed the emergence of what I call smart business and the strategic implications of becoming a smart business. For smart businesses, the game is now one of coordination among interconnected players, where data intelligence makes all the players smarter. In this strategic environment, traditional approaches to positioning, decision making, planning, and meeting customer needs are upended.

In part 3, I turn to the organizational implications of the new strategic environment. Drawn from my and my colleagues' work at Alibaba, as well as countless conversations with entrepreneurs and leaders in companies big and small, these chapters show that operating as a smart business requires a different process of formulating and executing strategy. These changes in turn mandate a different kind of organization, with different processes, systems, and roles for managers.

CHAPTER 7

SELF-TUNING

How to Make Strategic Processes Smart

One of the most important organizational processes a smart business needs to change is how it formulates and implements strategy.[1] Strategy no longer means long-range planning. It's not even short-range planning. It's not planning.

Fundamentally, strategy making is now a dynamic and fluid process, akin to learning. The classical approach of analyze, plan, and execute is much too slow and inflexible for today's environment. Instead of formal planning, strategy formulation is the constant and rapid iteration between vision and action. Constant experimentation creates feedback, which leads to adjustment of the vision, which in turn guides new experiments. Strategy is constantly updated in this iterative process. With the right infrastructure and leadership, this strategic experimenting process becomes core to the nimble, innovative, smart business.

In traditional strategic planning, management makes trade-offs between exploration and exploitation: both have costs that must be managed. In the most complex, dynamic environments, exploration and exploitation must be done in parallel and continuously, without interruption for assessment. Through strategic experimentation, a business must constantly absorb new information and test ideas and processes to adjust its strategies to the new reality and opportunities. Fortunately, with new technologies and infrastructure, the cost of experimentation has been dramatically lowered. But you must have your organization and strategy in place to experiment on a large scale. Your enterprise must be able to constantly adjust to new ideas and changes in the environment rather than simply manage them in the traditional fashion.

Learning and innovation have long been ideals of business development. Indeed, the very phrase *learning organization* has been around for roughly three decades. But, like customer-centricity, the learning organization has been more of an exception than a rule. Incentives and limitations inherent in the industrial-era model work against learning. Enacting a learning-organization culture in a traditional hierarchical organizational structure focused on execution and minimizing transaction costs is extremely difficult. The US military, for example, has long understood this limitation and inability to absorb and act on local knowledge and has struggled with various work-arounds to remedy these problems.[2]

Despite new technologies that have lowered coordination costs dramatically, made information transfer immediate, and automated some testing regimes, strategic planning has remained largely the same. Strategic planning departments provide strategic options and execution plans that are based on static analysis, and then management chooses the strategy. This process is ill-adapted to today's environment. Besides being slow and inflexible, traditional strategic planning makes little use of the data and machine-learning resources both inside and outside the business. These capabilities can speed and amplify the effects of strategy. If an enterprise datafies all aspects of customer interactions and partner activities, it can see the results of its experimentation, such as A/B tests, in real time. Then machine-learning algorithms can automatically make adjustments that increase systemwide efficiency and make exploitation of a successful strategic experiment efficient and even semi-automated.

Strategic planning departments or their successors can now focus their efforts on developing creative prototypes of products or processes—the exploration process—that can be fed into further experiments. I call this experimental strategic cycle "self-tuning," in an explicit nod to algorithmic design thinking from chapters 3.

Applying self-tuning thinking to strategy and even to the organization is no easy task. This chapter shows how Alibaba has been making this transition.

Dynamic Strategy: Strategic Adjustment in Real Time

In 2008, Alibaba identified its strategy for the next ten years as "fostering the development of an open, collaborative, and flourishing e-commerce ecosystem." But it wasn't until the last few years that we started realizing that in responding to the changes in the external environment, the organization itself had to evolve. We didn't know enough about what the future would look like a few years out to plan for it. Alibaba needed to constantly adjust and readjust to the environment in real time, without traditional management getting in the way.

Self-tuning means that learning becomes the central focus of an organization. The strategy-making process is one of generating, coordinating, and modifying experiments—a vastly different operation from traditional long-range planning. The organization seeks a coherent vision of the future, both in goals and in execution. It implements this strategy by experimenting on that vision throughout the business. When vision and the experiment intersect, success is imminent. At Alibaba, we have made great efforts in this direction, including studying what other internet pioneers have done. Our multiple businesses and continuing growth testify to our success in these early stages of experimentation, though there is much more to be done.

The Self-Tuning Learning Loop

Machine-learning algorithms are a productive analogy for a self-tuning organization; they embody learning loops that prompt self-adjustment. I discussed in chapter 3 how datafication, iterating algorithms, and smart products combine into the capabilities of data intelligence. Thanks to data intelligence, MYbank's loan product learns from borrower behavior, and the business continuously improves its lending decisions. The business's algorithms continuously update their lending rates according to feedback in the form of data such as loans accepted and time to repayment. MYbank's algorithms improve recommendations over time—their goal is to decrease the total default rate of the platform as a whole. (In computer science, the optimization goal of an algorithm is called the "objective function.") In chapter 3, I analyzed MYbank's product with a focus on how the lending business developed data intelligence. Now, I will extend the basic mindset behind data intelligence into a larger feedback loop, which organizations as a whole can apply to strategy formulation.

Adjusting through experimentation

Machine-learning algorithms are designed to generate, test, and amplify favorable outcomes. They exhaustively sift through an array of possible options; in MYbank's case, these options encompass all the possible variables that might affect a lendee's repayment. All of these possible outcomes represent hypotheses. Is default rate connected to the time of day when the loan is issued? Will this batch of users default? Machine-learning algorithms conduct experiments on enormous data sets, testing new ideas and recording the result. As the business grows, datafication continues and generates more information, with which the algorithms can generate even more options and experiments.

Experimentation does not occur at random. Engineers design algorithms to test various options economically, minimizing search time and computing cost. One of the chief techniques for economizing experimentation is to amplify what has worked in the past and replace less preferred options with different choices. Experimentation levels are moderated after machine-learning engines learn more and more about users through sustained interaction. MYbank's algorithms hone in on the risk tolerance of the lendee with each iteration, lowering the rate of recommendation of randomly generated products. The algorithms then apply this information to further experiments to amplify what worked.

As experimentation starts to converge on a result, the customer experience begins to improve as the adaptable product adjusts. MYbank's lending services get better and more responsive as they scale. It is no exaggeration to say that the algorithm engines shape, to some degree, user experience and even user behavior, in the case of more complicated data-intelligence products such as recommendation engines on the Taobao app. Much of the user delight with recommendation engines comes from finding new products and content they would not otherwise have found. Being directed to a new category or product both uncovers and shapes what a user finds interesting and what he or she will look for in future visits to the marketplace.

Taken as a whole, the experimentation process of machine-learning algorithms can be called "self-tuning." Self-adjusting functionality is baked into the algorithms themselves. No analyst or programmer needs to individually interpret user feedback, manually adjust the exploration ratio, commission an analysis, or deliberate on how best to guide users to more optimal behavior. Data intelligence takes care of much of the hard work, helping businesses adjust independently to a wide variety of environments, especially ones that change constantly. The most developed data-intelligence services can conduct experiments and make adjustments for each user in a rapid and massively parallel fashion.

Applying Self-Tuning Principles to Strategy

Products built on data intelligence are self-tuning, navigating with minimal human input though the complex, uncertain, and fast-changing landscape of user desires and requirements. But these products also herald a new trend that is often overlooked even by those quite familiar with artificial intelligence. The world's top internet companies, such as Facebook, Amazon, and, of course, Alibaba, are taking the self-tuning mindset behind data intelligence a step further, experimenting with how self-tuning principles can be applied to the entire enterprise.

To imagine how we might run a firm like an algorithm, recall that computer algorithms do not program themselves. Humans must decide their objective function, the overarching goal of the algorithm, and adjust how the algorithm prioritizes different directions toward that goal. (For example, the objective function of Facebook's news feed product is a combination of advertising revenue and user engagement, measured by metrics like the number of comments posted. By changing the relative weight of these two metrics, Facebook can make effective trade-offs between user experience versus income. I will return to Facebook's goal metrics in the next chapter.)

In an organization, the analogue to objective function is an organization's vision: as vision changes over time, the business model will evolve. As the rest of this chapter explains, the self-tuning characteristics of algorithms can shed light on how to structure and run whole enterprises in an increasingly complex and fast-changing business environment. As the organization collectively monitors the competitive environment, consumer engagement, and system-wide results, it intervenes when necessary, adjusting infrastructure, goals, and vision to shape a healthy, productive business. Such an organization is built for change and emphasizes planning and experimentation, not finalizing plans.

The Starting Point: A Vision of the Future

In most organizations, the vision and business model are fixed axes around which the entire enterprise revolves. They are worked out by the founder or founders, and once proven successful, they are rarely changed. The organization is essentially focused on realizing this fixed vision by executing, optimizing, and scaling the foundational business model.

In the traditional industrial economy, the vision or mission and the business model were often the same: build cars affordable to the masses, connect the country by railroad, provide electricity, and so forth. The vision or mission was less important when the future was more predictable. An organization's vision has progressively become more important as business makes the transition to a knowledge economy and as economic and technological change has sped up. Senior management needed a way of guiding employee actions, communicating goals with investors, and applying institutional knowledge to more markets and products. So, they started crafting a vision. They then generated new ideas to improve the current offering or to create new offerings, while still firmly situated within the frame of the existing business model and vision.

This traditional approach is clearly self-limiting, not only in a world of fast-changing customer preferences and offerings, but also in one of shortened enterprise life and rapidly aging business models and strategies. Today, vision is the heart of a firm's strategy. It must be clearly understood, trenchantly described, and regularly updated to bring together a network of suppliers, producers, partners, and customers. Vision sets the direction for the evolution of the whole network. Like *customer first*, vision has changed from nice-to-have to an operational must-have. It is the objective function for the organization and network.

I will discuss mission and vision in much detail in the next chapter, but for now, it is important to explain the difference between the two terms as Alibaba understands them. At the highest level, vision is an understanding of the world as it will be in the future. It captures the direction industries will evolve in response to societal, economic, and technological progress. Only on the basis of that understanding, within a landscape of change, can the firm articulate its direction and ambitions. Thus, vision, narrowly written, describes what the firm seeks to achieve and defines the scope of exploration. It defines where the firm fits into the future.

The mission of the firm, on the other hand, is the change the firm is driven to make in the world. It is the firm's reason for existing, and the clarion call by which it attracts talent and resources to its side. Mission and vision (as well as values, which I will discuss in the next chapter) are closely linked and influence the other: your view of how the world will change will necessarily affect how you might change that world. For some companies, mission and vision are treated as the same thing. However, I would advocate separating the two to achieve a balance between a relatively fixed *raison d'être* (mission) and a mutable, improvable view of the future (vision). Practically speaking, a successful firm does not normally iterate on its mission the way that

I advocate iterating between vision and action in this chapter. (Alibaba's mission, as I will describe in the next chapter, has basically remained constant throughout the life of the company: "to make it easy to do business everywhere.")

This chapter will focus on vision and how to steadily improve it through experimentation. Today, as I've described in this book, organizations are but one player in an interconnected, intelligent, evolving network. Whoever has the vision for the future will attract players into their network—the partners, providers, and consumers. The more connections the vision inspires, the more assets the visionary can mobilize. It is the only way to shape the future around you.

Why visionaries dominate

Jack Ma, Steve Jobs, Elon Musk, and Mark Zuckerberg are all known as visionaries. They have to inspire their employees, partners, and customers to mobilize the network to realize the vision. They are outspoken evangelists in a way that the leaders of GE, Toyota, and Merck have never been. The difference in the demeanors of these two groups is not coincidental.

Traditional corporate leaders do not shape the future; they run a machine. When we teach at Alibaba's School of Entrepreneurship, we show a slide of ten business leaders and ask our students to identify them.[3] They can easily pick out Ma, Musk, and Jobs. Communicating a vision to many people grants a form of celebrity and often requires a highly individualized value set and mission. But virtually no one can identify the CEO of Citibank, Toyota, or General Electric. Those companies don't need visionaries. They need executives who can manage operations. Such leaders are much more interchangeable.

In 2015, Lyft founder and CEO John Zimmer described to me how, when he started the company's ridesharing service, he worried about its ability to gain traction. Unlike other rideshare services, this one tried to connect several riders to minimize car use and to be more eco-friendly. But without a lot of riders, early adopters would have much longer trips and save little money. Zimmer was shocked at how quickly the service ramped up. Plenty of customers shared his vision and were willing to make short-term sacrifices to make it happen. In classic non-zero-sum fashion, as the number of customers increased, the service became more efficient and useful.

The web celebs described in part 2 are more than successful brand builders. These entrepreneurs continually demonstrate new visions of themselves, their looks, or the environment. More importantly, despite being just one individual, web celebs like Big-E have a vast network supporting them. Firms like Ruhan are visionaries within the wider network, shaping the future for themselves and for their partners as the apparel industry realigns around them.

Retuning the Vision

A clear vision shapes the future and directs the network's evolution, but the vision must continually incorporate feedback and evolve within the larger environment. More than a static vision, the firm needs a visioning process. As time passes, its vision has to be checked against reality and updated.

In a network, the boundary between the internal and external organization is blurred. More importantly, as I described in chapter 6, the strategies of different firms are interdependent, especially for platforms. Information from the environment must be taken in to retune the platform's vision. In this dynamic process, leadership needs to continually reshape its understanding of the future, thus influencing the future shape of the system. Steve Jobs used Apple's product launches, always spectacular affairs and self-conscious theater, to express his revised vision. That's why it is called Macworld: the event is an essential but often-overlooked way in which Jobs "managed" the Apple ecosystem.

Alibaba exemplifies this revisioning approach. When the company started in 1999, the internet reached less than 1 percent of China's more than one billion citizens. While many observers expected penetration to grow, they couldn't predict the precise nature of that growth. In response to this uncertainty, Alibaba applied an experimental approach to our vision. Rather than treat our vision as a given, the company instead posited a vision, given the best working assumption about the future and using all available information. We remained transparent about this approach. As the market evolved and new realities emerged, management regularly and profoundly reevaluated its vision, checking its intuition against reality and modifying the company's goals as appropriate.

In the early years, Alibaba directed its efforts to becoming, in the company's words, "an e-commerce company serving China's small exporting companies." This objective led to the initial focus on Alibaba.com, which created a platform for Chinese manufacturers to sell internationally. However, as the market continued to evolve, so did the company's vision. With the explosive growth of Chinese domestic consumption, Jack Ma saw the opportunity to expand our e-commerce offerings beyond China's export businesses to include Chinese consumers. The result was the launch of Taobao in 2003. However, Alibaba soon realized that Chinese consumers needed more than just a marketplace for buying and selling. They needed greater confidence in online shopping and assurance that their payments were safe. There were no credit cards in China at the time. Consequently, Taobao expanded its reach with Alipay in 2004, which became a runaway success and greatly sped up the penetration of e-commerce across the country.

We at Alibaba were not the only ones to create services to facilitate the marketplace. As described in chapter 2, other companies providing services, such as storefront builders and models, entered the growing marketplace. Building on this development, Alibaba expanded its vision in 2008: "Foster the development of an open, collaborative, and flourishing e-commerce ecosystem." The company started to offer more infrastructure services, such as cloud computing, finance, and logistics. With the rapid emergence of the mobile internet, Alibaba has further evolved our vision to its current version: "We aim to build the future infrastructure of commerce. We envision that our customers will meet, work and live at Alibaba, and that we will be a company that lasts at least 102 years." Note that we deliberately dropped the *e* from *e-commerce,* to reflect Jack Ma's belief that all business will become e-business. (For much more detail on the strategic choices made throughout Taobao's history, see appendixes A and B.)

Many outsiders view our vision statements as PR exercises that help the world understand the firm, not as actual descriptions of our business model. Nothing could be further from the truth. Alibaba's evolving vision reflects our top management's understanding of the future of commerce, as well as Alibaba's place in constructing that future. Only with the current vision articulated can the entire network and our organization begin to move toward that future.

Dynamic Strategy: Planning, Not Plans

As *vision* the static noun is inflected into the active verb of *visioning*, the strategic process must emphasize the dynamic. It is about the planning, not making a plan.

In many organizations, detailed, fixed plans form the core of their strategy. In Alibaba's case, rapid technology changes, shifting consumer expectations in China and beyond, and regulatory uncertainty make it very difficult to predict or plan for the future. In response, we have shifted the conventional focus on plans to a continuous process of planning. Rather than an elaborate plan that is executed meticulously, Alibaba continuously retunes strategy as circumstances change, in a very decentralized manner.

Within the company, there is a normal annual planning cycle, with a few iterations between business-unit leaders and the top management team in the third and fourth quarter each year. Leadership, however, recognizes and expects that this direction is only a starting point and will change. In my nearly decade-long capacity guiding the strategy team, I have never written a formal strategy plan for the company. But each year, we do have a ten-page presentation summarizing the key points of our strategic understanding. This presentation is often reviewed, and revised if necessary, whenever we discuss important business issues.

I remember an animated discussion at a top management meeting one day in April 2012. We reached consensus about the importance of data in the future and agreed that Alibaba should become the leading platform for data sharing. Later that same day, there was a scheduled meeting that included Alibaba middle managers. Jack Ma asked me to summarize the morning discussion during lunch and present the new ideas as our new "plan" to the whole group that very afternoon. This mindset might strike an organization accustomed to spending several months to create a three- or five-year plan as slightly unorthodox. For us, it is par for the course.

Moreover, such rapid iterations of strategy happen at every level of the organization. Whenever a business leader sees an important change or a new opportunity in the marketplace, he or she can initiate what we call internally a *cocreation* (*gong chuang*) meeting. It is called cocreation because Alibaba employees, including senior business leaders and lead implementers, codevelop new directions with customers.

Cocreation

Cocreation, typically kicked off with a full-day working session at Alibaba, involves four steps. First we set the "ground truth," identifying and laying out change signals based on data from the market or insights from customers or staff. In addition, we ensure that the right people are in the meeting and have the right dynamics to work together toward a solution.

Second, we get to know the user and their current situation in as much depth as possible. In this step, the participants dive deep into the merchant or consumer viewpoint to understand our users' evolving needs or pain points and to brainstorm potential solutions. For example, in a recent cocreation meeting for one business unit, Alibaba selected five consumers to join the meeting and divided the staff into smaller teams to each work with one consumer to understand their pain points. The teams then reported back to the larger group twice—once with the user present to ensure that the issues were understood correctly and the second time without the user to push to a deeper level of analysis and solution development.

Third, we base an action plan on the outcomes of the discussions. The action plans must identify a leader who can champion the issue or opportunity, the supporting team or teams that will put the ideas into action, and the mechanism for doing the work. The mechanism involves, at a minimum, the communication processes, the metrics for evaluating progress, and the timeline for execution so that the team can align its efforts. Often, this third step takes the most time and effort, because action plans are truly crucial for ensuring that ideas gets translated into reality. Figuring out who is in charge of making the action plan happen is a complicated and often-fraught process, but teams need to do the hard work to get results.

The fourth and final step of cocreation is user feedback. Teams must embed regular feedback into their development processes. At monthly or bimonthly check-ins at Alibaba, teams present user reactions to evolving designs, prototypes, or concepts to ensure that execution meets market expectations.

Taken together, the steps of cocreation highlight the iterative and distributed dimension of self-tuning. Business units can initiate cocreation sessions when they see a relevant market stimulus, without any central mandate or oversight. By creating a forum for regular exchange with customers and related parties within the company, Alibaba evolves with the market and makes optimal use of local knowledge. In effect, senior leadership relinquishes a degree of control to allow the enterprise to organically adapt to the external environment. In this way, self-tuning enterprises leave more room for products and even business models to be pulled by the market, rather than pushed via top-down decisions. All this effort also contributes to the continuous upgrading of the vision or strategy at the senior level, as decision making and its repercussions "trickle up" through the organization.

In summary, there are three key points in the strategy-making process for smart businesses. First, vision is critical. Second, smart businesses constantly retune their visions. Third, for smart businesses, strategy formulation is dynamic; it is about planning, not about static plans. What replaces traditional strategy formulation in a smart business is iteration through experimentation.

Applying Self-Tuning Principles to Business Models

When the vision and strategic plans are no longer fixed points but dynamic processes, so is the business model. Indeed, the business model as a whole is the most important arena for experimentation.

Experimenting with the Business Model

Previous chapters have discussed many examples of why Alibaba's eco-system consists of much more than retail in the traditional sense, from e-commerce platforms (Taobao, Tmall) to payment and finance (Ant Financial), cloud computing (Alibaba Cloud), and logistics (Cainiao Network). (See appendix A for more details on these businesses.)

To achieve such breadth and depth, we had to commit to business model experimentation from the outset. The decision in 2003 to venture beyond our core B2B business and found Taobao—just four years after our company's founding—was hotly debated within the company. A formidable rival, eBay, had already entered the Chinese market with much fanfare, but to the leadership team, the American-based company seemed to be operating in several ways out of step with the Chinese market. However, Alibaba did not give up on exploitation of our budding B2B business. To minimize downside drain, management set up the new venture as a startup, with separate funding. (In fact, Taobao was a fifty-fifty joint venture between Alibaba and Softbank.) The Taobao team spent its early days in an apartment, totally separate from the Alibaba offices, and experimented as it saw fit. By sequestering the new venture and its employees, Jack doubled down on experimentation.

At each juncture of its growth and evolution, Alibaba generated new business-model options, testing possibilities by letting them run as separate units. The most promising ones then scaled up. In 2006, seeing two new developing trends, B2C and SaaS (software-as-a-service), we started two new business units to experiment in those spaces. The Taobao Mall, which after a few iterations of the business model became Tmall, is a major part of the group portfolio today. On the other hand, AliSoft, which tried to catch the SaaS wave, entered the market too early and couldn't find a killer app with enough customers. The business was shut down in 2009.

Focusing on Exploration

Another driver of Alibaba's success has been its deliberate choice to keep experimenting with the business model in response to the environment. Rather than being content to transition into exploitation once the business model matures, Alibaba continues to engage in exploration as new conditions emerge.

For example, Taobao achieved more than an 80 percent share of China's e-commerce market within just four years of launch and became a national phenomenon by 2011. Many would take this leadership position as a signal of market validation and focus on optimizing and defending the successful model. Instead, we saw the still-unrelenting growth of China's internet population and the increasing sophistication of consumers and retailers as a signal of greater uncertainty in the marketplace and a risk to our current model. This is where human judgment comes in. Deciding when to keep exploring or switch to pure exploitation will define the culture and success of many businesses.

For Alibaba, leadership was inclined to conduct more experimentation and take more risks. Again, there was heated debate within the company on which direction to go and which business model to build up. Instead of making a simple top-down decision, we made a bold experiment: let the market pick the future winners. In 2011, Alibaba split the successful Taobao business into three independent and competing businesses units. Each unit would effectively make a different bet on the future of e-commerce in China. Taobao would focus on smaller brands and the consumer-to-consumer (C2C) market; Tmall on larger brands and the B2C market; and Etao, a new business unit, would focus on product search, aggregating information across different marketplaces and platforms.

Increasing your experimentation at the height of success runs contrary to established managerial wisdom, but for Alibaba, it was a necessary move to avoid rigidity and to continuously create options in a rapidly evolving e-commerce market. By early 2013, Tmall had won market leadership in fiercely competitive B2C markets—a successful experiment. Taobao maintains its dominant position in the C2C marketplace and has since given rise to innovative C2B businesses such as the web celebs—another successful experiment. Product search, on the other hand, proved not to be the future, and Etao has become a niche product.

Obviously, such experimentation comes with high financial and organizational costs. I remembered the tremendous pressure we faced when we split Taobao into three units. It was very hard to tell employees that while they were competing against each other in the market, they also belonged to the same company. But being straightforward about what we were doing was also very important. Employees needed to know that the experiment was taking place and what we were trying to learn. Discerning the real drivers of each business's development is also very difficult. The time spent setting up, communicating, and letting the businesses duke it out might have been inefficient, but the costs are worth it. In a rapidly changing environment, getting your vision of the future right and securing the fit of your strategy with the evolving environment are the most important objectives. The significant investment in experimentation is well worth the cost and the risk. For Alibaba, our experiments clarified the direction of e-commerce in China and kept providing the resources that fueled the growth of Taobao and Tmall—as exemplified by our stunning Singles Day successes.

Returning to the Vision

Through business-model experimentation, Alibaba has not only arrived at a clearer vision of the dynamic environment in which we operate. Our vision has profoundly shaped the evolution of our environment.

For smart businesses, leadership and the entire organization should be structured to experiment and report results, even those that are unsuccessful or have unintended consequences. The organization must be minutely attuned to its network and market. The vision, the objective function of the "algorithm" that is the firm, may need to be recalibrated, improved, or changed altogether. A vision, just like algorithms, needs to be guided and modified by constant human inquiry to make sure both customers and the overall ecosystem are evolving in healthy ways. Recall from chapter 4 how Alibaba kept adjusting its search algorithms to promote a balanced and robust market for both buyers and sellers, and how our recommendations product changed after the 2013 transition to mobile.

As our vision of the future changed, our platforms set the direction of China's e-commerce sector. Tmall has evolved from a higher-end marketplace on Taobao to the entrance point for the world's global brands to enter China through Tmall Global. Taobao has come a long way from its origins as a digital flea market; it now enables consumers to shop for anything imaginable, and incubates highly innovative firms such as the web celebs. At the same time, Alibaba's enabling business models, such as Ant Financial for finance and the Cainiao Network for logistics, have set new expectations for security and computing online and offline. Our dominance today is a result of consistently improving upon our vision, and then daring to allow our businesses to capitalize on a new and improved view of the future.

The Foundation as a Change-Seeking Culture

Faced with market fluctuations and disruptions that regularly reshape the landscape, an organization with a self-tuning strategy sets aside the idea of a fixed vision and business model. Instead, the organization regularly recalibrates all its components to the environment by continuously experimenting throughout the organization. The goal is that the firm's vision will begin to converge through a process of action and recalibration—in other words, self-tuning. Self-tuning thus implies that the organization is always learning and innovating. Consequently, change is the natural outcome and an essential feature of the organization.

Setting Expectations from the Beginning

With all this retuning and experimentation, a culture that not only facilitates but even encourages change is fundamental. Reactions to change depend heavily on the mindset of the organization. At Alibaba, the embrace of change is wired into its DNA. The company has created a language and an expectation of change through its six core values, one of which is precisely "embracing change." Jack Ma regularly emphasizes this theme in his communications with employees, as does the rest of the leadership team. Leadership is totally forthcoming with employees about anticipating change and adaptation at every level from the day that new employees join the company.

By creating the expectation of change, Alibaba's employees have come to see it as part of business as usual. "If you have not changed bosses five times in a year, you haven't seen real change" is a well-circulated adage. *Customer first* is the first of Alibaba's six core values. Since customer needs are a moving target, you have to change to meet their needs. Otherwise, you will simply be wiped out by competition. "To be prepared for change," Jack Ma emphasizes, "is the best plan." You have to evolve with the external environment, no matter how fast you have to do it, and change must be hardwired into your organization's culture.

To build this culture, you need the right people. A key consideration in Alibaba's hiring decisions is a candidate's willingness to change. Experience has shown that technical skill alone is not a sufficient metric to identify the right talent. Rather, when assessing candidates, interviewers regularly ask about the biggest change a candidate has experienced and how he or she dealt with it. In this way, Alibaba only brings on board new employees who are ready and able to change. I will expand this point in detail in the following chapter.

Institutionalizing Change

Organizational change must be institutionalized and normalized. To be good at change, an organization must regularly engage in it. Traditionally, organizational change is conducted through infrequent, but major transformations. However, if an enterprise regularly adjusts itself to the external environment, it has less need for risky one-shot overhauls.

An extreme example occurred in 2012, when Alibaba experimented with a rotation program for its twenty-two main upper-level managers across the business. While rotational programs are not uncommon at more junior levels, Alibaba focused its program on the senior-most levels of each business unit (i.e., shuffling around all leadership except the C-suite). There was some concern about the potential risk this program would bring to continuing operations. However, the program proved quite successful, as it required managers to institutionalize and transfer knowledge to transitioning colleagues, thus preventing siloing and parochial thinking. The program not only helped further develop the skills of top talent, but also demonstrated throughout the entire organization the leadership's commitment to organizational flexibility. Alibaba now runs a regular program rotating a portion of senior leadership every year.

Alibaba continuously focuses on developing and maintaining an organizational flexibility that tracks the environment, especially as the company continues to grow. As Ma has explained many times in internal meetings: "Strategy and organization go hand-in-hand. Every year we change the organizational structure in tandem with changes in strategy."

I mentioned above how Taobao was split into three business units in 2011. Two months later, the whole group was first split into seven business units and then further divided into twenty-five business units in the following sixty days. The objective was to make the whole company as nimble as possible, so that each business unit could move quickly on its own. Remarkably, after three major reorgs, each business unit finished its strategy, annual planning, and budgeting process in three months. Then, in late 2013, Alibaba launched an all-in-mobile initiative to become a mobile-first company. In addition to normal reorg, the company drafted 5 percent of engineers from all business units—often some of the best—and moved them to the mobile initiative. Though there were growing pains, most employees understood that these changes represented a conscious effort on the part of the company to adapt to the environment and to prepare for the future. All this would be impossible without a culture that embraced change.

Many people talk about experimentation, innovation, and organization change, but the cost is simply prohibitive. Internet companies like Alibaba can do this because they have built the right culture and the right infrastructure. I will elaborate on culture and infrastructure in the next chapter.

The Supple Organization

Taken together, a transparent change culture and flexible organizational structure play an important role in shaping employee perceptions about what an organization should be. The prevailing idea that organizations should be stable, fixed structures with clear reporting lines is the product of a stable and predictable environment. Facing a much more dynamic and uncertain landscape, Alibaba has prepared itself to evolve quickly by making change a part of business as usual for its employees and providing the clarity and infrastructure to support it.

Our company has thus gradually embraced the self-tuning ethos. We work to apply an evolutionary approach to all levels of the company. The vision, the business model, and even our organizational structure are regularly recalibrated to the environment through experimentation. Most fundamentally, our learning processes do not occur in a top-down, deliberative chain. They are spread throughout the organization and are self-directed. The organization is no longer viewed as a means to amplify and cascade leadership's intentions. Information, be it user input, environmental changes, or effective or ineffective responses, flows freely through the organization, and every actor can respond. With the vision articulated by leadership acting as its magnetic pole, the organization moves organically.

Taken together, a focus on exploration, experimentation, and iteration across the business mandate a reconceptualization of organization and management. The firm becomes a collective machine for continuous iteration, much like an enormous algorithm whose objective function is the needs of the customer. The machine engages with its environment, its partners, and its clients, obtaining rich feedback, which it uses to further oil its gears and run more effectively. Management doesn't tell the machine what to do; it merely makes sure everything runs smoothly.

If managers no longer direct and control, and the organization is self-tuning, then what is the role of management in a smart business? What should the firm itself look like, and how should managers design their organizations? We turn to these topics in the next chapter.

CHAPTER 8

FROM MANAGING TO ENABLING

How to Retool the Organization

When computers can do the routine but energy-intensive knowledge work more efficiently than humans can, and the network can coordinate effective responses to consumer demands, what do organizations do? To be sure, a smart business—its operations, algorithms, and products—must be designed by humans. Yet once these elements are in place, the machines can do the heavy lifting. However, computers cannot create new products and services, much less engage in the visionary experimentation of the previous chapter. Innovation and creativity are the crucial human input that keeps an organization growing and thriving. Organizations of the future will focus on continual innovation. They go beyond computer calculations to intuit customer needs. In response to new technology, the people in an enterprise create original products and services or reimagine existing offerings that will be even more efficacious for humans.

In the industrial age, organizations aimed to improve the efficiency of resource utilization. In the knowledge age, they optimized knowledge usage and management. Now, in the new age of smart business, an organization's goal is to improve the efficiency of innovation founded on human insight and creativity. The success rate of innovation itself is the new game.

Think about that for a minute. Businesses have been talking about becoming more innovative for some time. However, today we are facing an innovation imperative that requires companies to come up with winning innovations quickly, consistently, and continuously. To meet this imperative, business must depart sharply from traditional management theory and practice.

Since Frederick Winslow Taylor and the idea of scientific management, management's job was to know exactly what workers should do. Managers needed to prepare and motivate workers and ensure that they did the work as efficiently as possible. It was about planning and control. No longer.

When Alibaba realized in 2013 that it had to transform itself into a mobile internet company—the all-in decision described in chapter 4—the transformation was a momentous task that could not be planned or controlled. It was not just the challenge of reengineering software to operate Alibaba services on mobile devices. The entire business had to be reinvented. What worked on a website might not be appropriate for the mobile market; website-based software certainly did not take advantage of the new opportunities that mobile offered. While company leaders could see the outline of the future, they could not accurately or easily foresee its details or direct its development. They faced the daunting but requisite task of mobilizing the whole organization to innovate quickly and figure out what the markets wanted.

Alibaba's leadership lacked a road map for success in the mobile environment. However, our company's experience with creating an online retail industry and, later, a logistics operation suggested a path. In those cases, we created a platform and tools that others used to build their businesses as they saw fit. They innovated and transacted; some made money and some went out of business. Now we had to do it internally. When Alibaba moved to mobile, we had to get our teams to innovate and experiment at a furious pace so we could learn what the market rewarded. We had to create the internal platforms, tools, and methods to ensure that market responses would immediately affect our internal activity and resource allocation.

This was a learning process, and we did not hit the gate running. However, armed with opportunity, vision, and increasingly relevant and powerful frameworks and tools, such as those described in this chapter, our mobile teams exploded with energy. Team after team came up with new forms of advertising—banners, live streaming, videos. They created apps or features that helped users learn new subjects, find products, and get together with communities of like-minded viewers to advise each other. The team members watched what other mobile or social networking companies around the world were doing and tried to take them to the next level on the Taobao mobile app. Some things worked and some didn't, but the creativity and churn has been tremendous.

This kind of initiative, independence, and innovation is not what is expected of a typical employee; nor can it be managed in the traditional way. Many employees like, or are trained to like, coming to work, executing orders or policies, and going home with a paycheck. (This still seems to be a mistaken stereotype of the typical Chinese worker.) They focus on exploitation, i.e., trying to get better at what they have done so they can be more efficient. But they are not scanning the horizon (internally or externally) for new ideas or cross-fertilization and are not eagerly experimenting to see what works. Increasingly, today's enterprises need to infuse their work with exactly this kind of initiative, independence, and innovation. Management's job now is to enable these qualities.

How to Enable the Organization

A firm's approach to innovation is not dissimilar to the path through which a business becomes smart, facilitating network coordination and leveraging data intelligence. Internally, the organization connects employees with different discipline expertise relevant to customer needs. At the same time, using data intelligence, the organization must provide internal platforms and data resources that make workflows smarter. For example, a company should comprehensively organize product development and deliberately institutionalize organizational memory. It must create smart metrics for employee and product performance. In practice, doing any of these things requires that internal workflows occur online, are softwared, and rely on live data.

As described in the previous chapter, the organization is no longer a vessel for conveying orders from the top. It is a vacuum sucking up information about its environment and then generating and coordinating effective responses. The job of leadership is not to manage this experiment, but to make it possible and boost its success rate. These new methods stand in direct contrast to traditional management techniques and philosophy. Within Alibaba, I use the term "enabling" (*fu neng*) to refer to the organizational methods for managing experimentation. (Readers interested in more background on enabling may consult appendix C.)

"Enabling" is a technical term within Alibaba because it mandates technical work. An enabling organization undergoes the complex task of creating the conditions, environment, and tools so that people within the organization can more easily reach their goals. Through enabling mechanisms, management provides the necessary conditions to tackle business problems through innovation as opposed to the execution of tried-and-true procedures. This means managers must now focus on things like articulating the mission and providing the environment that attracts the right collaborators, supplying the tools for them to experiment and scale successful ideas, and providing a market to assess the innovation's success. Instead of micromanaging the firm, management creates the organization's architecture to run itself.

The practice of enabling, a very concrete approach to organizations, requires specific values and technical infrastructure. Note that enabling is not a touchy-feely encouragement of employees. It is very, very difficult, and the overall costs of running organizations through various enabling practices have previously prohibited the techniques from being applied to organizations at scale. The techniques have similarities to those traditionally used in the arts, movie making—the Hollywood model—or journalism. Technology has lowered these costs so that organizations can experiment with this new innovation-oriented paradigm. While no one has found all the right answers yet, smart businesses are making steady progress in this direction.

This chapter will examine what managers in a smart business do differently on three dimensions: people, infrastructure, and mechanisms. I will show you what enabling looks like and how to do it. If you're a manager, most of your job now will be about understanding the type of people the organization needs; appealing to them; and designing the architecture for the interaction between groups of creators and their work, all to make innovation more effective.

People: Who You Need and What to Do about Them

Smart businesses require people who combine creativity with technological comfort and business savvy. Different businesses and missions will have particular requirements, but when automation can do much of the routine, punch-the-clock type of work, employees or associates need to advance the overall mission or invest in the craft of their activity. They draw on their internal resources and training and seek inspiration, ideas, and support from wherever they can find them. The employees may seek advice and input but not direction. With their initiative on the line, they must see the results of their contribution.[1]

Management's first function is finding the right people for its business. This requires different recruiting, vetting, and incentive systems than the ones most companies use today. Commensurate financial rewards for high performers are necessary but not sufficient. A compelling mission, an empowering environment, and a distinctive culture are also necessary for success. Each of these is a very tall order for organization leadership.

Start with Mission and Vision

In the previous chapter, I discussed how a firm should formulate its vision and, to a lesser extent, mission. Once formulated, firms must use their mission and vision to motivate the organization. In the Chinese business world, Alibaba is well known as an uncommonly mission-focused enterprise (see the sidebar "Alibaba's Mission, Vision, and Values"). Alibaba's mission, from nearly day one, has been "to make it easy to do business anywhere." This phrase is not merely a slogan. It is a genuine belief on the part of the founders, and it has deeply affected nearly every important decision that the company has made.

ALIBABA'S MISSION, VISION, AND VALUES

Our Mission

"To make it easy to do business anywhere."

Our founders started our company to champion small businesses, in the belief that the internet would level the playing field by enabling small enterprises to use innovation and technology to grow and compete more effectively in the domestic and global economies.

We believe that concentrating on customer needs and solving their problems—whether those customers are consumers or merchants—ultimately will lead to the best outcome for our business. We have developed a large ecosystem for online and mobile commerce that enables participants to create and share value on our platforms. Our mission over the long term, not the pursuit of short-term gains, guides our decisions for the ecosystem.

Our Vision

We aim to build the infrastructure of commerce for the future. We envision that our customers will meet, work, and live at Alibaba and that we will be a company that lasts at least 102 years.

Meet @ Alibaba

We facilitate hundreds of millions of commercial and social interactions among our users, between consumers and merchants, and among businesses, every day.

Work @ Alibaba

We empower our customers with commercial infrastructure and data technology so that they can build businesses and create value for the benefit of all.

Live @ Alibaba

We strive to expand our products and services so that we become central to the everyday lives of our customers.

102 Years: Built for the Long Term

We were founded in 1999. To last 102 years means we will have spanned three centuries, an achievement signifying that we will have stood the test of time. We build our culture, organization, business models, and systems for long-term sustainability.

Our Values

Our six values are fundamental to the way we operate and how we recruit, evaluate, and compensate our people:

Customer first: The interests of our community of consumers and merchants must be our first priority.

Teamwork: We believe that teamwork enables ordinary people to achieve extraordinary things.

Embrace change: In this fast-changing world, we must be flexible, innovative, and ready to adapt to new business conditions to survive.

Integrity: We expect our people to uphold the highest standards of honesty and to deliver on their commitments.

Passion: We expect our people to approach everything with fire in their bellies and to never give up on doing what they believe is right.

Commitment: Employees who demonstrate perseverance and excellence are richly rewarded. Nothing should be taken lightly as we encourage our people to "work happily and live seriously."

Consider the wording of the preceding mission statement. By definition, business has to be easy for everyone if the mission is to be fulfilled; business cannot just be easy for the most convenient or profitable of clients. In the early years of Alibaba's wholesaling platform, our B2B business focused on serving China's small and medium-sized enterprises (SME). This focus differentiated Alibaba from the competition, but the leaders' decision to focus on SMEs was not based on a calculation meant to entice investors. Their mission mandated that they serve the majority of clients.

To do that, they needed a business model that could rapidly scale to help everyone do business, everywhere. This mission continued into the days of Taobao, where business grew to include not just retail, but also dozens of related functions. If business is easy everywhere, then business for ISVs and models and photographers must by definition also be easy. Looking back, our mission planted the seeds for network coordination: without large-scale coordination, it would be nigh impossible to make all business easy. And the data created through wide-scale network coordination also laid the foundations for data intelligence.

After my many years of working closely with Jack Ma, I cannot emphasize enough that Alibaba's mission and vision are not slogans written for shareholders. They are genuine beliefs that affect the entire makeup of the company. They are the yardsticks by which we measure our strategic decisions. In the context of this chapter, our company's mission and vision attract people who resonate with our values. This resonance is one of the main functions of a genuinely expressed mission and vision.

Most people are not fully satisfied by material incentives. They want their personal passions to connect with the mission of the company. For the type of people whom smart businesses want to attract, motivation comes from personal achievement and the social impact of their creation. They are self-motivated. Monetary rewards are still important, but in today's war for talent of this type, money is certainly not enough. Something more intrinsically inspiring is necessary. Asked to explain why he started his space transport company SpaceX, Elon Musk described how it was part of human nature to dream of space traveling, and that he thought being born on Earth and planning to die on Mars, although not on impact, was a great idea.[2]

All the important business leaders of the last two decades have emphasized the importance of mission, vision, and values significantly more than have chief executives of the past. Whenever he talks about Alibaba, for instance, Ma always starts by saying Alibaba is a company driven by mission, vision, and values.

A good mission and vision not only encourage the support of network partners, but also help build the organization's reputation as a recruiter and increase internal support. Employees are very proud of the profound changes Alibaba is bringing to startups, SMEs, and consumers in China. Especially once we launched our Rural Taobao initiative, many employees who had grown up in rural areas jumped at the opportunity to leave their comfortable urban posts at Taobao to join the new rural business unit. Promoting economic development in their homeland is an enormously powerful force that drives company employees and associates. Similarly, Google's legendary motto "Don't be evil" and Facebook's famous "Break things" have great resonance among their employees.

Monetary compensation, including options, emphasizes rewards after the work is done. But the practice of enabling is more concerned with stimulating interest and passion with the right challenges. Only passion through internal interests, not instructions from superiors, can override the continuous frustration inherent in any innovative effort. With passion, an innovator can accept an uncertain (but possibly very large) upside for entrepreneurial work. Hence a core function of the organization is no longer assigning work and monitoring progress, but matching staff interest and expertise with customer needs. The firm needs to be agile enough to pinpoint and engage with customer needs and then deploy the employees who would be the most excited about the problem to tackle it together. Combined with commensurate rewards for excellent performance, this strategy energizes creative workers better than does simply giving them a commanding salary.

One purpose of Google's 20 percent time, where engineers get to spend 20 percent of their time on any project of their choosing, is to monitor staff interest and figure out where it could be applied to customers. Indeed, Google has acknowledged that this practice isn't really a formal policy as much as a motivational attitude by company leadership that encourages staff to be creative and do what they think is important.

Culture: Ensuring a Good Fit

Alibaba's strong mission and vision have also given rise to a truly unique culture that is enticing to potential employees, especially in the earliest years of Taobao. Taobao began as a place of great imagination, where workers were involved every day in envisioning the future of online commerce in China. Thus, the company took a page from Ma's favorite books as a child: Jin Yong's Chinese martial-arts novels.[3]

Every employee picked a nickname taken from these novels, assuming a superhero-esque alter ego as he or she traveled through the mythical landscape that was Taobao. (It would be as if every employee at Google picked a name from a Marvel comic, so that official work emails would thus begin with "Dear Lois Lane" or "Dear Wolverine.") The practice of picking nicknames continues to this day. All new employees, upon entering the company, must pick a nickname, which is used for most internal communications, even with HR and back-office staff. Many employees do not know the real names of their closest partners in the office.[4]

The whimsical and even cute culture of Taobao persists within the company today. Strong beliefs about equality run throughout the enterprise, and many of the common hierarchical terms for managers within traditional Chinese companies are not used at Alibaba. For example, in a typical Chinese workplace, lower-level employees usually refer to executives on the vice president or senior vice president level by their last name appended with the Chinese term for "President." It would be unthinkably discourteous to use the executive's full name, much less first name. At Alibaba, there has only ever been one "President": President Ma. And even in the past few years, Ma has cautioned employees not to use the term. Instead, he prefers to be called "Teacher Ma," harkening back to his original line of employment.

A strong culture, by definition, does not appeal to everyone. Any anthropologist will tell you that culture works to segregate as much as it does to bring people together, and Alibaba is no different. The firm has a special class of HR workers who are assigned randomly to interview employee candidates. They are informally dubbed the "chief olfactory officers" (in Chinese, *wen wei guan*). Their job is to "sniff out" the match between candidates and the strong corporate culture. When staff members disagree on a candidate, chief olfactory officers can have significant input on the final hiring decision.

Organizations can uphold a strong sense of community through a tight recruiting and vetting process. Zappos has long made news with its policy that pays people US$2,000 to leave after their first two weeks of paid training if the company does not seem to be a good fit for them. Google has a long and complex process to evaluate candidates, ensuring that they not only are technically qualified but also fit the culture and interact well with the team. For many years, cofounder Larry Page insisted on making the final decision on every offer. Alibaba's HR team continues to stand by its job of sniffing out new employees even as business teams put more and more pressure on HR to speed up hiring and to "avoid unnecessary overhead," because hiring is the single most important thing a company can do to preserve culture.

Today's enabling companies rely on culture more than traditional companies did. But the idea of culture is complex. Broadly, culture is the set of behaviors and common understanding that connect and perpetuate a group, forming the basis of how it navigates its environment. In the past, companies considered company culture the same way they viewed the "customer-first" mantra: clearly a great goal but not an issue that supersedes the considerations of the balance sheet. Traditionally, remuneration was clearly the most important incentive system for employees. Organizational culture was a second-order lever that managers could use to encourage or discourage certain types of behavior or that could help drive internal and external marketing efforts.

But in smart businesses, culture is fundamental. What the organization is committed to doing and how the organization does it is truly the starting point. People join the group, the culture, that they feel an affinity with. And an enormous part of the appeal of the organization is being a member of that culture and working together with like-minded people.

The attention to culture is very apparent within Alibaba. The company moves fast, requiring emotional and social maturity, and individual success often rests on an ability to speak directly to colleagues and to executives in power. Some would say you need to be able to argue to survive at Alibaba. (A sense of humor is a real asset, as well.) For people whose sensibilities are unlike those of our employees, the experience can be tough. But people who fit in with the group love working at the company.

Culture has always been a competitive advantage between firms, but it is even more so when the work is mostly creative. Innovative work is demanding and uncertain, but with the right culture, it can become exciting and fun for the right people. For firms that want to enable creative workers, fostering internal culture is a business challenge no less important than product development, sales, or marketing. They need to make the culture explicit so that it attracts people with a similar vision. Ultimately, an effective shared culture rewards those who find the culture a good way to accomplish their goals.

Indeed, the atmosphere of the organization itself can be the best reward. Creative workers are much more serious about the culture and are willing to make sacrifices for a mission, a vision, and the values they believe in.

Building the Right Infrastructure

An organization's atmosphere doesn't emerge from the ether; it arises from deliberate organizational design. To enable people instead of managing them, organizations need to build the right infrastructure services that can support innovation instead of relying on managers to plan, direct, and control resources.

Traditional management roles or services, such as HR, payroll or accounting services, and logistics management, need to be available on an organization-wide platform so that they can be accessed throughout the organization. Typical internet companies have layers of horizontal service platforms, ranging from solid tools that improve coding and development efficiency to various HR services available throughout the organization. The function of these many services is to offer network coordination and data-intelligence capabilities within the organization. I refer to these services collectively as *infra-structure*. Our experience at Alibaba has shown us that it is imperative for organizations to offer these services on demand to their workers.[5]

Creative people want to see their ideas become reality. Anything that makes this transformation easier or saves people from what they consider distractions is valuable. Making such infrastructure services accessible to everyone is not dissimilar to having food and laundry services available to employees, as many internet companies are known for doing.

But HR, accounting, logistics, and the like are only the tip of the managerial iceberg. Much traditional vertical-management work is also being transformed into internal services that are easily accessible on the organization's internal network. This is much more extensive than simply being able to download and fill out new employee forms and skip a trip to HR. It subsumes significant managerial activities like resource allocation and evaluation, which I will discuss later in the chapter in the section on metrics.

A Common Technology Infrastructure

At Alibaba, we learned from experience how important a common technological infrastructure was. The first B2B subsidiary of Alibaba Group was known for having a more traditional culture and for being less innovative than its offshoot Taobao. The business model— a digital yellow pages in which businesses could pay for placement in the lists—had become fixed early on. All efforts to build new businesses or revenue streams atop this base had fizzled. In 2012, when top leadership rotated, Jeff Zhang, the vice president of product and engineering from Taobao, was transferred to lead the older B2B business unit.[6]

Almost immediately, Zhang realized that the B2B unit's technology infrastructure was built like that of a traditional industrial company, unlike Taobao. It was vertically integrated, with little sharing or cross-pollination between products or teams. There was the technology that supported the yellow page listings, another technology silo that reached out to new businesses, and yet another one that dealt with sourcing support. No platform united all the unit's operations. Many technical teams were unable to create products that would interact or communicate with each other due to organizational barriers.

To make matters worse, every time anyone in the B2B business unit wanted to try a new idea, the person had to build it from the ground up. He or she couldn't just access the existing technology and add new features. Trying anything new took enormous time and resources and hence required approval from the top. The cost of experimentation—which also meant the cost of failure—was prohibitive.

Zhang decided to tear up the entire technical infrastructure of the business and reconstruct it as a horizontal platform. This change caused significant disruption and cost. But having the right structure and technological platform made all the difference. People could start trying new ideas easily, taking advantage of existing knowledge, tools, and code. Soon, much more innovation started bubbling up.

A common technology platform and infrastructure where learning and experimentation can be tried, applied, and adjusted across the system is an essential first step. The common tech platform has become an important organizational principle at Alibaba. Over the last few years, through round after round of hard work, Alibaba has moved all the computing work of any of its businesses onto the same cloud-computing infrastructure. This achievement not only saves millions in capital costs annually but also makes the support of new business launches much easier. Systems, software, and business know-how can now be readily shared. Another recent major project has been to consolidate all coding and development work across departments and acquired businesses onto the same platform. This platform, called Aone, will be explored later in this chapter.

Consolidating code is only the beginning. Ambitious organizations can directly embed many duties of traditional management into the infrastructure. HR management, resource allocation, project coordination, budgeting, and other aspects of financial management all become services provided by the platform. These services are accessible to people and units without direct oversight. The most significant of these is resource allocation—with the right rules in place, resource allocation becomes almost automatic. There is little arguing about a budget. If a prototype takes off in the market and needs more resources to scale up, the resources, both people and money, are provided largely automatically. As the firm builds the infrastructure and as more knowledge becomes widely accessible through APIs and other sharing tools, contributors in the firm's internal network see their ideas compete for resources in both internal and external markets.

Unified Metrics

From an organizational point of view, a crucial part of infrastructure as described above is a smart version of a key performance indicator (KPI) system. KPIs are one of the most important methods in traditional management. A KPI describes what is expected and rewarded, as dictated from the executive suite, and is executed through hierarchical levels. Many technology companies have developed versions of a real-time, online, user-centered, and objective evaluation system more in tune with their goals, in contrast to a traditional KPI system. For simplicity, I will call it the *metrics evaluation system*, although there are many versions throughout the industry.

The metrics evaluation system quantitatively measures, monitors, and evaluates a product or a desired outcome. This evaluation is constantly compared against well-defined value and optimization objectives, which, though determined by upper management, are evaluated transparently and in terms of market performance. The system usually has three main components: metrics research, an online monitoring system, and a system to design and run A/B tests.

People working on metrics research try to ensure that the strategic targets of different teams are consistent with the ultimate mission of the organization and to define these goals mathematically. The goals are then translated into computational measurements, for example, conversion rate, or user engagement.

The monitoring system—usually in the form of a scorecard or dashboard—presents the status and real-time changes of a product across a variety of dimensions. In leading internet companies, this product could be as large as an entire business or as small as the features of a mobile application or an algorithm. As the product evolves, the monitoring results will set off instant parameter adjustments, design changes, or other decisions. For example, monitoring the traffic to a particular button in Mobile Taobao gives a clear indication of how the category or SKUs accessed through that button are performing over time.

Engineers use the A/B test system to design scientific experiments that test and evaluate different "features," which correspond to versions or functions of an offering. A product or a feature will only be put on the market when scientific testing confirms the offering's improved performance with users. A/B testing makes product development quicker and more objective. In a scenario where the user base is large or interactions are frequent, a statistical outperformer can be identified in minutes and many alternatives can be tried in parallel. Throughout the industry, A/B testing is a revolutionary way to make experimentation easy, quick, and continuous. I still remember my shock in 2006, when I learned how relentlessly Google tested every aspect of its search result page.

Under metrics, the monitoring, evaluation, and governance of an organization can be semiautomatically completed in real time in a transparent, objective way. Clear, impartial assessment is the same principle underlying the self-tuning organizations discussed in the previous chapter. For example, Facebook's news feed uses two main goal metrics—user engagement and advertising revenue—to interact with more than a billion active users globally. These two metrics impact every part of the platform that connects to the news feed and thousands of related data collection points. Each data point captures the decisions made by relevant operating, design, or computation teams. Team members can compare their own actions (captured in datafied form) to the overarching goal metrics in real time. When team members see that they are not meeting a target or that a metric is going in the wrong direction, they modify their design or algorithm. Thus, the granular relevance of all the company's and employees' actions becomes clear in the context of larger organizational goals.

For example, if a Taobao team wants to improve user experience, it knows that this metric might be related to improving ad matching accuracy, decreasing ad exposure, or improving the interaction process. The team can experiment on all these dimensions simultaneously to determine which dimension performs best. Tmall's personalized recommendation software provides similar infrastructure for wide-scale experimentation. During the Singles Day shopping festival, the system that optimized every interaction was constantly iterating to make sure that the best matches were happening all day long. The optimization goal metrics even varied across different times of the day to achieve the overall best operating results.

Metrics evaluation systems fundamentally improve the management and performance evaluation as practiced by traditional organizations. Every improvement of a product, every contribution of a team, every innovation attempt, can be scientifically tested and accurately measured, instantly and transparently. They are KPIs made smart, displaying the accessible resources and the outcome of your work. Metrics evaluation systems provide a new dashboard for the CEO; he or she can see each team's contribution and can change the parameters if needed to optimize the whole system. Accountability becomes clear.

The use of metrics also explains the weakening of the hierarchical structure and administration systems in pioneering companies like Google and Facebook. Metrics evaluation systems can comprehensively and instantly calculate the influence of a small innovation on the whole system and its constituent parts, in order to coordinate resources between similar or conflicting innovations and achieve global optimization. Companies can make evidence-based decisions and select among different evolutionary paths.

When quantitative metrics cannot tell the whole story, peer review and input from committees of experienced and neutral colleagues can provide supplementary information to evaluate performance. Sometimes, the automatic quantitative system cannot effectively evaluate contributions, for example, within a small team whose interactions with users are not easily quantifiable. The same might be true for some innovations whose value is spread across the platform or the organization, or for innovations that have major long-term effects, like foundational technical infrastructure.

In some ways, metrics make management easier—such a system encourages experimentation, can incorporate system-wide effects, and provides results and feedback in real time. All of this, of course, assumes we get the system right. But getting the metrics right is extremely challenging, which is why metrics research is such an important function. As the entire system begins to reflect the business in increasing granularity, management becomes more and more focused on architecture building rather than hands-on management of individual tasks.

Integrating the Technology Infrastructure and the Metrics Evaluation System

In Alibaba's experience, the productivity gain from developing a common technology infrastructure is huge compared to traditional management practice. But if innovation is the goal, firms must change the way they are built. The architecture of the firm must be overhauled with smart-KPI metrics, as discussed above, and with a technological infrastructure that captures organizational knowledge and provides tools for further learning and innovation. These two elements, the metrics evaluation system and the technological infrastructure, must be woven together.

For example, as a data-driven company, Alibaba has a multilevel infrastructure, including a data-storage and data-processing platform powered by Alibaba Cloud. To name a few, Alibaba Cloud's AI and machine-learning platform contains PAI, a collaborative platform for code, algorithms, and models; Aone (discussed later), which includes project and process management software; and even more platforms and tools specific to different business units that offer access to business analytics, user research, and design functionalities. Alibaba's infrastructure also contains systems of standards, protocols, and specifications that help coordinate connections and sharing outside the company.

A comprehensive infrastructure can minimize the cost and time of innovation and can scale an innovation efficiently. Every day at Google, Facebook, or Alibaba, a small algorithm improvement can bring in millions or even billions of dollars in revenue. By arranging and aggregating components of existing software using a well-oiled infrastructure, developers can test and quickly deploy an innovative idea as if they were playing with Lego blocks.

Therefore, the innovation platform for an enabling organization of the future is not a separate or independent platform constructed and maintained by a third party, but a common foundation established and enriched by all participants. Much like the organization model described in the previous chapter, the platform is self-tuning. It evolves over time.

Building the Internal Mechanisms That Enable Network Innovation

Recent progress in network theory and sociology have emphasized the importance of networks in supporting innovation. Networks effectively foster ideas, allow broad sharing, and generate persistent feedback. Businesses wanting to encourage innovation need to turn their hierarchy-driven structures into networks. Thus, the best way to increase collaboration is to design a flat and networked organization. Under such an architecture, everyone can interact on an even and productive playing field.

The need for collaboration mechanisms has been particularly evident during the past several years of Alibaba's rapid growth. Since the expansion of Taobao's APIs and large marketing events such as Singles Day, the business has rapidly expanded to encompass many teams and external actors. For example, in 2016, the technical teams at Cainiao Network had to coordinate more than two hundred projects just to prepare for that year's Singles Day. With so many projects, managers had to split the work into five tiers of priority. The projects involved hundreds of employees and countless external partners.

Creating software and internet products that can respond nimbly is a staggering technological challenge, even if Alibaba's work weren't spread across an unusually diverse mix of industries and business units. To solve these complex coordination problems, Alibaba created an internal coding and project management platform called Aone (Alibaba One Engineering System). Aone offers a complete suite of tools to support the entire engineering workflow and product life cycle, from project management to code building, quality assurance, and software release. In Aone's stable and transparent coding environment, all colleagues involved with a project can monitor its progress and ensure that no details are overlooked.

Before Aone, people who tested code for bugs and failures faced a nerve-racking endeavor. The quality-assurance team had to confirm a slew of details manually, checking with engineers repeatedly just to make sure that the code was ready for release. Now, with Aone, all coding and testing happens in the cloud. Code is constantly updated and shared with all the relevant employees. Past code and past projects can be easily accessed and compared with current projects. Managing code changes through an open, accessible, and coordinated platform smooths communication between teams and drastically reduces program build time and cost.

The Aone platform improves coding efficiency and serves as a comprehensive record of employees' activities, meetings, and work product—a record stored and accessible across the organization. More than twenty thousand employees across the world use Aone daily; in dozens of business units, at least half of all employees access the platform every day. Every week, 1.5 million-plus lines of code are scanned, and some one hundred new products and features are tested for bugs and integrity. This infrastructure enables people with different expertise to collaborate efficiently and to focus on their most important task: creativity.

As time goes on, the whole knowledge base of the company—its collective thinking—will be implanted in this internal platform and database. If an employee wants to know why a product was designed a particular way five years ago, the person can find a historical trace, read past discussions, and see coding changes. If employees face some problem or need to do some coding, they can search the database and most likely find a relevant piece of code that can be modified for their use. The knowledge, competencies, historical changes, and other resources can be endlessly recycled, repurposed, and expanded. People across the organization can see what others are doing and tease out opportunities to build on others' work. The internal organization is not in a matrix anymore; it is not siloed by function or business unit. The experience and other tools from people and units throughout the company are now available to all.

Web-Based Interactions

Platforms like Aone are useful for building software and consolidate user responses in the form of data or direct feedback. Keeping this information in one accessible place during coding and project management greatly decreases the time and effort involved in improving and iterating product features. This communication and feedback can easily extend outside the organization.

A good example of this external sharing is Alibaba's AutoNavi digital mapping business. (For more on AutoNavi, see appendix A.) AutoNavi is one of China's largest digital mapping and navigation service providers. In addition to its consumer-focused mobile app, it also integrates mapping functionalities with applications across China and car manufacturers. The coordination involved in creating its mapping software can be complicated and requires close communication with car manufacturers to ensure that its technology is successfully embedded into vehicle hardware.

Like most companies, AutoNavi originally used a suite of separate engineering solutions and environments. This state of affairs decreased team productivity. When AutoNavi had to work with various car manufacturers, all of which were using their own engineering solutions, workflows slowed to a crawl because of the repeated manual checking throughout the engineering cycle. AutoNavi had to collect bug reports (usually sent in the form of Excel documents whose formats differed from partner to partner) and programming logs (delivered via email or thumb drive) from various partners, including vehicle manufacturers, systems integrators, and providers of embedded speech-recognition software. AutoNavi's team then had to regularly reformat, collect all the information, and manually upload it to Aone's system during software development. To make matters worse, the team then had to individually communicate the results of its work to each of these partners. The situation was untenable.

Aone's solution was to create a common channel for partners to directly upload their bug reports and programming logs. The Aone platform mandated standardized data formatting through a single interface, automatically conveying bug reports to associated engineering workflows. All partners knew how to structure and upload their data, and information flowed smoothly. AutoNavi's teams could continue working regularly from within Aone—all the data the team needed updated automatically, without manual support. By creating an interface for external partners, Aone greatly decreased communication and engineering costs and laid the foundation for network coordination. Its approach reflects the softwaring principle that I discussed in chapter 4. The key is to streamline feedback and ensure that all actions and responses are continuously recorded online.

Even within the company, Alibaba is moving away from traditional ERP management software and developing its own web tools for people to easily interact and provide feedback online. For example, in HR employee reviews, 360-degree feedback is a costly process in traditional management. Enabled with internal web tools, you can give feedback much more easily. You can instantly share on a mobile device your impressions from interacting with anyone in the organization.

To become smart, an organization has to replace its IT structure with an open web-based infrastructure very similar to an open-source environment like Linux. The infrastructure must have common standards, APIs, and a searchable depository for the accumulated information. As discussed, APIs are crucial because, as interfaces, they allow a form of plug and play: they ensure that any new or changed coding will be interoperable with everything else on the platform.

All the tools necessary for everything the organization does must be available and transparent to all in the company. Changes in software or code are marked the same way that changes are marked on an edited document whose comments and revisions are embedded. Successes, mistakes, and failures are viewable. This common platform, across the enterprise and even the entire ecosystem, embeds its collective knowledge and competencies.

Transparency

As discussed in the previous chapter, Alibaba operates through constant experimentation. This experimentation requires a commitment to transparency—a commitment that goes hand in hand with the infrastructural solutions discussed in this chapter. To make good decisions that consider the larger context and the organization's vision, everyone in the organization must have the information they need to stay up-to-date on the market and to react accordingly.

An organization's commitment to transparency must extend across all levels to facilitate better cross-pollination of ideas. What's more, all levels and business areas can provide their own insights into how the environment is evolving. If information or results are hidden or hoarded, the organization can miss subtle shifts in its market and cannot adjust accordingly.

Transparency throughout the organization also contributes greatly to coordination across the network. When the basic software code is available to all users and is standardized to work with all the other software in the enterprise, people can take the bits they want, rework them to their own purposes, and deploy them to their potential customers, knowing that the software will interact smoothly with the technological infrastructure. When workflows themselves occur online, people can evaluate the contributions with minimal politics.

Because people can easily share data, code, and metadata in a transparent environment, the work and, hence, innovation are facilitated. When everyone's contribution is viewable, their work can be recognized and respected and the environment encourages healthy competition. An open platform is part of the organization's collaborative internal culture. Only such a platform can consistently and fairly reflect everyone's contributions and increase learning and collaboration.

In the early days, Larry Page frequently ran all-hands meetings at Google to review every project people were working on and ranking their importance. This practice let everyone know what was going on and encouraged people to contribute to (and compete on) the projects then deemed as having the highest potential impact for the company. The previous chapter described Taobao's cocreation meetings, an intensive process in which company teams get together with users, design prototypes, and gauge user reactions.

But transparency sounds more uniformly positive than it can be in day-to-day experience. When we introduced a public online forum at Alibaba, we were astounded by all the negativity that came out.

People suddenly let us know what they thought, what we had done stupidly, who was overrated, or which leadership ideas were useless. In one famous episode, when Jack Ma announced the appointment of a new chief technology officer (someone who had initiated the Alibaba Cloud project with much controversy), a litany of public criticism ensued. Ma wrote a long letter replying to the complaints, and even that letter received many negative reviews. On the face of it, these attempts at openness might appear to only air dirty laundry and stink up the entire room. But in actuality, we have found that this kind of open communication on important issues does make the staff confident in the company and its decision making.

Most creative workers enjoy intellectual debate or have strong opinions about issues. Leadership must do the difficult but necessary work of learning to deal with varying opinions and assuring people that they can speak freely. With time, we have learned to gauge which issues are significant and lie outside the usual rumble. Not everything mentioned on our forum turns out to be a true problem. But in retrospect, almost every major issue in the company's history has, in fact, surfaced in some corner of our online forum. The challenge is not merely to find the signals in the noise. It is to stay open-minded and humble enough to truly listen and reflect when serious problems arise.

While people in any given organization will differ, the amount of talk and negativity that becomes transparent represents a significant change from traditional hierarchies. It is important to carefully consider mechanisms that dampen destructive talk and encourage healthy discussion. Our online forum features a system of "sesame" seeds—we are Alibaba, after all—that rewards meaningful posting and encourages genuine socialization. HR and managers at Alibaba have learned not to behave like bureaucrats: an impersonal response to a high-profile issue within the company can lead to hundreds of sesame deductions from indignant employees.[7]

Overall, the benefits of transparency outweigh all the uncomfortable risks. At its most basic level, transparency encourages collaborative innovation and building on previous efforts. Every new piece of information, be it an achievement or a failure, can be accumulated on the platform and enriched through iterations. This cumulative knowledge establishes barriers to competitors and defines the organization.

The Future of the Organization

If smart businesses function as self-tuning organizations with few managers and these managers aren't directing or controlling, then it's fair to ask, what is the future of the organization?

In the age of innovation, traditional corporations based on management will give way to the organizations of the future—organizations characterized by the core value of enabling their creative workers (see table 8-1). The principle of enabling will redefine organizations

TABLE 8-1

Comparison of traditional, management-focused organizations and enabling organizations

	Traditional organization (focused on management)	Smart organization (focused on enabling)
Structure	Tree or hierarchy	Platform, networked
Information movement (internal)	Integrated from the bottom up, and diffused from the top down	Fully connected, synced, and coordinated in real time
Information movement (external)	A single dedicated communication channel	Fully connected, synced, and coordinated in real time
Decision process	Centralized, executed from the top down	Centrally coordinated by a global metrics evaluation system, locally self-adaptive
Resource appropriation	Centralized, hierarchical breakdown and allocation	Locally self-sufficient, elastic, based on external environment, provided by common infrastructure
Collaboration mechanism	Specific job definitions, difficult interdepartmental collaboration, inefficient information sharing	Self-organized collaborative networks based on a platform, transparent and sharable, collaborative competition, globally optimized to work across the network, iterative and evolving
Value orientation	Profit driven	Innovation driven, focused on growth
Risk perception	Focused on minimizing risks, avoiding mistakes; information and data strictly controlled, not shared	Focused on transparency, efficiency, and freedom of innovations; trial-and-error approaches; inability to innovate is the biggest risk

and their operation. Managers will provide infrastructure, mechanisms, and a situation-appropriate culture to coordinate networked, creative workers. These workers will innovate more effectively in service of their customers, and in doing so realize their dreams and values. As stewards of business ecosystems, enabling organizations will ignite and accelerate innovation even outside the firm itself.

The main function of an organization is no longer internalizing and utilizing resources or even optimizing management efficiency. Smart organizations improve innovation efficiency by facilitating internal and external collaboration. Although the form of such future organizations is still in its incubation stage, table 8-1 summarizes some of their nascent characteristics. At the very least, one takeaway from all of these organizational changes is clear: innovation and experimentation will be the test of any firm's survival. And in a world that prizes innovation, human creativity and data will become the key factors of production for the future.

The previous two chapters have described how the key elements of smart business, network coordination and data intelligence, are to be used within the firm. From one perspective, self-tuning through data intelligence supercharges exploitation, allowing good ideas to scale up while freeing up precious resources for exploration. Enabling through network coordination expands the scope of experimentation and provides the conditions for effective creative work. From a different angle, network coordination and data intelligence can work together to datafy the organization through a metrics evaluation system, where all parts of the organization are connected, recorded, and optimized digitally in real time. As we have seen again and again through this book, the yin and yang of smart business work together to transform business practices and the organization as a whole.

We have come a long way from Singles Day 2017 at the beginning of this book, tracing the implications of smart business through strategy, operations, and the organization. In the final chapter that follows, I will summarize the many lessons from Alibaba's experience, and discuss what smart business means for you as an individual.

CHAPTER 9

THE FUTURE OF SMART BUSINESS

What It Means for You

Alibaba's approach to business seems counterintuitive, but understand it, and you arrive at valuable insight into the future of strategy. Through the course of this book, I hope you have come to understand what makes Alibaba unique, and why our business offers definitive lessons for the future. In this final chapter, I will summarize and tie together all the concepts of the preceding chapters and help you see how the ideas apply to you as a leader and as an individual in a changing world.

Each chapter of this book has introduced and discussed actionable concepts for the future of business strategy. In part 1, I discussed how the core logic of business is changing to reflect the two new drivers of value creation: network coordination and data intelligence. In part 2, I detailed how businesses that operate with those two drivers make profound changes in their strategic thinking and operations, from automated decision making to C2B realignment to positioning within a business ecosystem. In part 3, I further expanded on what a transition to smart business entails for strategic planning and the organization. Specifically, smart strategy is experimental and self-tuning, and smart business embraces an enabling organizational structure. Each of these new facets of smart business expresses a different and related aspect of the same fundamental sea change.

The business world is in a very interesting transition period. On the one hand, the digital revolution has been going on for so long that, to paraphrase a common Silicon Valley saying, the horizon is clear but the distance is unknowable. Yet, clarity about that horizon is very unevenly distributed. Most people cannot see it. In this book, I am not predicting the future. I am simply telling you what is happening now at the forefront of internet companies and in China, the world's richest petri dish of innovation. I recognize these changes as the end of the beginning.

To summarize these changes, I will first return to the metaphor of the double helix, which captures the value unleashed when networks and data are marshaled together at the same time. Then, I will retrace our steps throughout this book, weaving the many concepts into a cohesive whole, and offering some big-picture observations about key strategic themes that have run throughout this book. Finally, I will advise readers on how to harness the great promise of these exciting times.

Yin and Yang: The Power of Network Coordination and Data Intelligence Combined

Despite the unique evolutionary path of Alibaba, it should be clear by now that the new business model we have developed has much broader global implications. To paraphrase Schumpeter, revolution often comes from the periphery, unencumbered by switching costs or legacy burdens and beyond the headlamps of incumbent powerhouses.[1] China has indeed come from behind very fast, and Alibaba Group is in the forefront. Current leaders across the world of business have already achieved success through these strategies, and the leaders of the future are beginning to implement the smart-business toolkit.

Network coordination and data intelligence are fundamental economic forces shaping the future of business. Firms can and should implement these mechanisms and strategies as sources of competitive advantage in products, services, and organizations. In much of this book, I have described both these forces in isolation. But even though strength in one area is enough to make a strong and even very valuable company, the companies with the largest competitive advantage will deploy both network coordination and data intelligence.

As described earlier, the network is the yang to data's yin. The two forces are interconnected and mutually dependent. Because networks and data drive each other's growth, the cycle of value that the two create in tandem provides greater and greater competitive advantage. With either network or data, you can outcompete the competition. With both, not only do you outcompete, but your competitive advantage also constantly builds on itself. The synergy of network and data is what makes smart business so powerful and, in many ways, so dangerous for the competition.

Combining the yin and yang of smart business creates a new framework for value creation and value capture in the future. Because these fundamental forces are not going away, the technologies, strategies, and organizational forms engendered by network coordination and data intelligence are here to stay as well. The most insightful strategists will quickly grasp the underlying logic and apply it to their businesses. New innovations, from advances in AI to innovations in coordination technology like blockchain, are likely to spread and reinforce the principles put forth in this book.

Coming from the East, I can see the whole picture of both yin and yang. The Chinese viewpoint illuminates a business frontier partly obscured in the West, but the new rules of the future are emerging. The fundamentals are already embedded in the genetic code of leading internet companies: the twin DNA strands of network coordination and data intelligence, the double helix for smart business. Chinese firms that use widespread network coordination and Western firms that have developed data intelligence are competing and cooperating all over the world. As leaders learn from each other, East and West will merge to define the future of business.

The Feedback Loops of Smart Business

Yin and yang. The double helix. Smart business reinforces itself, growing to greater heights of competitive advantage through loop after loop of feedback. Let us now pull together all the concepts of this book into a self-reinforcing cycle of value creation.

Feedback loops have appeared throughout this book in different incarnations, from smart financing at MYbank to automated decision making on the Taobao app, to Big-E's previews and flash sales and Alibaba's organizational dynamics and strategy. Feedback is a prerequisite for learning, and fast feedback loops speed up learning. Automated real-time feedback loops, like those used in data intelligence, put learning on steroids and create an unprecedented advantage. Algorithms and data intelligence steadily come to reflect the business and its operations. More broadly, in a world of smart business, feedback loops operate throughout every relationship and action in the network by means of data intelligence and live data. The more your business utilizes feedback loops, the smarter your business will become.

The idea of the feedback loop carries a slew of prescriptive implications. When network coordination and data intelligence begin to affect how business operates, certain things change. As we have seen in chapter 5, fostering direct connections with customers mandates that the creation of products and services becomes part of the same feedback loop. This is the essence of C2B. But once a certain part of the firm starts to operate using a C2B mindset, all the other functions of the firm must also work in a C2B and on-demand fashion. The feedback loops need to operate between the customer (or at least, the product and service designed for the customer) and all the other functions of the business. Otherwise, the firm cannot stay agile and adaptive. It will be unable to effectively serve the customer and likely outcompeted by firms better able to ply network coordination, data intelligence, and feedback loops.

For network coordination, however, the firm's operations and resources are not limited to the firm itself. As chapter 6 described, the smart business firm exists in a network and must determine its positioning relative to other players and their potential for future growth. Interdependence in the network is amplified by feedback loops between firms through technologies such as APIs. These feedback loops illustrate why the ecosystem metaphor is so important. The design and structure of feedback loops within an individual firm are inextricable from the firm's relationships with its partners and platforms. As described in chapter 5, Ruhan's Layercake software coordinated feedback from social media platforms, manufacturing partners, and e-commerce analytics to ensure the quick and accurate design and production of clothing. Ruhan operates through feedback loops on top of more feedback loops.

These feedback loops, omnipresent throughout the ecosystem, have even deeper implications for the organization. As I described in chapter 8, by creating internal platforms and infrastructure for sharing knowledge and capabilities, organizations can increase the scope and success of innovation. Internal metrics evaluation systems encourage experimentation by providing results and feedback in real time. The organization's role is not to manage its workers, but to create the tools and conditions that enable workers to quickly string together experimental products and services, test the market, and scale the ideas that elicit positive response. All these organizational improvements strengthen the core feedback loop of user response to the firm's decisions and actions.

The organization's approach to innovation optimization, viewed from a different perspective, is not unlike the way a business becomes smart. The organization aims to facilitate network coordination internally between employees of different functions and teams, aligning capabilities and people around user problems. At the same time, it should exploit data intelligence to improve workflows by creating an accessible database of organizational memory and developing smart metrics. In practice, this accessibility requires that internal workflows occur online, are softwared, and rely on live data. The organization must become smart in the exact sense that I have used throughout this book.

Besides enabling innovation, leadership must continually adjust its vision by experimentation as described in chapter 7—creating yet again another feedback loop. Second, using the framework of points, lines, and planes (chapter 6), leadership must clearly understand where the organization's capabilities and value proposition fit into that vision. A firm whose people keep the vision clear in their minds will understand the firm's role in creating that future. The technologies, mindsets, and strategies of smart business will earn firms more and more success, but it will take tremendous experimentation and other work to learn how the core capabilities of the network and data can be best utilized in different situations.

The Ecosystem and Its Strategy

Using Alibaba's experience, I've shown that networked operating models and organizational structures bring many subtle and nonintuitive changes to the traditional perception of how to conduct business. One of the biggest changes having implications for both the firm and the individual is the ecosystem mindset.

In chapter 6, I defined an ecosystem as a smart network that evolves to solve complicated customer problems through the combination of three roles for its constituent firms: point, line, and plane firms. Although the term *ecosystem* has been overused in the last few decades, from a strategic perspective, this ecological metaphor is still very useful in stressing that strategy for platforms and individuals is reactive, not planned and interconnected, not isolated. It evolves through an interplay of point, line, and plane firms, through the combination of network coordination and data intelligence.

The history of Taobao clearly shows what I mean by *evolve* and the appropriateness of the ecosystem metaphor. Taobao did not begin from day one with the vision of creating an online economy composed of all the actors involved in the retail industry. Instead, a series of small decisions to support the work of others gradually snowballed into an ecosystem strategy. Platform firms must commit to building the infrastructure for the success of other firms in the ecosystem. More importantly, they must be willing to experiment, iterate, and, as explained in chapter 2, let roles develop and evolve instead of systematizing their growth too quickly.[2]

Though business ecosystems are still rare in the world, they will rapidly proliferate, become the most important part of the new economy, and affect nearly all the readers of this book. The most innovative firms of the future will fashion new ecosystems to tackle previously unsolvable business challenges, akin to how Taobao has created a comprehensive online economy in a country that once lacked any nationwide retail industry. Innovators will build new ecosystems by creating new forms of efficient, widespread coordination powered by intelligent data engines that combine and build on the efforts of many types of participants in the network. These innovators and all of the participants in the network will drive the new economy.

What You Can Do

So what do all these big changes mean for you? Even if you are not an ambitious entrepreneur or the CEO of a big company, you and everyone else will have to adjust their roles within organizations and in society in general to prosper or even just to survive. I want to leave readers with three small kernels of wisdom gleaned from my years of trying to understand the changes brought on by technology and how individuals should adapt to these new and sometimes bewildering times:

1. Correct decisions today rest on your view of the future.

2. Creativity will be the only source of value creation.

3. The individual is more powerful today than ever before.

To act effectively today, you need a vision of tomorrow.

We live in a world of quick and expansive change. Conventional wisdom tells us that the faster things change, the harder it is to predict the future. Yet my experience has taught me that times of drastic change are precisely when individuals need to think clearly about the future. Whoever has a clearer view of the future will bet correctly and will potentially win big, while those without such a vision will definitely make missteps. And because change comes so quickly, a misstep today could make it very hard to catch up tomorrow.

Because success today requires a view of the future, you must do whatever you can to arrive at a clear picture of where your industry will be in five or ten years. My view of the future, as advanced in this book, consists of network coordination and data intelligence, but you need to envision how these new forces will affect your business and the ecosystem in which it operates. This difficult task demands substantial effort and attention to your environment. But finding your own place in the future is the most important work you can do.

I believe that vision—or visioning, as I described it in chapter 7—is a craft, not an inborn talent. To improve, you need to put effort into staying at the forefront of industry and science, continuously integrating new information, and, most importantly, relentlessly experimenting. In the last two chapters, I discussed the importance of iterating between vision and action. Using actions to test your vision is the single best way to check and improve the quality of your vision. If you keep working at your capacity to envision, you will enjoy a huge edge over others very quickly.

To have a vision does not mean you have to be a visionary like Steve Jobs, Elon Musk, or Jack Ma. Everyone can learn to perceive the future, no matter what job you are doing. Once you have a vision of tomorrow, you will be able to imagine where you fit into that future. From there, you can determine what action to take today and how to incorporate relevant feedback that prods you to self-tune.

To create value, you must be creative.

In 1969, the incomparable Peter Drucker coined the term *knowledge worker*, anticipating how the work of managers would consist of measurement and planning and how corporations would manage knowledge to develop the skills and competencies of the workforce. Driven by modern scientific disciplines, knowledge changed from a private good to a public good. In Drucker's terminology, business was experiencing a knowledge revolution, its third revolution after the industrial revolution of the nineteenth century and the managerial revolution of the early twentieth century. The key factor (of production) for the individual worker to create value within the firm was to use the person's knowledge to work.

At Alibaba, we see a fourth revolution brewing: the creativity revolution.[3] In this revolution, innovation and human creativity will become the key capability for producing value in the future economy. I have made this point quite clearly in chapter 8. There is a huge debate raging in industry and in policy circles about the impact of AI on the workforce and jobs. The debate suggests that routine work, even information processing and calculation, will have decreasing value. But what about work that is nonrepeatable, requires complex knowledge and reasoning, or creates something completely new? Such creative work will have increasing value.

In a world where competitive advantage revolves around networks and data, the pathways by which humans create value will change.

Without creativity, people cannot design new business models that rely on new mechanisms for coordination and cooperation. Data intelligence, too, requires an enormous amount of human creativity, not only in the design of algorithms and smart products, but also in the application of machine-learning technologies to complicated business questions and the widespread implementation of these technologies throughout internal and external networks. The pure execution of tried-and-true methodologies will create less and less value in a world driven by smart business and C2B. So, be creative.

In the networked future, where powerful and intelligent online markets structure the economic activity, anyone with unique value to contribute will find a way to apply that value in the service of themselves and others. More importantly, the impact of creativity can now be quickly amplified across networks through data technology. This observation brings me to my last piece of advice.

The individual is more powerful than ever before.

In the traditional industrial economy, organizations operated like well-oiled machines, and a person's place as an individual cog was more or less fixed. As assembly lines proliferated in the workplace, the individual's place in society diminished. There was little room for development or change. Creativity operated at a narrow, local level.

Network technologies such as the internet have changed all that. This book has shown that the large platforms prosper only because they better enable points or individuals to grow and succeed. In the other direction, individuals can increasingly access and utilize capabilities and other assets that they do not own themselves, as long as the assets are available within the network and are empowered by platforms. The web-celeb Big-E is the quintessential example. In less than a decade, she first metamorphosed from a regular in-house model at a large magazine with little freedom and limited earning power, into a freelance model charging top rate in the open market of Taobao, and, finally, into a brand owner who makes a serious fortune as a web celeb. This transformation could not have happened in the age of business before platforms, ecosystems, and smart business.

The key to maximizing individual potential is correct positioning, as described in chapter 6. Whether you decide to be a point, a line, or a plane, you can take advantage of network capabilities and network effects to grow at a speed that would be unimaginable on your own. Overall, the principles of smart business apply to individuals just as they apply to firms. Be flexible. Think carefully about your positioning within any organization or any network, and explore how data technologies can maximize your contributions. Choose the role and partners that give you the most leverage and bring the greatest future potential.

This is an exciting time to be alive. Counterintuitively, the individual has more potential than maybe at any other time in history. Just as advanced technologies appear to take over the world, these technologies are coalescing to emancipate individual creativity from the fetters of static organizations. Do not be afraid of the technologies that define the current era. They need not swallow the individual, but instead can propel you forward toward greater heights.

So Much More to Come

I was born in 1970, in a third-tier city in China. China was still in the middle of the Cultural Revolution, and I had barely enough food. Luckily for my generation, we grew up as China was beginning the economic reforms that started in 1978 as the country opened up to the wider world. I was able to go to the United States for my PhD program through a scholarship offered by the State University of New York at Binghamton in 1991. I still remembered vividly how shocked I was when I first visited a supermarket in Binghamton: it was paradise on earth.

Little did I know then that fifteen years later, I would join Alibaba and participate in a journey that transformed the global retailing industry. In early 2000, China had very few large department stores. Consumer logistics was nonexistent. People still paid in cash for everything and were leery of buying even products they could see and feel. Because of Alibaba and China's other internet firms, the situation has completely changed in less than twenty years. Now, mobile shopping, same-day delivery, and trust between strangers has become the norm for the new generation of young Chinese. The speed of change astounds me to this day.

So much change in a brief two decades, yet so much more in the coming years. Google, Facebook, Amazon, Alibaba, and Tencent were all created just a couple decades ago, and now they all rank in the world's top ten companies by market cap. I regularly speculate with colleagues as to which will be the first trillion-dollar firm.

We live in a time of exponential change. Everything I have described in this book will soon be conventional knowledge. Change will be disruptive. But it will also bring massive opportunity.

I sincerely hope the framework presented in this book helps guide your actions to great success. As the adage goes, the best way to predict the future is to create it. I am excited to see the future that tomorrow's business leaders will create.

ALIBABA AND ITS AFFILIATED BUSINESSES

The Founding of Alibaba

Alibaba was launched onto the world stage by its explosive IPO in 2014, more than a decade after Jack Ma founded the company. (See figure A-1 for Alibaba's history at a glance.) Considering that China is now the world's second-largest economy, observers may have a hard time recalling how far and how quickly the country has come since its economic reforms in the 1970s. Before then, China's government centrally planned the country's socialist economy, orchestrating the work of millions of communes across the vast Chinese countryside. With Deng Xiaoping's market reforms, China did an about-face, embracing capital markets and free enterprise with a fervor. Yet it was not until the 1990s that the private sector truly began to emerge as a driving force in society, becoming an attractive destination for workers accustomed to cradle-to-grave labor assignments and lifetime socialist benefits. In 1992 alone, 120,000 civil servants abandoned the security of their cushy government posts to jump into the sea of free-market entrepreneurship.

At that time, the United States was already experiencing the first exciting ripples of the dot-com boom: the Mosaic browser was released in 1993, and David Yang and Jerry Filo started the website that would become Yahoo! the following year.

In 1994, Ma had been working as an English teacher since his graduation from the university in his hometown of Hangzhou, once the capital of the Song Dynasty and in 1994 a small city with a population of 2.5 million. (Hangzhou has since ballooned to over eight million people, and is now the second-most important city after Shanghai in the Yangtze delta economic zone.) That year, when he visited the United States while working as a translator, he encountered the web for the very first time. As Ma recalls, he first began to search online for beer, and found American beer, Japanese beer, and German beer. Only when he realized that Chinese beer had no results did he catch a fleeting glimpse of an enormous business opportunity.

On his return to China, Ma started his first company, the China Yellow Pages, in Hangzhou, but he later had no choice but to sell the company to China Telecom. As he learned more about the internet, Ma realized that this new technology could potentially open and expand Chinese trade to the outside world by bringing the country onto the information superhighway. Yet on the whole, China seemed uninterested. Although he helped to create the web portal for the Ministry of Foreign Trade in Beijing, Ma's big ideas met with cool disinterest from most of the trade officials.

Ma returned to Hangzhou and, in 1999, brought a dozen friends together to found a new e-commerce site aimed at small and medium-sized enterprise (SME) exporters. He named the site Alibaba, from the *Arabian Nights* story. At the time, Chinese trade was indeed booming, but most of the volume of outgoing goods had to pass through official channels, in a practice exemplified by the Canton Fair. Held twice a year, the Canton Fair was the largest and longest-running trade fair in China, jointly run by China's Ministry of Foreign Trade and the Guangdong provincial government. For enterprises that could make their way into the fair, business was exceptional. But in the multitudes of SMEs from across the country banging on the gates, Ma saw an enormous opportunity. Alibaba was the SMEs' *open sesame.*

Like many other entrepreneurs at the time, Ma had dreams of becoming another Yahoo! or the other emerging Silicon Valley dot-coms, but he had little to support those aspirations. After being rejected by thirty-seven venture capitalists, Ma met Joseph Tsai, a Taiwanese Canadian then working at a Swedish investment company. Ma convinced Tsai of Alibaba's potential and, with Tsai's help, landed a round of US$5 million led by Goldman Sachs in October 1999. Early the following year, Japan's Softbank made an additional US$20 million investment. Tsai joined Alibaba as one of its first employees.

But within eighteen months, the dot-com bubble burst. Having burned through much of its cash, Alibaba cut out all extraneous business projects and focused on its core product, letting SME exporters pay for premium placement on its B2B marketplace. This so-called Gold Suppliers product, combined with a tireless direct-sales workforce that signed up thousands, kept Alibaba afloat. In 2002, the company began to turn a profit. Yet the truly revolutionary story of Alibaba was just beginning. (See table A-1 for a summary of Alibaba's milestones.)

TABLE A-1

Alibaba's timeline

Year	Milestone	Chinese internet users (millions)
1999	Alibaba.com founded	9
2003	Taobao launched	80
2004	Wangwang and Alipay launched	94
2007	Alimama launched; Alibaba.com lists in Hong Kong	210
2008	Taobao Mall launched (name later changed to Tmall)	298
2009	Alibaba Cloud founded	384
2010	AliExpress launched	457
2013	Cainiao Network and Small and Micro Financial Services Group (later Ant Financial) set up	618
2014	Alibaba goes public in the United States	649

China's Retail Opportunity

In 2003, Ma started a secret project, a domestic consumer website he named Taobao in Chinese ("hunting for treasure"). At the time, China's retail industry was nearly nonexistent.[1] Taobao's challenge was nothing short of constructing an entire retail industry from the ground up.

Many readers are familiar with Taobao's victory over eBay in China: in barely two years after Taobao's founding, the young company's market share exploded from 8 to 59 percent while eBay's plummeted from 79 to 36 percent. By 2006, eBay announced that despite enormous investments, it would pull out of China. Since then, Taobao has kept its dominant position as China's largest e-commerce platform. It taught China to trust strangers with their money, and it penned pages in the history of world business. But many observers miss the key point of the story of Taobao. By emerging in a vacuum, the platform had to re-create every layer of modern business in an online environment, from sales to marketing to operations to logistics, and later even further up the supply chain.

This dearth of poor retailing infrastructure in China can be seen from its low penetration of commercial real estate. Per capita, China's retail space has consistently lagged behind most developed nations. As of 2011, the United States' retail space per capita was 45.2 square feet, Australia's figure was 22.6, while Japan's extremely mature economy had already reached 16.4. China, on the other hand, possessed a mere 12.9 square feet per capita, of which "a large portion of current stock will become obsolete."[2] Due to China's extreme social and geographical diversity, macrolevel statistics only tell part of the story, with infrastructure such as real estate spread unevenly across the country. The nation does not lack for retail demand. Rather, China has suffered from all kinds of infrastructural deficiencies, from transportation to communication to finance.

For most of the modern period, China had no national markets in the traditional sense of the term. Because producers of consumer goods could not reach anything like a national market, most brands were satisfied to achieve local reach, which normally means within a province or across several neighboring provinces. (The market within a province is nothing to be sneezed at, as many Chinese provinces are larger in population and physical size than many European countries.) China's diversity, too, is often underappreciated. The country's customs and climate vary enormously from north to south, east to west. It has fifty-six recognized ethnicities, many with their own languages, and eight major religions. The geography is tremendously varied, and there still yawns a huge rural-urban divide. Consumer powerhouses such as McDonald's, Nike, and P&G, or their Chinese counterparts, do a thriving business, but brands do not achieve the homogenizing influence that they do in many less-diverse countries. The majority of China's consumers have been vastly underserved for decades.

As the natural result of such a discrepancy, e-commerce has stepped in to fill the gap that traditional business has left empty. E-commerce in China has grown much faster than has offline retail. New Tao brands have emerged on Taobao to fill the aforementioned space. Where China had no nationwide advertising media, e-commerce stepped in. Where China had no nationwide distribution networks, e-commerce again ponied up. Where China had no nationwide consumer logistics services, e-commerce incubated the network, and the same process is currently occurring for SME finance and manufacturing.

If only on the surface, then, Alibaba's story is the complete transformation of China's inefficient retail industry. But it did not, à la Amazon, become an enormous retailer, build a logistics fleet, and squeeze out small businesses across the country. Instead, Alibaba began from day one with the mission "to make it easy to do business anywhere" by exploiting internet technologies. Alibaba's central conceit as a business is to enable others to do business, beginning with a platform mindset from day one. Today, Alibaba operates platforms on which a panoply of third-party service providers offer resources and functions, from software solutions to store operations, logistics, marketing, advertising, and payment. Alibaba's strategic vision demands large-scale collaboration and the construction and operation of vast, connected business systems.

Throughout the rest of this appendix, I will summarize each of Alibaba's main businesses, beginning with its core marketplaces.

Our core commerce business comprises platforms operating in four areas: retail commerce in China, wholesale commerce in China, cross-border and global retail commerce, and cross-border and global wholesale commerce. (Unless otherwise cited, information and statistics in this appendix come from Alibaba's SEC filings.)

Retail Commerce in China: Taobao, Tmall, and Juhuasuan

In this book, I have used *Taobao* as a catchall term for Alibaba's retail platforms. Our China retail marketplaces have become an important part of the everyday life of Chinese online consumers. Our high penetration rate of China's online shopping population is evidenced by the 443 million annual active buyers we had in the twelve months ended December 31, 2016 (out of the 467 million Chinese internet users that have experienced online shopping), as well as more than ten million annual active sellers and one billion-plus listings of products and services in at least 150 categories.

Though these retail platforms share much of the same technical infrastructure, they are split into several related retail businesses: the Taobao marketplace, Tmall (including Juhuasuan), and Rural Taobao.

The Taobao Marketplace

Taobao launched in May 2003. Through the website www.taobao.com and the Taobao app, consumers come to the Taobao marketplace, a commerce-oriented social platform, to enjoy an engaging, personalized shopping experience, optimized by our big-data analytics. Through highly relevant and engaging content and real-time updates from merchants, consumers can learn about products and new trends. They can also interact with each other and their favorite merchants and brands on Taobao.

Merchants on Taobao are primarily individuals and small businesses. They can create storefronts and listings on Taobao for free. For buyers, Taobao offers wide selection, value, and convenience. Taobao's e-commerce offerings are arguably the most diverse in the world, from branded and nonbranded mainstream products from across the world to boutique and artisan brands within China, fast-moving consumer goods, custom-made products, fresh foods, local services, and educational courses, to name just a few. The platform comprises multiple special channels that cater to the diversity of China's sophisticated consumers. The channels include home improvement and renovation, cutting-edge fashion, auctions, crowdfunding, and second-hand trading.

By the numbers (monthly active users), Taobao was China's largest mobile commerce destination in 2015, boasting more than 150 million daily visitors. Young people are its core constituents, with around 70 percent of buyers born in the 1980s and 1990s; over a third of Taobao sellers were born after 1990. In addition to its transaction value, its social activity is profound, creating some ten million instances of product sharing and twenty million reviews daily.

Tmall

Launched in April 2008 and spun off into an independent platform in June 2011, Tmall was the largest B2C platform in China in terms of gross merchandise volume (GMV) as of 2016 (according to iResearch). Tmall caters to consumers looking for branded products and a premium shopping experience. Numerous international and Chinese brands and retailers have established storefronts on Tmall. It is positioned as a trusted platform for consumers to buy both homegrown and international branded products and products not available in traditional retail outlets. By March 2017, the platform featured more than 100,000 brands.

Rural Taobao

By the end of 2016, around 590 million people in China resided in rural areas, according to the National Bureau of Statistics of China. Consumption in the rural areas is highly constrained by dispersed geography and infrastructure limitations, due to the prohibitive cost of cost of distribution. We aim to increase the level of consumption and commerce in rural China through our Rural Taobao program. By March 2017, we had established service centers in some 26,500 villages to give rural residents greater access to goods and services and the ability to sell what they make to the cities.

After villagers place orders at service centers, the goods (e.g., consumer goods, electronic appliances, and agricultural supplies) are delivered to county-level stations and then distributed by local couriers to service centers in the villages for pickup. Coordinated by the Cainiao Network, almost all packages can be delivered from the county-level station to a village service center the next day.

Cross-Border and Global Retail Commerce: AliExpress, Tmall Global, and Lazada

AliExpress

AliExpress is a global marketplace targeting consumers from around the world to buy directly from manufacturers and distributors in China. In addition to the global English-language site, AliExpress operates sixteen local language sites, including Russian, Spanish, and French. Consumers can access the marketplace through its websites or the AliExpress app. The most popular AliExpress consumer markets are Russia, the United States, Brazil, Spain, France, and the United Kingdom. In the twelve months ending in March 2017, AliExpress had approximately sixty million annual active buyers and had generated GMV of US$10.1 billion.

Merchants on AliExpress pay a commission, typically 5 to 8 percent of transaction value. We also generate revenue on AliExpress from merchants who participate in the third-party marketing affiliate program and those who purchase pay-for-performance marketing services. In the twelve months ending in March 2017, AliExpress generated US$7.2 billion of transaction value.

Tmall Global

In February 2014, Tmall launched an international extension of its platform. Called Tmall Global, the platform addresses the increasing Chinese consumer demand for international products and brands.

It is the premier platform for overseas brands and retailers to reach Chinese consumers, build brand awareness, and gain valuable consumer insights in forming their overall China strategy without the need for physical operations in China. For example, Costco, Macy's, Chemist Warehouse, Victoria's Secret, LG Household & Health Care, and Matsumoto Kiyoshi have storefronts on Tmall Global.

Lazada

We acquired a controlling stake in Lazada, a leading operator of e-commerce platforms across Southeast Asia, in April 2016. Lazada operates e-commerce platforms in Indonesia, Malaysia, the Philippines, Singapore, Thailand, and Vietnam, with local language websites and mobile apps in each of the six markets. The company offers third-party brands and merchants a marketplace solution with simple and direct access to consumers in these six countries through one retail channel as well as quick and reliable delivery. It also sells products owned by its retail operations. In the twelve months ending in March 2017, Lazada had approximately twenty-three million annual active buyers.

Wholesale Commerce in China and Globally: 1688.com and Alibaba.com

We operate a China wholesale marketplace, 1688.com, which matches wholesale buyers and sellers in categories such as general merchandise, apparel, electronics, raw materials, industrial components, and agricultural and chemical products. A significant number of merchants on our China retail marketplaces source their inventory on 1688.com.

We also operate Alibaba.com, a global English-language wholesale marketplace founded in 1999. Its offerings span thousands of product categories across forty-plus industries, and it is China's largest global online wholesale marketplace in 2016 by revenue, according to iResearch. By March 2017, buyers on Alibaba.com were located in more than two hundred countries and regions all over the world.

Alibaba.com comprises a suite of tools and services enabling wholesale buyers, which are companies of all sizes from around the world, and suppliers, typically SMEs engaged in import and export, to find each other and do business. These services include premium tiered membership for suppliers, seller and buyer verification, trade assurance, inspection services, and logistics solutions, all built on a comprehensive payment and financing infrastructure. Buyers and sellers enjoy an increasingly seamless and secure online workflow across borders.

Finance: Ant Financial and Alipay

Ant Financial Services provides digital payment services and other financial and value-added services to consumers and SMEs in China and across the world. The services include payment, wealth management, lending, insurance, and credit systems. Ant Financial Services uses its technology and customer insights to help financial institutions, ISVs, and other partners on its platform to enhance the user experience and improve their risk management capabilities. During the twelve months ending in March 2017, Ant Financial Services, together with Paytm (an Indian e-payment company 40 percent owned by Ant) and Ascend Money (an e-commerce company based in Thailand invested in by Ant), served over 630 million annual active users globally.

Alipay, a wholly owned subsidiary of Ant Financial Services, provides payment and escrow services for transactions on Taobao, Tmall, 1688. com, AliExpress, and some of our other platforms. Alipay is the principal means by which consumers pay for their purchases on our China retail marketplaces. Except for transactions paid with credit products such as credit cards, where Alipay charges the merchant, neither Alibaba Group nor Alipay charges any payment fees to merchants doing business on our platforms. Instead, the group pays Alipay a fee for the payment and escrow services it provides on our marketplaces, pursuant to a commercial agreement with Ant Financial Services and Alipay.

Ant Financial Services partners with more than two hundred financial institutions around the world. It and its partners also provide wealth management, lending, insurance, credit systems, and other services to merchants and consumers in the Alibaba ecosystem. The services include working capital loans to SMEs, consumer loans, and logistics-costs insurance for goods returned. More than 0.8 million restaurants, fifty thousand supermarkets, three hundred hospitals, and one million taxis now accept Alipay as a payment method across China. By 2015, Alipay's barcode-based point-of-sale payment solution was accepted in more than seventy thousand overseas retail stores in seventy countries and regions, and tax reimbursement via Alipay is supported in twenty-four countries.

Ant Financial received approval from the China Banking Regulatory Commission on September 29, 2014, to set up a private bank called MYbank (Zhejiang E-Commerce Bank Co. Ltd.) together with Shanghai Fosun Industrial Technology, owned by Fosun International, and Ningbo Jinrun Asset Management. MYbank will fully utilize online and big data analytics to serve the financial needs of small and micro enterprises, as well as individual consumers. It opened for business in June 2015. As of the end of 2016, MYbank managed 61.5 billion RMB in assets (US$9.46 billion), and had 32.9 billion RMB (US$5 billion) in outstanding loans. As of December 2016, the online-only bank has served nearly three million small businesses, giving more than 87 billion RMB (US$13.4 billion) in loans to these businesses since its founding. Its borrowing costs are equivalent to most Chinese banks. Its net operating margin, at 3–5 percent, is significantly higher and its loss rate, at 1 percent, is significantly lower.[3]

Logistics: Cainiao Network

Cainiao Network is a joint venture that Alibaba formed in May 2013 with other shareholders engaged in logistics, retail, and real estate. These shareholders included four major express courier companies in China. Cainiao Network does not deliver packages itself. It operates a logistics data platform that exploits the capacity and capabilities of logistics partners to fulfill transactions between merchants and consumers on a large scale.

Through its platform approach, Cainiao Network integrates the resources of logistics service providers to build out the logistics ecosystem. Cainiao Network operates with ninety domestic and international partners, including fifteen strategic delivery partners. By March 2017, Cainiao Network's fifteen strategic express courier partners employed more than 1.8 million delivery personnel in six hundred-plus cities and thirty-one provinces in China, according to data provided by the courier partners. Collectively, they operated more than 180,000 hubs and sorting stations.

Cainiao Network uses technology and insights from its data to improve efficiency across the logistics value chain. The proprietary data platform provides real-time access to data for merchants to better manage their inventory and warehousing and for consumers to track their orders. In addition, the data platform helps logistics service providers improve their services. For example, these providers can utilize data to optimize the delivery routes used by express courier companies.

Cloud Computing: Alibaba Cloud

Founded in 2009, Alibaba Cloud aimed to make the technologies that grew out of Alibaba Group's own cloud-computing requirement—to operate the massive scale and complexity of its core commerce business—available to third-party customers. In 2016, we expanded our cloud-computing services to Japan, Korea, Germany, the Middle East, and Australia to provide customers worldwide with greater access to our diverse offerings. By March 2017, Alibaba Cloud had approximately 874,000 paying customers. The company was China's largest provider of public cloud services by revenue in 2016, according to the global market intelligence firm IDC.

Alibaba Cloud offers a complete suite of cloud services, including elastic computing, data storage, a content delivery network, large-scale computing, security, management and application services, big-data analytics, and a machine-learning platform. Products that differentiate Alibaba Cloud from its domestic peers include proprietary security and middleware products and large-scale computing services and analytic capabilities provided by our big-data platform. These products enable customers to build IT infrastructure quickly online without having to work on the premises. During the November 11, 2017, Singles Day shopping festival, Alibaba Cloud successfully processed a peak transaction volume of 325,000 orders per second.

The Wider Ecosystem

Surrounding our core e-commerce marketplaces and key businesses (Ant Financial, Cainiao Network, and Alibaba Cloud) are several new initiatives and businesses. Powerful network effects and synergies between our core platforms and these new businesses will drive the future growth of Alibaba's online economy, moving us closer and closer to fulfilling our mission of making it easy to do business anywhere. Let's look at some of these new businesses.

Digital Media and Entertainment: Youku Tudou and UC Browser

Taking advantage of our deep consumer insights to serve the broader interests of consumers, we have developed an emerging business in digital media and entertainment through two approaches. First, we developed two key distribution platforms, Youku Tudou and UC Browser. Second, we created diverse content platforms that provide TV dramas, variety shows, news feeds, movies, music, sports, and live events.

Youku Tudou, a leading multiscreen entertainment and media company in China, is among the most recognized online video brands in China. UC Browser is one of the top three mobile browsers in the world and, by May 2017, was the number one mobile browser in India and Indonesia by page view market share, according to StatCounter. In March 2017, our digital media and entertainment businesses had more than half a billion mobile monthly active users, including overseas users.

Mapping and Navigation: AutoNavi

AutoNavi is a leading source of digital maps, navigation, and real-time traffic information in China. Besides providing these services to end users directly, AutoNavi also operates a leading open platform in China that powers many major mobile apps in different industries such as food delivery, ride services, taxi hailing, and social networking with its location-based services. The company delivers fundamental services to major platforms in the Alibaba ecosystem, including our China retail marketplaces Cainiao Network and Alipay.

Local Services: Koubei and Ele.me

In 2015, Alibaba and Ant Financial Services set up the joint venture Koubei, a leading local services guide business in China. Koubei operates online-to-offline (O2O) services in conjunction with Alipay by generating demand to local establishments such as restaurants, supermarkets, convenience stores, and other offline lifestyle establishments. The service gives consumers a closed-loop experience, from acquiring information on mobile to finding the store to claiming discounts to payment. For the three months ended March 31, 2017, Koubei generated RMB74.7 billion (US$10.9 billion) in GMV settled through Alipay with merchants.

In March 2016, Alibaba jointly invested with Ant Financial Services in Ele.me, a leading food delivery company in China. Consumers using the company's food delivery app can order meals, snacks, and beverages on a mobile device. Through a delivery network of employed and outsourced personnel, the company's service covered more than fifteen hundred districts and counties in China in March 2017. Under a cooperation agreement, Ele.me fulfills food orders generated from the Taobao and Alipay apps.

THE EVOLUTION OF TAOBAO AS A SMART ECOSYSTEM

Alibaba's retail platforms tell an unprecedented story in the annals of business history. In barely ten years, a fully functioning retail economy emerged in an online environment, complete with an array of business functions and associated independent actors. This book's core arguments and case studies have sampled from the history of Alibaba and Taobao. However, readers interested in the larger strategic evolution of the marketplace may wish to examine the platform diachronically.

This appendix will track the growth of Alibaba's e-commerce marketplaces (exemplified by Taobao, the first and still the biggest marketplace, though henceforth I'll use the name *Taobao* to include related retail platforms such as Tmall for larger brands and AliExpress for international markets). Throughout this book, I have discussed episodes and examples from Taobao's rich operating experience. In this appendix, I will reorganize this material chronologically and fill in important gaps, in the hope that a historical description of Taobao's growth will help readers better understand the book's conceptual framework and how a smart business network evolves. (To avoid repetition, I will refer readers to the pertinent chapter when discussing material from earlier in the book.)

Four Stages of Growth

This book's core analytic framework—the combination of network coordination and data intelligence—devolved from years of observing the unplanned growth of the Taobao platform. Taobao was not built step by step on a design conceived of by the central office. Consistently, Taobao leadership responded to developments pioneered by users in its marketplace. In this way, what started as a basic marketplace grew organically into a very complicated ecosystem.

Taobao exemplifies the business organization that I call an *ecosystem*, a smart network of disparate business actors that evolves to solve complicated customer problems. Its growth occurred in four stages: building the online marketplace, building the coordinated network, the emergence of smart business, and exponential growth through smart business.

Taobao's and Alibaba's retail ecosystem is still evolving. Its future is a smart, globally coordinated network that Jack Ma calls "the Alibaba economy." Let's look at these evolutionary stages, by years.

Building the Online Marketplace
2003 to 2005

As described in chapter 2 and appendix A, Taobao emerged in a relative vacuum of technologies and services that would enable online retailing. Taobao's early task was very simple: get more people to buy online. Consequently, Taobao initially focused on putting the core constituents of the marketplace online: products, merchant-consumer interactions, and transactions. After this effort, Taobao became a functional online marketplace. It was a very simple version of what would later be understood as network coordination. Taobao got all the basic parts of the marketplace online, where they could interact through our platform. At this stage, Taobao lacked data intelligence, although the most basic online product database and bare-bones product categories laid the foundation for later datafication and for market mechanisms for matching buyers and sellers.

From the beginning, Taobao had a clear purpose: populate the marketplace, and establish mechanisms that facilitated direct connection and interaction among users. Initially, the Taobao website was essentially an online bulletin board. All users were created alike: everyone had come to do business in some way, whether that meant wholesaling or reselling, selling goods from their homes or presenting goods of their own creation. Slowly, sellers began to specialize and expand into multiple product categories.

Our internal KPIs for the first three years of the business were the buildup of three critical masses: products, merchants, and buyers. We also worked to forge connections between the constituents of the market. The Taobao forum allowed groups of consumers and merchants to connect and discuss common challenges. This community was especially useful in spreading know-how and helping newcomers to learn the ABCs of online selling. The Wangwang instant-messenger application connected consumers and merchants so they could discuss product offerings or transactions. And the assignment of credit ratings to sellers helped tremendously in overcoming the lack of trust in an online environment.

Infrastructure

At this early stage, much of the company's effort was consumed in creating the most rudimentary features of the website: displaying product information, allowing core communication, and enabling all facets of the online transaction process, especially the transfer of money. The most important infrastructure features created in this stage were communication and payments capabilities.

- *Instant messaging:* The Wangwang instant-messenger app connected consumers and merchants (chapter 2).

- *Payments:* The introduction of Alipay and escrow transactions brought into the system trust and liquidity, essential building blocks of a market (chapter 2).

Building the Coordinated Network 2006 to 2008

With the basic ingredients for growth in place, the Taobao marketplace began to tackle the many challenges created due to increasingly sophisticated transactions on the website. It had to offer more functionality, most of which could not be handled by the platform alone. As needs surfaced, new or existing participants found ways to satisfy them. Individual actors began specializing or exploiting their own skills by becoming service providers.

In economic terms, as more and more actors joined the network and as product offerings and categories proliferated, growth of various functions and categories began to jump-start self-reinforcing network externalities. They sprouted from every surface of the marketplace, powering the market's growth engine. This stage demonstrated Taobao's potential for exponential expansion, as yearly GMV grew tenfold from 10 billion to 100 billion RMB (US$1.54 billion to US$15.4 billion).

Network coordination

With the basic infrastructure of the Taobao forum and Wangwang as springboards, Taobao's many business users began to grow their businesses in ways unplanned by the platform. External partners migrated to the platform, new supporting functions emerged, and other business roles gradually became formalized. By opening storefronts to outside software development, Taobao set a precedent for further third-party involvement in the platform and for strategic incubation of new roles and submarkets. The following elements of network coordination got the marketplace off the ground:

- *Early organization:* New connections between sellers both online and offline began to create some of the marketplace's first externalities through knowledge spillover.

- *Early supporting functions:* Examples include the Taobao University lecturers, experienced sellers who shared their experience and best practices, and the earliest ISVs. Certain functions within individual storefronts gradually became formalized, such as the Wangwang customer-service representatives (chapter 2).

- *Early subnetworks:* ISVs and Tao models emerged on the platform and would later incubate separate markets within the larger Taobao ecosystem. The breakneck growth of logistics capabilities drove infrastructural growth and investment across the country (chapter 2).

Infrastructure

With the core interaction of the platform up and running, Taobao began to focus its energy on creating the infrastructure to support the next stage of major network expansion. The most important key mechanism created in this stage was support for logistics. Logistics providers were already emerging, coaxed onboard by the needs of the growing marketplace. But Taobao began to put a priority on building the infrastructure for these providers to efficiently do business and make connections across the network.

As product categories exploded, Taobao began to construct the technical scaffolding that would allow for flexible growth. This support included the following tools and mechanisms:

- *Logistics:* Systems for tracking orders and shipping improved customer experience and made merchant operations easier (chapter 2).

- *Reputation systems:* The platform instituted products and mechanisms for reviewing transactions and quantifying credit for both buyers and sellers, to ensure trust in all parties to the transaction.

- *Category expansion and datafication:* Datafying new products, such as airline tickets or lottery tickets, and offering them for sale on Taobao drove the growth of the platform (chapter 4).

The Emergence of Smart Business 2009 to 2012

In 2005, Alibaba Group acquired Yahoo! China as terms of its agreement with Yahoo!, one of the Group's largest investors. Over time, teams and technology from Yahoo! China integrated into the platform. By 2009, the stage marking the true beginning of smart business in the Taobao marketplace began. The already complex network was reinforced by data-intelligence technology brought into the network by teams from Yahoo! China working on search. In these crucial years of the platform's growth, the forces of network coordination and data intelligence began to build off each other.

The network expanded in breadth and depth. Taobao witnessed phenomenal category expansion, expanding into new markets. At the same time, the network incorporated even more actors and business functions. More professional merchants, including sellers of offline brands, began to operate on the platform, prompting the founding of the Taobao Mall, which would eventually become Tmall. Fueled by search and ad technology, the ecosystem incubated completely new organisms, such as the Tao brands. These brands were started by entrepreneurs on the platform without relying on any brick-and-mortar presence. Many grew to become recognizable national brands.

Taobao's yearly GMV exploded from 200 billion to 1 trillion RMB (US$31 billion to US$154 billion). The double helix of smart business was complete, and it formed an extremely powerful engine for growth.

Network coordination

The influx of advertising technology was a powerful new catalyst for the network's growth. Taobao's growing advertising network brought traffic from a multitude of external websites, large and small, into the Taobao ecosystem, cementing the platform's market dominance in China. Three developments were particularly responsible for Taobao's growing dominance:

- *Network expansion:* The affiliate marketing ad platform Taobaoke allowed Alibaba to outmaneuver search giant Baidu for control of product search (chapter 2). As countless smaller websites began to rely on Taobaoke for income, their traffic poured into Taobao, rapidly growing the network and feeding seller demand.

- *Specialized third-party roles:* These functions include affiliate marketers on external websites organized through Taobaoke; product recommenders (*daogou*) who earn commission from sales on curated lists of products from across the platform; and all manner of ISVs, from customer-relationship-management software providers to logistics management to search optimization to call-center outsourcing (chapters 2 and 6).

- *New organisms:* These include the Tao brands (online-only brands built from scratch by entrepreneurs) and Taobao partners, or TPs (a special class of ISVs that run storefront operations) (chapter 6).

Data intelligence

Search and advertising technologies were the first bona fide data-intelligence engines in the Taobao system. As search products and metrics steadily improved, advertising helped sellers monetize and find new clients. The development of the Taobao application programming interface (API) also enabled the growth of countless service providers. By bringing efficiency and fostering new connections to the marketplace, the following new technologies formed the second DNA strand of the double helix, ushering in Taobao's first true stage of smart business:

- *Ad technology:* The merging of Yahoo! China brought search and advertising technologies to the marketplace. By allowing the platform to effectively allocate resources, advertising revolutionized the ecosystem, making it smart, globally optimized, and highly lucrative (chapter 4).

- *Evolution of search:* Improving metrics and incentives for sellers, such as including statistics on customer satisfaction, made the entire platform more efficient and scalable and enhanced the consumer experience (chapter 4).

Infrastructure

As described, integration and investment in advertising and search technology provided crucial infrastructure for the ecosystem. But beyond this data-intelligence infrastructure, the growth of the network and the technical demands of data intelligence caused Taobao and the rest of Alibaba to feel the pain of operating such a complex website. This stage saw consistent investment in all levels of technical infrastructure, chiefly the following innovations that developed Taobao's smart infrastructure:

- *Cloud computing:* These internal cloud-computing resources that would later become China's largest provider of cloud-computing services, Alibaba Cloud, were originally developed to ease untenable pressure on Alibaba's finances created by escalating computational loads. Moving Taobao's various businesses into the cloud brought technical efficiency, coordination, and security (chapter 3).

- *API technology:* Taobao's API (the tools that streamline communication between different software modules) enabled parties to coordinate with one another using live data. Many external developers began to offer software and data-driven services for merchants. Partners can cooperate easily and automatically through the online protocol, dramatically decreasing costs of coordination. At the same time, the API enabled free flow of data on the network, completing the live-data feedback loop. By facilitating both network coordination and data intelligence, the API was crucial in the evolution of Taobao (chapter 4).

- *Jushita operating cloud:* As sellers began to coordinate with increasing numbers of outside partners, it became clear that data security was a significant problem for clients and the entire platform. To protect the privacy and interests of both merchants and consumers, Alibaba invested in an enclosed environment for data sharing and processing, calling it Jushita ("tower of collected stones"). Merchants and ISVs can safely deploy data-driven software and applications within the Jushita cloud environment.

Exponential Growth through Smart Business 2013 to 2017

As reflected by the richness of product offerings on the Taobao app, the Alibaba ecosystem has grown stronger and stronger in the mobile era. The coordinated network keeps expanding, creating important new roles through social commerce, such as new content creators. At the same time, data intelligence has spread to every corner of the network, growing both more powerful and more effective. This growth is exemplified by the transition from search to recommendation throughout the platform, as well as new upgraded uses for AI technology, such as fraud detection, customer service, and automated design.

The combination of these two forces has made the Taobao app flexible, dynamic, intelligent, and powerful. The continual emergence of new actors and business models, chiefly the web celebs, testifies to the health and vitality of the Alibaba ecosystem and to Taobao's continued strength in network coordination and data intelligence. As manifold networks of retail, finance, and logistics grow smarter and better coordinated, the entire ecosystem unfolds into new heights of prosperity.

Network coordination

Since 2013, the borders of the ecosystem have quickly outstripped the Taobao platform itself to crisscross the Chinese internet, social media, the most rural corners of the country, and even the wider world. Inspired by the success of e-commerce and shopping festivals like Singles Day, manufacturers and brands from inside China and abroad have flocked to the platform. Offline merchants, too, have begun to link up with online platforms and mobile payments. In China, this area of coordination, in which online networks increase purchases in physical establishments like stores and restaurants, is known as O2O, online-to-offline. The following developments continue to expand Taobao's reach:

- *External marketing networks:* The Alimama ad exchange and ad network has grown into a new mobile marketing ecosystem that spans nearly every channel and website known to the Chinese netizen.

- *Social media:* The rise of social media has driven the expansion of social commerce, as social platforms such as Weibo offer unprecedented opportunities for brand building (chapter 5).

- *Complex new roles:* A second wave of ISVs, powered by Alibaba Cloud's computing and data resources, has migrated to the platform. Manufacturing solutions such as the Tao Factory are beginning to connect merchants to China's untapped productive resources. Besides the web celebs, new entrants such as live-streaming influencers and content creators now thrive on Taobao, making money by working with merchants (chapter 5).

- *Penetration into the countryside and across the world:* The rapid expansion of Rural Taobao and Tmall has sped integration of partners across China and around the world. These two businesses have brought a plethora of partners into Taobao's smart ecosystem, from agricultural resellers, local and municipal logistics players, and village-level operators across rural China to international shipping companies, bonded warehouses, and other internationally focused partners around the world.

Data intelligence

Machine learning, large-scale computing, and data intelligence now operate continuously throughout the network, rapidly improving the consumer experience, production efficiency, and merchant margins. More importantly, data intelligence is spreading beyond Alibaba's core e-commerce businesses to associated platforms like finance and logistics. Taobao benefits as these platforms grow smarter and better coordinated. The double helix continues to rotate onward and upward as the following elements of data intelligence improve:

- *Comprehensive AI technology:* A suite of artificial intelligence technology affords improvements in personalized search and recommendations, security and fraud protection, customer service, business coordination, and more (chapter 3).

- *Finance:* From Ant Financial's smart microloan business to comprehensive credit scores and other financial infrastructure, Alibaba's ecosystem and the entire country are witnessing an explosion of financial technology driven by data intelligence (chapter 3).

- *Logistics:* Alibaba's affiliated data-driven logistics platform, the Cainiao Network, works through a network of fulfillment partners to make these partners' operations smarter and more efficient.

Infrastructure

The most important infrastructural breakthrough in this stage was Alibaba's persistent focus on mobile. Beginning in late 2013, Taobao completely restructured its marketplace from the ground up to fit the new world of mobile. Taobao's infrastructural improvements in this stage can be summarized as follows:

- *Mobile:* Taobao entering the world of mobile mandated a new and robust infrastructure for mobile transactions and operations. These investments in mobile technology have driven great externalities across the network and ushered in a new period of intense competition across the industry (chapter 4).

- *Comprehensive AI technology:* Alibaba's technical stack (the various applications that coordinate network operations) supports real-time, hyperscale data processing for fundamental marketplace functionalities such as search, recommendation, and security.

- *Cloud computing:* Alibaba Cloud and its own mini-ecosystem for developers now provide powerful data storage and processing for the network's various partners as well as an increasing number of industries beyond e-commerce.

Now let's look chronologically at how Taobao grew from a small forum of amateur users into the massive online retail force that it is today.

Stage 1: 2003–2005

The Birth of Taobao

In 2003, Jack Ma assembled a group of eight employees to begin work on a secret new project. Alibaba had been in business for four years. Its B2B platform was profitable and growing quickly. But Ma had bigger designs on the Chinese market: he wanted to reconstruct China's antiquated and poorly developed retail industry.

In May of that year, Taobao was born. It began as a small, cute, and unassuming forum for selling goods. Ma and his fellow coworkers uploaded as many items from their own apartments as they could to rapidly populate the platform and give the appearance of activity. Little did they know at the time that their little forum would become the world's largest online marketplace.

In the first few years of its life, Taobao successfully fought off the incursion of eBay, the world's top e-commerce marketplace, into the Chinese market. Many other books have discussed Taobao's tactics for beating eBay. Here, I want to discuss Taobao's larger strategy for developing a more robust and flexible business network. Much of this strategy is only discernable in hindsight as the cumulative result of a multitude of small decisions, many of which were made to fit with Alibaba's values and beliefs about the connected future of the e-commerce industry.

Taobao began by taking advantage of eBay's greatest weakness. eBay's markets are rigid by design. The company makes its money through listing fees and commissions: if buyers and sellers connect but do not eventually make transactions through the platform, eBay makes no money. Thus the core logic behind eBay's marketplace is to mediate much of the interaction between its users to prevent buyers and sellers from making free connections. Transactions must be tightly controlled, and sellers primarily have to deal with eBay itself. The marketplace is a clearinghouse for products and mostly idle consumer goods waiting to be transacted. It is not a solution for enabling more-complex business activities.

In China, buyers and sellers had needs that the rigid structure of eBay could not satisfy. The country had given birth to an enormous number of small sellers without business and access to consumers. Buyers didn't want to bid on only a few unique products; they wanted access to a vast universe of products from across China. And sellers wanted access to that multitude of sellers and the chance to compete on products and services. More importantly, China's retail industry was extremely undeveloped. As the marketplace grew, sellers also needed solutions that would improve their businesses.

Taobao's strategy was to build a bustling two-sided market, catering to both buyers and sellers. In 2003, employees did everything they could to fill the market with as many products as they could find. The next year, the goal was to bring in as many sellers as possible. Finally, with a critical mass of sellers, Taobao began 2005 by attracting buyers to a website that advertised itself as selling anything you could possibly imagine. In retrospect, this transformation was a classic exercise in building a platform through network externalities and using two sides of the market to build off each other. More sellers brought more buyers; better sellers brought better buyers.

Finding products to sell was often an exercise in tedium, as employees resorted to any tactics they could to catalog as many SKUs as existed in China. The platform attracted sellers through Ma's famous policy of keeping Taobao free. Opening a storefront was free. Listing products was free. With no entry barriers, apart from the time and energy needed to learn how to use the website, sellers flocked into the marketplace. And as soon as buyers realized that Taobao housed every product on the face of the earth, they came in droves as well.

The constant flurry of activity that resulted knit a market out of a dense web of interactions. Bringing ever more players onto its platform and allowing them to connect and do business with one another engendered increasingly complicated coordination technology and systems substantially facilitated by Taobao. That coordination capability enabled progressively more advanced business models.

From Warmth to Trust

Despite its growing popularity, Taobao was not just a forum. It was a marketplace, and markets are not sustained by mere social interaction. They require means of exchange and other tools and structures to authenticate, safeguard, and enable healthy transactions and trust. The offline market economy took thousands of years to develop—from bartering beans for hides to credit card transactions for something produced halfway around the world. Taobao was faced with the same challenges, except in an online environment.

Taobao's two technological keys that bootstrapped its market evolution were Alipay, Alibaba's platform for secure escrow payments, and Wangwang, Taobao's chat feature. By convincing consumers that online buying was safe, Alipay provided the foundation of trust that allowed Taobao's transactions to proceed smoothly. Wangwang enabled sellers to build rich interactions with buyers and to offer differentiated services. Some sellers even became famous for the humorous exchanges they had with customers!

Any discussion of the early years of Taobao would be incomplete without mention of Alipay and escrow payment. In 2003, China lacked trust on a multitude of levels. There were no checking accounts, credit cards had just been introduced to a very small user base, and no trusted back-end settlement protocol existed. Early transactions on Taobao were small-scale and local, mostly restricted to offline trading in the same city. After connecting online, buyers and sellers would meet in person, inspect the goods in question, and physically exchange money. Transactions were slow and costly. More importantly, the setup was a recipe for fraud and cheating. The early days of Taobao abound with stories of sellers who scheduled a meeting with a buyer and arrived promptly with their products, only to find that before they could react, the buyer had driven past them on a bicycle, grabbed the product out of their hands, and pedaled swiftly away before anybody was the wiser. Clearly, the direct physical swapping of goods and money was not a recipe for safe, nationwide, frictionless trading that might lead to explosive growth.

The escrow solution solved these problems. Buyers would first entrust their money to Alipay, in the early days by wiring to Alipay's bank account. Alipay would then hold the payment in a secure account until the buyer received the good he or she had purchased and confirmed its quality. Thereupon, Alipay would reward the seller with the earnings. For buyers unfamiliar with and suspicious of e-commerce, escrow provided the peace of mind needed to trust their hard-earned cash to a transaction with a stranger, no matter who the merchants were or where they were located. For sellers, escrow payment greatly broadened their client base. Now, instead of several thousand buyers from the same city, sellers could sell to hundreds of millions of consumers across the country. Trust had been built to undergird the marketplace, and the gates were suddenly thrown open to all. From this humble beginning, Alipay later built an online payment network that connected with all the online banking services in China and hence became China's major online payment gateway.

Your Credit, My Credit

After escrow payment, Taobao's next step was to establish credit ratings to digitalize reputation and thereby inspire good service and better performance. In an online setting, reputation is an asset like any other, albeit invisible and difficult to transfer. Taobao was by no means the first e-commerce platform to use such rating systems to quantify reputations; eBay pioneered credit ratings in online marketplaces, with a standardized reputation score system applied in the same way to every user. But Taobao's employees quickly realized this reputation system pioneered by eBay was insufficient.

The central problem was that users engaged in both buying and selling behavior. In the early days of Taobao, all conversations and transactions occurred through a central forum. Users who wanted to buy goods found items and contacted other users. Essentially, any user could buy or sell as he or she wished. When a transaction was completed, the user's credit score would improve. However, this design meant that a user who had bought a lot of items but had no selling experience seemed just as credible as, if not more credible than, an experienced seller. There was room for fraud: the signal of reputation within the market was ineffective.

For Taobao to become a major retailing platform, amateur sellers had to begin to operate like professional sellers. Taobao decided to separate reputation scores into buyer and seller scores. A user who had sold many items would not have a high buyer score unless the same user had similarly bought a lot of items, and vice versa. Furthermore, buyers and sellers would rate each other after the transaction was complete. In Chinese e-commerce, transactions are only completed when the buyer confirms delivery of goods.[1] The buyer's confirmation not only alerts escrow payment systems to send the money to the seller, but also allows the buyer and seller to rate each other.

By splitting credit scores, Taobao also separated the buying and selling roles institutionally and technologically. For any selling activity, the credit score served as a concrete incentive to provide quality products and good service, as sellers with better scores attracted more buyers. Good buyer scores also supported the evolution of a healthy ecosystem, because the presence of good buyers encouraged the entry of more sellers. These credit scores were only the first step of deeper and broader differentiation in the market—a prelude to the inclusion of more and more roles in the platform and hence to a more and more complex ecosystem.

Settlers in a Virtual Marketplace

At first, the new inhabitants of this new market were all alike. Taobao's early employees spent their days on the Taobao forum talking to sellers and facilitating transactions. Sellers were buyers, and buyers were sellers: in the first few years, when consumers had not yet grown accustomed to online buying, many sellers bought and sold from each other. The Taobao offices played host to a steady stream of local merchants discussing platform design and marketing tactics, suggesting rules and other features, and criticizing and complaining about shortfalls and imperfect user experience.

But soon, Taobao experienced the natural evolution of markets that in an offline setting might have taken decades. Roles began to separate, evolving new forms of cooperation and competition. Like cells dividing, the market grew more complex. I just described how credit scores established two roles characterized by very different behaviors. However, Taobao leadership quickly realized that buyers and sellers alone were not enough to sustain a functioning marketplace. Sellers needed more support to effectively engage in the complex practice of commerce.

The earliest of these new roles to appear was the customer-service representative. One of the biggest differences between Chinese and Western e-commerce is the role of in-house customer service. Whereas websites such as Amazon and eBay only have official customer hotlines, every storefront on Taobao has its own account on the official Taobao instant-messenger, Wangwang. The site puts a human face on each storefront: customers can ask about offerings or dicker over price. They can even chat about other things if they want. And as described earlier in the book, Wangwang customer-service representatives use an unusually informal tone, even calling customers "dear," injecting warmth into an otherwise impersonal experience.

As explained in chapter 2, besides the traditional function of polite, helpful pre- and post-purchase service, the customer-service roles on Taobao differ in that customers expect service to be available 24/7.

Taobao's customer service has provided employment opportunities for tens of millions of Chinese people, including students, people with low incomes, people with little education, and people with physical disabilities that make working in the traditional economy difficult.

The Web We Weave Together

Most sellers in these early days were young, inexperienced in the retail industry, and often unable to adequately execute the difficult task of operating an online store. Early sellers were often individuals, at most a very small team, learning on their feet. They rarely manufactured (much less designed) their own products, often procuring goods from wholesale markets or factories around the country, in itself a challenging task in the still underdeveloped Chinese economy. While doing business on Taobao and processing transactions through Alipay was free, sellers had to learn to use the growing array of tools provided by Taobao for managing a storefront and connecting with customers. Thus, some sellers saw an opportunity to provide supporting services for quickly growing merchants.

With more sellers selling to more buyers, the ecosystem began to grow in complexity. But, in marked contrast to eBay, Taobao showed an impressive ability from the very beginning to engender connections and even organizations outside its official purview. Precisely because the world of e-commerce in China emerged without models or precedents, whereas eBay was born within the well-developed US retail environment, Taobao's value as a marketplace quickly began to spill over. Sellers formed informal networks as more and more service providers flocked to the platform, driven by its ever-increasing potential business value.

Even in the first few years, sellers began to openly organize into local clubs and other associations, forming unofficial business forums and unions. These early spaces, offline accessories to the online marketplace, allowed sellers to connect, sharing knowledge and helping each other adjust to the new world of online selling. Some of these forums were localized, where sellers in one city or province would meet periodically. Sellers of all ages and backgrounds, from different product categories and industries, came together in search of business opportunities and improved performance.

Gradually, dedicated online forums for sellers emerged, among them the most famous being Weiya and Paidai. At the same time, a new breed of sellers began to distinguish themselves from the rest of their contemporaries. Whether through innate aptitude or pure happenstance, these sellers swiftly apprehended the mindset and strategies needed to succeed in those early, chaotic years. The group, however, did not conceal its knowledge or hoard the fruits of success. Instead, these sellers found meaning and even material reward from sharing their experience, for example, by organizing lectures online and offline; sharing techniques and tricks for better online marketing, including customer service and dispute resolution; and working with factories to improve supply-chain management. And as one might expect, many other sellers were willing to pay for the valuable, trustworthy information from their experienced peers.

After Taobao quickly realized that this group of lecturers performed an important service for sellers, it created the so-called Taobao University, a department within Taobao to certify and support the Tao U lecturers. Taobao's goal was not to manage and standardize the rapidly growing market for education. By encouraging sellers to self-organize and cooperate, Taobao gave the most active instructors a platform for growth. Tao U lecturers quickly gained prestige and recognition and, with Taobao's support, expanded the range of possibilities for earning money from their lecturing. Over the next decade, the lecturers exerted an often-overlooked but immensely important force throughout the market. Lecture after lecture spread waves of knowledge that helped sellers, especially the smallest and least experienced sellers, perform better in new and unfamiliar surroundings.

Stage 2: 2006–2008

Category Fission

By 2005, more and more sellers had joined the platform, bringing with them ever-more items for sale and attracting an enormous number of buyers. The platform's growth was exploding. With that explosive growth, Taobao had already begun its evolution from a simple online marketplace into a retail platform. Starting in 2006, Taobao began to build the core resources and mechanisms that would support its later growth in network coordination and data intelligence.

At first, Taobao's breakneck growth brought practical design challenges. With an ever-growing array of buyers, sellers, and products, how should the platform allow these various groups to find and interact with each other? How should the network that connects buyers and sellers be designed to grow?

I have discussed how the website changed from a forum to a full-fledged market, but I have paid less attention so far to the design and infrastructure of the website, and hence, the market. The first incarnation of Taobao looked like a forum, but in actuality it was a very flexible database of product information. That database's core functionality was to datafy products by encoding their characteristics into data, which allowed buyers to browse, find, and buy items on Taobao. The database thereby enabled Taobao to live up to its early reputation: you can find anything you can imagine.

The product database essentially created a series of "boxes" in which sellers could slot in their items, from apparel to food to electronics. This database acted like an index, almost like one you would find in a library, listing each product along with a predetermined set of features such as size, material, and brand. The platform could in theory create an infinite number of boxes with an infinite number of features attached to each box. Because growth in product categories necessarily implied growth in types of sellers, the expansion of the product database drove the expansion of the network. Each time a new box appeared, so too would a new group of sellers flock to the market, in turn attracting a new swath of consumers.

Early in the marketplace's evolution, a certain practice called "category splitting" became quite common among Taobao's employees to achieve growth. For example, in the women's apparel category, employees would notice a type of product that was particularly popular, e.g., dresses. By creating a subcategory of dresses like "miniskirts," employees enabled buyers and sellers to find each other much more easily. Browsing efficiency increased, which naturally improved sales. At the same time, sellers could further specialize their products and gained better and better access to precision volume, increasing conversion rates and business. From the platform's perspective, more categories meant that transactions from more and more industries were going online. Taobao thus expanded the boundaries of the marketplace through datafication.

For category managers, as long as the website was growing, splitting categories was an easy and effective way to drive business growth. In the words of one of Taobao's early category managers, "split a category, and GMV spiked." Separating and defining categories had such an effect because, even as early as 2005, the growth in buyers greatly exceeded the growth in sellers. In those first earlier years, the main channel that consumers used to find products was the category listings. Give buyers a new category to explore, and they would buy like gangbusters. And for sellers, each new category meant greater specialization.

At the same time, category splitting laid the groundwork for the platform's future data intelligence. The data produced as a side effect of category splitting became richer and deeper, and category managers could see when demand for certain categories was growing quickly. But there was a bigger problem with the category system: increasingly fine-tuned differentiation between products ultimately did not improve efficiency. As Taobao expanded, it became immediately obvious that the existing categories were far from adequate to keep up with the dizzying variety of new products and new consumer demands.

Fundamentally, the category managers' decisions were imperfect human decisions. By the time the market had grown to include millions of buyers, even the category managers had to admit that their job was next to impossible. How could one or two employees responsible for an entire category with up to hundreds of thousands of storefronts hope to select products efficiently? Splitting categories without restraint or principles would eventually mean efficiency losses and would perhaps even hurt the marketplace. The network had grown, but it needed stronger tools of data intelligence to keep up its efficiency.

Logistics

As the e-commerce industry began to pick up, Taobao's consumers, merchants, and employees quickly had to cope with a pressing social problem: the sorry state of Chinese logistics. As China's economy modernized and opened up in the 1980s and 1990s, industries emerged from nothing. But the development of supporting commercial infrastructure often lagged behind. Logistics, especially courier service, was no exception. Though China's national postal service covered the country, its service even to this day is often too slow for effective commercial use. International couriers such as FedEx and DHL sent packages into and out of China, but not to any significant degree within the country. For the better part of two decades, businesses had little choice when it came to consumer shipping. (This lack of delivery infrastructure was one of many factors that prevented Chinese firms from creating companies and business on a national scale before the 2000s.)

Beginning in the late 1990s, several entrepreneurs from a county called Tonglu, located in Zhejiang Province to the southwest of Hangzhou, began to offer courier service for companies and individuals in the commercial corridor around the Shanghai River delta. These companies very quickly began to expand across the country to fill a nascent need for quick and affordable delivery. More importantly, as these companies expanded in the booming years after the turn of the new century, they also caught the wave of e-commerce.

When Taobao was founded in 2003, it unwittingly stepped into a complicated, shifting map of courier service providers across the countries. The so-called Tonglu Mafia, all from the same county in Zhejiang, founded four of the largest companies. SF Express, a high-end express-delivery service originally founded to handle deliveries between Guangdong Province and Hong Kong, began to expand quickly into the rest of China's high-end market. Another dozen or so smaller players operated throughout the country, staking various regional claims while aiming for national dominance. How was a growing e-commerce marketplace to decide how to work with this many companies operating at vastly different scales and levels of expertise?

By the time the basic structures of Taobao's marketplace had solidified in 2006, company leadership quickly saw that the complicated state of the logistics industry created serious difficulties for both buyers and sellers. Because of regional differences across China and a convoluted system of franchising within the logistics industry, pricing and service quality varied drastically across geographical regions. Even in the same area, different logistics companies could offer very different quotes for the same service. Sellers operating on Taobao had to contract their own logistics partners, which operated independently from the website.

The situation for consumers was a minor nightmare. Even once the seller had quoted shipping prices and times, consumers had to use badly designed and unstable websites created by the logistics companies to access tracking data related to their purchase. The problems spawned by this innocuous-sounding arrangement could be truly treacherous. For one, because the logistics companies possessed less-than-stellar IT capabilities, rapidly escalating traffic from Taobao consumers checking delivery statuses soon gave rise to regular server crashes and blackouts. More dangerously, often exploited by hackers, security vulnerabilities hidden in the logistics companies' web pages were stealing user information, engaging in phishing, or even infecting consumer computers with Trojan viruses.

Taobao needed to provide better consumer experiences on fulfillment, but what to do? It could emulate Amazon, well known throughout the industry for developing in-house logistics capabilities. But the cost and difficulty of managing a fulfillment fleet was not feasible given the exponential growth of Taobao's platform model. In 2006, Alipay experimented with an optional service whereby sellers could send pricing inquiries to logistics companies. The idea was to make prices more transparent and standardized. (Alipay also intended to reserve the right to fine logistics companies if they did not meet their promised standard of service, including time to fulfillment.) The service didn't take off. Only two major providers and one minor company located in Shanghai were willing to work with Taobao, most likely because it meant ceding no small amount of control to an outside party. Sellers had little incentive to use the optional and very limited service, and consumers felt little impact when they did use it.

In response, Taobao took a different approach. It would embed the act of fulfillment into the core transaction flow of the platform and, in doing so, would implicate third-party logistics companies into the larger ecosystem.

To understand what this new approach meant, consider Alipay's escrow system. In Chinese e-commerce, once the consumer finishes a purchase and completes the checkout, the money paid is held in

Alipay's system until the transaction completes. The flag for completing the transaction is again incumbent on the consumers, who confirm that they have received their item as requested. Once Alipay receives that confirmation—and only when it does so—the merchant receives payment. The fulfillment process is deeply intertwined with the escrow system. Many situations where the consumer is not satisfied and refuses to complete the transaction have nothing to do with the seller. For example, the parcel never arrived or it was damaged in transit.

Taobao's retooling of the transaction flow embedded shipping into the escrow workflow. In 2006, Taobao consolidated transaction software and product under a single team, including portions of Alipay transactions, and required sellers to enter a package tracking number into Taobao's system after shipping physical goods. Without a tracking number, consumers could not complete the transaction. By integrating tracking numbers, Taobao pulled tracking information from the logistics companies, allowing consumers and merchants alike to track their parcels en route. This change had profound implications for the platform, for consumers, and for the logistics companies.

At first, the vast majority of the logistics companies were less than willing to share core operating data with Taobao. But six months after the first company successfully integrated its fulfillment platforms with Taobao in 2007, that company's delivery volume spiked. The others took notice and warmed to the idea. By the end of 2008, all of China's major logistics companies had integrated with Taobao. Though sellers still had to contract with logistics companies on their own, the process became more standardized and consumer complaints decreased. More importantly, from the perspective of the platform, logistics companies had been integrated into Taobao's core mechanisms. The ecosystem had expanded. As Taobao began to experience exponential growth, the logistics companies that were now connected to the platform rode the same wave of growth.

From Yahoo! China to Alimama

Utilizing Yahoo! China's technology, Taobao founded Alimama, a marketing technology platform, in 2007. The platform first brought advertising into the Taobao ecosystem. Alimama's advertisements came in three general forms. First, keyword-based ads embedded in Taobao search pages allowed sellers to post ads within the Taobao marketplace. Second, Alimama created an ad exchange that allowed ads to be posted to external websites. Third, the Taobaoke platform created a market for affiliate marketing, quantifying and paying for ads on third-party websites, that drew traffic in from every corner of the web. (See the later discussion of Taobaoke in this appendix.)

Online advertising differs from offline advertising in its precision and ability to quantify behaviors and reactions. If a user views an ad you have posted through Baidu, Baidu will record that impression. If a user clicks on an ad from Taobao and eventually goes on to complete a transaction, Alimama's advertising engine will alert you. More-advanced advertising technologies can also give ad buyers a clear picture of who their audience is, the audience's preferences and interests, and even what sorts of products people might be interested in. It is next to impossible to measure the exact impact from, and return on, offline advertising expenses. By contrast, online advertising directly measures and tracks connections between sellers and buyers.

Yahoo! China possessed yet another important technology that had significant influence on Taobao's ecosystem: search. Not surprisingly, in 2008, Taobao began to continuously upgrade its rules for popularity search. For example, the upgraded search assigned more weight to sales, picture click rates, and conversions. Taobao began to encourage certain seller behavior through its design of search algorithms, encouraging the healthy growth of sellers.

Stage 3: 2009–2012

The New Fusion: Search and Ads

In combination with ads, search took on a new meaning as a metaphorical internal combustion engine for the platform. By 2009, many sellers had begun using Zhitongche, Alimama's keyword-based advertising product. Bidding for search keywords meant exposure to buyers, which meant more sales and improved metrics. Improved metrics meant better search rankings, and again more exposure to buyers through search. Combining search and ad products in this way brought explosive growth for enterprising sellers.

To understand how the combustion engine works, consider how retail products are positioned on Taobao. To avoid cannibalizing offline sales and even damaging the brand, the average company in China does not sell the exact same goods in online and offline channels. Every retail channel needs a dedicated product strategy to deliver a distinctive experience for the customer—an experience that is customized for each channel. In the average Taobao storefront, a seller will typically offer at least three tiers of products, which are differentiated mostly on margin: "exploding" items, margin-driven items, and showcase items. (In women's accessories, for example, an "exploding" pair of tights might be priced at a 1.6 ratio to cost, while margin-driven and showcase items might instead offer a ratio of 1.8 and 2.1, respectively.)

Besides contributing to the bottom line in different ways, each of these tiers of products has a specific function within the store and on the platform. Margin-driven items are easy to understand; these are the higher-margin items that every retailer wants to sell. Showcase items are often placed in a store to shape the general brand identity and positioning, with many sellers keeping very low quantities in stock.

The most interesting of these categories is the exploding tier, a term that originally arose on Taobao in the early years of the platform and soon grew to represent the basic operational strategy for SKUs in associated categories. Exploding items (*baokuan*) are cheap, but with quality surpassing their price. In fact, they are often priced at a level that would in and of itself be unsustainable for the seller. The attraction to heavily price-conscious customers is obvious, but exploding items are not offered to exploit economies of scale. They work to build reputation for a store and gain higher weight in search algorithms.

In e-commerce, placement and traffic is chiefly determined by reputation, which is quantified by historical sales volume and product review scores. The best way to quickly accrue reputation is to offer a high-quality product at low-quality prices, thereby attracting a critical mass of customers and positive responses. The ensuing reputation data in turn boosts the placement of, and traffic to, the store, ensuring that more and more consumers can visit the store. From then on, the seller's job is to drive traffic into conversions of its higher-margin items.

This tripartite tier of items works in Chinese e-commerce because of the technological mechanism by which reputation accrues and how it influences operating strategy. In an offline shopping mall, a store is perfectly within its rights to display a high-quality product sold at a low price in its window. Odds are, it will attract consumers, but the long-term payoff for the brand will probably be limited. But online, a store's very placement in the online mall is inextricably tied to its reputation and performance. It is almost as if the aforementioned store, after selling numerous sale items, could move closer to the escalator.

Many sellers quickly learned that they could use advertising and search to quickly grow their brands. First, they would invest in advertising, funneling traffic into stores to purchase exploding items. Sales activity would boost storefront metrics and afford better search placement, which in turn brought more traffic and sales. Sellers who understood the system could quickly take advantage of the platform's resources of data intelligence to grow their businesses.

As time went on, this internal combustion engine, too, began to impair the ecosystem's long-term growth, as larger sellers grew larger and larger, creating imbalances on the platform. Thus, Alibaba would invest in recommendation technologies in later years to promote more-balanced seller growth across the platform.

Taobaoke: The Growing Network

The growth of advertising technology was in many ways the beginning of Taobao's most important period of explosive growth and the first of many factors that allowed the small Taobao ecosystem to exert influence on the business environment outside the platform. In addition to external advertisements hosted through Alimama's exchange, Taobao's other network of affiliate marketing, Taobaoke, also did considerable work in expanding the network.

Taobaoke began as a fairly simple idea. If I bought a piece of clothing or a household good that I particularly liked, I could recommend the product to my friend. If the friend bought it, I could earn a small commission from the seller as a way of saying thanks for helping the merchant gain a new customer. In 2008, when the Taobaoke product first went online, this logic of affiliate marketing was already established in markets like Japan and the United States, with the prime example being Google AdSense. This platform allows websites to embed advertisements on their web pages and monetize the ads' content. If a visitor to the website clicks on one of Google's ads, the website earns a small commission. For many small websites that lack the resources to develop advertising and sales teams, AdSense provides a crucial lease on life.

Taobaoke differs from AdSense in one fundamental way: the Chinese commissions are based on sales, not clicks. (In technical terms, this is the difference between cost per click and cost per sale.) If a visitor to a small media portal is looking at an article on what sort of porridge to brew for weight loss and radiant skin, the individual might see a link to Taobao selling cloud-ear mushrooms. If that user clicks on the link and looks at the page but doesn't end up buying a product, the website gets nothing.

This mechanism design completely changed the incentives for external websites. It was not enough to ensure that an ad got an enormous number of clicks: users needed to enter Taobao and actually buy products for the website to earn its commission. In practice, it was most profitable to guide as many people into the Taobaoke platform as possible in the hopes that some fraction of them would end up buying. Thus, Taobaoke encouraged savvy webmasters to drive traffic to Taobao.

As a result, when Taobaoke was introduced into the Taobao ecosystem, it brought far more than extra business for sellers. It expanded the boundaries of the entire network and opened up Taobao to countless external sites across the internet. As smaller websites began to rely on Taobaoke for more and more income, their traffic poured into Taobao, rapidly growing the network and feeding seller demand. These new sources of traffic meant more and more business for the store owners that participated in Taobaoke's commission program. As more consumers entered the Taobao ecosystem, they became even "stickier" buyers, purchasing from more and more sellers. The network grew thicker and denser as it expanded.

Tao Brands: The Origin of Species

In just a few years, Taobao experienced the natural evolution of markets that in an offline setting might have taken decades. Roles began to separate, evolving new forms of cooperation and competition. Like cells dividing, the market grew more complex. One of the most interesting and exciting examples of that complexity was the Tao brands, brands incubated and grown completely online. (See the sidebar "A Case Study of UNIFON.")

The Birth of Singles Day

In late 2009, employees at the newly separated Tmall sat down to brainstorm how to bring their new marketplace into the mainstream. Tmall was positioned as Alibaba's platform for large and established offline brands, but many of those brands did not see a compelling reason to join the marketplace. A sale might be a worthwhile carrot to lure these flocks of brands to the platform.

Traditional Chinese retail cycles focused around the Chinese New Year in January or February, as well as changing seasons across the country. After copious research, the staff decided that the month of November would serve as an ideal bridge between fall and winter seasons in various categories and regions of China. This was the opportunity to create a new megasale, a Black Friday for China. Except, there was one problem. Between the National Day holiday on October 1 and late December (when the rarely celebrated Christmas can be invoked as a pretense for sales), China had no important holidays analogous to an American Thanksgiving Day.

The search persisted to no avail, until somebody suggested November 11, known among some young people as a tongue-in-cheek holiday for the lonely, unattached masses: Singles Day, named for the depressing singularity represented in the date's numerical written form.

And so, Singles Day was born. The first year, with little preparation and only twenty-seven sellers participating, 52 million RMB worth (US$8 million) of goods were sold in a single day, to the utter stupefaction of all involved. Clearly, they were onto something: in 2010, the new holiday's sales numbers continued to skyrocket, racking up 936 million RMB (US$144 million), more than the entire volume of products sold in Hong Kong in a single day.

Yet even as Taobao and Tmall were growing at a bewildering pace, e-commerce had still not entered the average retailer's field of vision. For the offline brands that comprised an increasing percentage of sellers on Tmall, e-commerce was still only a minor part of their operations, often handled by a small portion of their marketing staff. On Singles Day in 2010, when demand first greatly exceeded the volume of goods that sellers had prepared ahead of time, many companies had to scramble to divert products from other channels. Yet despite the huge sales numbers created on Singles Day, physical retailers and malls still felt e-commerce was beyond the horizon.

But by 2011, the e-commerce tide was clearly coming in. Many local Chinese brands at all levels, and even foreign brands, had begun to open stores on Tmall. To avoid conflict with their offline channels, these brands began to offer differentiated goods only available online, or special packages and assortments for online consumers. Tao brands (e.g., UNIFON) also came of age around then. That year's Singles Day saw 3.36 billion RMB (US$517 million) in transactions, including the first time a brand's sales broke the 10 million RMB (almost US$2 million) ceiling in a day. (That apparel brand, GXG, in fact shattered the ceiling, selling 44 million RMB worth [US$7 million] of products.)

In the same way that coastal inhabitants know that an offshore earthquake presages a tsunami, everyone could see what was coming. When the curtain closed on Singles Day in 2012 with nearly 20 billion RMB (US$3 billion) in transactions, the phones began to ring. Indeed, the next day, I received a call from a traditional retailer who asked me almost verbatim, "Tell me again, how do I get online and start selling?" The sea change of e-commerce had arrived, and by 2012, everyone could see that those who hadn't grabbed a spot on the boat might end up sleeping with the fishes.

A CASE STUDY OF UNIFON

The Tao brand UNIFON (in Chinese, *Yunifang*, literally, "imperial mud atelier") demonstrates the incredible growth that Taobao's brands could achieve. In a mere decade, it transformed itself from a small online store to a public company boasting the largest sales volume of facial mask beauty products in the world. Less common in the United States, facial beauty masks are a mainstay of Asian cosmetic regimes—the facial mask category in China is expected to be a US$13 billion market by 2019. Demand for this core product brought enormous growth opportunities for UNIFON. In 2007, the brand was merely a small Taobao storefront run by two part-time workers. Annual revenue was less than US$100,000. Ten years later, the brand employed more than eleven hundred people, had created several lines of original beauty products, and had made more than US$300 million in revenue.

In 2008, the year after UNIFON had begun creating its facial mask product, the Taobao marketplace entered its first period of exponential growth driven by mature market mechanisms, technological infrastructure, and the sustained growth of many online merchants. That wave of growth inspired a group of entrepreneurs across industries to marshal the potential of the internet to build new and innovative brands. Many of these new consumer brands have gone on to produce long-lasting businesses and have gone public. UNIFON's success story as a brand and then as a company is emblematic of the brands that emerged on Taobao in this period.

2007–2011: First, Survive

A popular Chinese folk legend holds that in ancient times, the emperor's household prized rare types of mud for their cosmetic properties. The substances were so valued that tributes to the emperor would include certain soil extracts for the benefit of the imperial harem. In 2007, UNIFON began to extract essential ingredients from a unique mica slurry mined from Hunan Province in southern China. To precisely isolate the finest minerals from the mixture, the company used a traditional levigation process commonly used in traditional Chinese medicine to prepare certain medicinal ingredients. (In levigation, an insoluble substance is ground to a fine powder under wet conditions. As finer particles remain suspended in water while heavier particles sink, repeated wet grinding can effectively extract the finest particles from a slime or mud.)

UNIFON initially focused on developing a line of washable mud masks. With the rise of the consumer class, a new set of young, educated, and affluent consumers began to demand more varied deep-cleansing products. But at the time, the only beauty brand available in China that offered deep-cleansing solutions was the imported Italian brand Borghese. (Moreover, Borghese products were only available in select offline channels.) Though the mud mask was a niche product in the cosmetics industry, market opportunity was ripe. UNIFON's mud mask line quickly earned credibility with Taobao's youngest and most fashionable users. Early on, 17 percent of the brand's consumers came from Shanghai, China's most fashionable and Westernized city. In two years, the brand had built a strong user base.

In April 2010, Taobao partnered with one of China's hottest television talk shows, *Day Up*, to showcase several online-only brands. UNIFON's founder Dai Yuefeng was a guest on the show, promoting UNIFON as a natural and local cosmetics brand perfectly suited to the new fashionable Chinese consumer. Sales boomed after the show aired. By 2011, UNIFON had shifted the focus of its online operations from Taobao to Tmall, Alibaba's e-commerce platform for established brands. Successful cross-category marketing campaigns on Alibaba's flash-sales platform, Juhuasuan, catapulted the brand to greater heights. Annual sales revenue broke US$100 million.

2012–2017: From Startup to Mature Brand to Public Company

Starting in 2012, UNIFON began to exploit Alibaba's analytics products and stores of big data, keeping a close watch on market trends to determine which product lines would prove the most popular among consumers. The company launched a series of disposable facial masks featuring designs created in partnership with some of China's most popular cartoons (the beaver Ali) and TV shows (*Little Daddy*). This new product series allowed the brand to capture different sections of the young consumer market. Successful marketing work across Alibaba's various platforms, from Tmall to Juhuasuan to Alimama, brought new waves of growth, and during Singles Day 2012, UNIFON's flagship store was ranked number one in sales in the beauty category.

By 2013, the brand's commercial success impelled the company to upgrade its internal organizational capabilities. UNIFON's parent company, Yujiahui, completed three rounds of investment, led by the largest RMB fund in China (Shenzhen Capital Group Co., Ltd.), the Shunwei Fund (led by Lei Jun, Xiaomi's founder, who later became a director of Yujiahui's board), and the Qianhai Fund. Yujiahui brought in several mid- to senior-level executives from cosmetic giants such as P&G, Unilever, and Shanghai Jahwa, as well as from internet titans such as Alibaba and Tencent.

With talent and capital to spare, the company created a series of cosmetic brands aimed at different sectors of the Chinese market. UNIFON invested in R&D and brand development. The firm also moved decisively

---

Stage 4: 2013–2016

A Mall That Evolves: The New Mobile World

In the fall of 2013, a sense of crisis had set in among Alibaba's management. Mobile penetration was skyrocketing, and Tencent's killer app WeChat was steamrolling its way across China's smartphones. Yet across Alibaba, nearly all its products, platforms, and policies were designed for a world of PC computing. Both inside and outside the company, comparisons were made to companies like Nokia and Motorola, whose insensitivity to changing market conditions caused those companies' precipitous decline from market leadership to obsolescence.

In late October of that year, Alibaba's business units were restructured and resources were diverted from PC-era product lines. Management moved to redesign its marketplace and product line for a mobile environment. Taobao's technical and product teams began to tackle the enormous technological and infrastructural challenges of

to establish deep partnerships with overseas cosmetics brands, including Johnson & Johnson, Dr. Ci:Labo (Japan's number one medical cosmetic brand), and Leaders (South Korea's only listed cosmetic company). It worked to help them enter the Chinese market through e-commerce. It also acquired the Taiwanese brand Wellfon.

Between 2014 and 2016, Yujiahui's revenue growth rate surpassed 50 percent year over year. In 2016, the company achieved more than US$1 billion in sales revenue across all brand divisions. In 2017, the company sold four hundred million-plus sheet facial masks; since 2013, the company has sold more than one billion single pieces. Some twenty million users have purchased the company's products.

In November 2017, Yujiahui's application was approved by the China Securities Regulatory Commission for public listing on the Shenzhen Stock Exchange. When the company went public in February 2018, it became China's first A-share IPO from the e-commerce industry, and the second from China's cosmetic industry.

---

converting a PC-based platform into a mobile application that would perform equally well on myriad devices across developmentally disparate areas of China. These reforms, though difficult at the time, ushered in a new wave of growth for the marketplace. Now, the vast majority of Taobao users are now completely acclimated to mobile shopping and payment, as evinced by the enormous share of transactions (more than 90 percent) that were completed on mobile devices during the first hour of Singles Day in 2017.

For PC users, the Taobao customer experience was overwhelmingly dominated by search, static category lists, and the occasional curated promotion page. The Taobao app, on the other hand, became, and still is, a multifarious collection of banner ads, live streaming, flash sales, recommendations from power users, written articles (the Taobao Headlines), social networking, crowdfunding, crowdsourcing, and more. In this one app, a user can find a cornucopia of product channels, from worldwide brands to deep discounts to fresh food to luxury goods. Sellers, products, and even business models drastically differ in different sections of the app.

Most importantly, data intelligence operates pervasively behind the scenes, in the app's operation and in its constantly evolving structure. The Taobao app, like the ecosystem as a whole, is constantly changing and getting smarter and smarter. It is like a virtual mall where every storefront is customized to the customer and where even the layout of the mall itself can be rearranged. Flash-sale channels, for example, rank their products dynamically according to the customer. Even before a consumer begins browsing a particular channel, data intelligence is already working behind the scenes to guide the buyer to his or her desired product. To give another example, many of the pictures that users see to guide them into categories or specialty channels are already highly personalized. Different users that encounter the same channel will see different pictures.

Deeper network coordination and more-robust data intelligence drove GMV growth but, significantly, also incubated more and more new functions within the mobile ecosystem. In Taobao's PC era of growth, the platform evolved from a forum of buyers and sellers to a marketplace composed of all sorts of supporting functions for merchants. The growth of these ISVs and the development of market mechanisms and technological infrastructure to support their growth proceeded organically as the market developed. After 2013 and Taobao's transition to mobile, the marketplace continued to evolve. Even more roles and business models flocked to the platform. Taobao created another series of mechanisms and infrastructure for a new generation of ISVs.

The first group of new players in the mobile marketplace evolved from affiliate marketers and product recommenders that had done business on the platform for years. These new players operated by collating products on behalf of sellers and earning commissions. (Their offline analogue are buyers in the fashion industry.) In the mobile era, more and more of these aggregators began to exploit social media platforms to find and circulate their product listings. The distinction between recommenders and the group of users normally called influencers began to blur—very quickly, social media influencers and websites started to make money off commissions from Taobao. Taobao categories like Ai Guang Jie ("Love Window Shopping") and You

Hao Huo ("Good Find") provided specialized virtual "racks" where these marketers could showcase their wares.

Behind many of these affiliate marketing channels, a common infrastructure for payment settlement allows entrepreneurs to make money on commission. When a third-party writer (a new type of ISV) creates marketing copy, they inevitably embed links to Taobao products in their articles. Conversions that occur from these links generate commission on a cost-per-sale basis, with 20 percent going to the writers and 10 percent going to the platform. For many sellers, this commission is a acceptable marketing spend, especially for traffic that, thanks to data intelligence, can be more accurate than other traditional search and advertising channels.

Astute readers may notice that this payment infrastructure resembles the Taobaoke product described earlier. (Taobaoke allows affiliate marketers to earn commission from sales generated through the links they circulate.) The infrastructure between Taobaoke and these affiliate marketing platforms is in fact one and the same: the spread of cost-per-sale commission models to new types of content is a hallmark of Taobao's evolution in the mobile world. Much like the API, which continues to facilitate network coordination on Taobao to this day, new uses of Taobaoke's infrastructure also shows how core platform infrastructure continues to expand and be reused in new situations for the benefit of different users.

From Search to Recommendation

Certain sections of the platform showcase product content that is completely based on recommendation. These sections take data intelligence even further.

Flash-sale channels were once operated by Taobao employees, who curated the content in the channel through negotiations with merchants or by selecting from standard pools of product. Yet as Taobao's mobile technology improved, the Taobao app began to focus on purely algorithmic channels. In those channels, the products shown to consumers are completely chosen by data intelligence, from specialized recommendation-based areas aimed at higher-spending consumers to individual items displayed at the very bottom of the Taobao app's main screen. (This item recommendation area, dubbed "Guess What You Like," is nothing to sneeze at. In an industry where area within an app is worth more than real estate, "Guess What You Like" is extensive, easily displaying more than a hundred precisely related products for users who are willing to continue scrolling.)

These recommendations are now ubiquitous throughout the Taobao app. When a consumer enters a store or views an individual item, the system will also recommend other goods from the same store. At the bottom of the user's shopping cart, other items purchased by consumers who bought the same item will also appear as the user views their cart. After checking out, the user will see extra recommendations for products from other categories and sellers that might interest the consumer. When a user opens a recent order to check a delivery status, if he or she gets bored and scrolls down past the order information, there is ample data intelligence waiting with more recommendations. In many internet products, such as search, advertisements are intrusive and even detrimental to the user experience. However, because the Taobao app is already dedicated to shopping, product suggestions placed in relatively unobtrusive locations are not distracting to the consumer. (After all, the person is browsing, ultimately, to buy.) Consequently, the Taobao app works hard to turn every possible nook and cranny of the app into smart products, helping merchants create as many selling opportunities as possible. Through these merchant actions, consumers encounter, in increasingly smarter ways, the goods they are most interested in.

Data intelligence operates everywhere behind the scenes of the Taobao app, often in areas that the user might not expect. Consider, for example, banner ads, one of the marketing mainstays of e-commerce websites. In years past, advertising copy and visual advertisements were the province of a multitude of designers within the industry. Some designers are employed in-house by merchants, but many operate independent companies that provide specialized services for e-commerce operators. Year-round, these companies are busy with design work, but when large sales occur (and, especially, Singles Day), many of these designers find themselves overwhelmed with a spike of demand for work product. Enter Alibaba's AI banner-design software, LuBan, named after ancient China's most famous craftsman. This software uses existing product information and pictures, as well as those uploaded by merchants, to automatically generate effective and aesthetically pleasing banner ads. During Singles Day 2017, LuBan created four hundred million banner ads—that's eight thousand per second. Coupled with the Taobao app's personalized ad engines, LuBan ensures that just about every consumer sees different advertisements even for the same product.

From Retail to Content

Starting in 2014, Taobao began to move further into content, reaching out to writers, online content producers, and established media outlets and publishers. In addition to retail products in the narrow sense, Taobao fostered an environment where users could consume content related to retail. The offerings and business models in Taobao's new, mobile incarnation came to take a very different form than did those of its PC predecessor, which tended to focus on commerce more narrowly defined.

The first type of content to appear on the Taobao app was sponsored articles collected in a prominently placed section of the app called Taobao Headlines. These feature-length articles are written by third-party affiliate marketers about certain industries or certain categories of product, for example, "Full-Length Winter Coats for Short Girls" or "In the Battle of the Toners, Who Wins, China or France?" The authors may not get high marks for their refined aesthetics, but Taobao Headlines aren't meant to be literary masterpieces. The articles, a form of indirect advertising copy, make an effective marketing tool for sellers. (Authors get paid using Taobaoke infrastructure for commissions, as mentioned above.)

The Taobao Headlines section of the Taobao app builds data intelligence into the design of its channel the same way other specialized sections of the Taobao app do. The first application of data intelligence comes even before consumers enter the channel. As befits a headline, the channel gateway on the front screen of the Taobao app previews a rotating selection of articles. Which articles are displayed on the front screen is based on the user's previous buying history and browsing behavior. Once the user enters the channel itself, the order in which content is displayed is also customized, much like search results. Yet because the Taobao Headlines channel is matching consumers to content rather than to product information, its algorithms naturally must consider more facets of the consumer to effectively pair user and article. More-sophisticated algorithms and data technology maximize matching efficiency and drive sales, generating commission income for a growing cohort of content producers. The result is that the Taobao Headlines channel is itself an intelligent product whose value constantly evolves in response to consumer behavior and feedback.

After the success of written content in 2014 and 2015, Taobao continued to move into video content in 2016, comprehensively investing in video technology across all parts of the app. In China, technology for online video began to boom around 2015, and live streaming soon took the platform by storm. From the mobile app, users can browse live streams featuring social media influencers, Chinese celebrities, industry experts, and representatives from brands and merchant storefronts. These live streams might take consumers on tours of factories and storehouses in China, might show viewers what buyers around the world are buying at discount outlets, might feature singing and dancing—the sky is the limit. What most attracts China's netizens to these live-streaming sellers is the opportunity to ask direct questions of brands, catch deals and sales specially designed for live-stream viewers, and even tease and flirt with the streaming host. For merchants, live streams support brand marketing and increase consumer engagement.

Video now appears all across the Taobao app. Product detail screens—previously static text and images—now often commonly feature short videos produced by the brand. Especially in categories where the look and feel of a product are important, such as in apparel and cosmetics, video content greatly enhances the consumer experience. Buyers can even upload short videos (generally a few seconds long) when leaving reviews for products they have bought, for example, capturing how a pen writes on paper or how easily they assembled a coat rack. Although video on social media websites is not a new technology, allowing any user to upload created content at scale, when the platform hosts hundreds of millions of active buyers, is a significant technical challenge. (Not surprisingly, ISVs specializing in video production now do a thriving business for merchants on the platform. New point positions abound in a mobile world.)

Taobao has even partnered with well-known directors and production companies across China to run sales in the form of short original videos. In 2016, Taobao quietly introduced a "secret" area in the app called the Taobao Loft, which users can access by swiping downward on the home screen after ten o'clock every night. The app's "second floor" originally featured an online video series, *One Thousand and One Nights*, created exclusively for Taobao. Each episode tells the story of a different person enjoying a different midnight snack at a magical restaurant and reliving the past. At the end of each fantastical video, viewers can buy the featured food from merchants on the platform.

The series was a runaway hit and became a classic case study in Chinese marketing circles. More importantly, it also sold a prodigious amount of food. The first episode tells the story of a young woman from Qingdao (in the north of China) working far from home in Shanghai. One rainy night, unable to catch a cab, she happens upon a magical restaurant that is larger inside than it appears from outside. The chef serves her a certain fish dumpling from her hometown and calls her by name, wishing her a happy birthday. The fish dumplings, made with mackerel native to Qingdao, are unheard-of outside the city. The flavors of home bring back memories of home cooking and childhood.

In the first two hours after the video went live, consumers bought two hundred thousand dumplings. Throughout the sixteen-episode run of the series, users again and again demonstrated unexpected appetite for the flavors of the stories. A merchant selling imported Iberian ham, normally an expensive and extremely niche product, sold out of the store's entire stock by midnight after the product was featured in an episode. (When China's Spanish consulate got wind of the story, an embassy official directly called Taobao's marketing team to learn more about the series. Understandably, the phone call left the young, unprepared employees in a state of apoplexy.)

But more than just creating a huge volume of sales for a few merchants, the video series reminded users that Taobao offers more than just business or commercial products. It reminded users that Taobao began as a forum, a place where you could find anything under the sun, sold by anyone, anywhere around the world. *Nights* sought to bring users back to a Taobao they only vaguely remembered, a Taobao a decade removed, when the merchants were less "professional" but more genuine, where each product came with a genuine story, and where you might shoot the breeze online with a stranger in an afternoon lull at the office when neither person had anything better to do. It meant a return to a Taobao that felt small and warm, where new things were happening and where the scent of the future wafted through the virtual air.

Taobao continues to evolve. The only limits of the platform are the limits of technology and the limits of your imagination.

CONCEPTUAL FOUNDATIONS

A Unifying Theory of Strategy

My view of strategy encompasses both traditional strategic thinking and future creative concepts. Traditional notions of strategy are built on economies of scale. Structured in a line or chain, a firm aims to control inputs and maximize efficiency, thus lowering the cost of outputs and raising its own value. The factors of production were capital, machinery, materials, and the labor and management to run it all. Because these factors were expensive and hard to assemble, they granted important competitive advantage. Formerly, long-term planning, good strategy, and effective organizations maximized competitive advantage. Building a successful firm took time, as did the production of many of its goods. Similarly, business failures or the decline of a firm's products also happened slowly. Thus there was more economic stability, and the future of businesses was more predictable. Strategic thinking and other tools, such as Michael Porter's five forces analysis and SWOT (strengths and weaknesses, opportunities and threats) analysis, were designed to help business leaders navigate in this environment.

As some traditional industries became overcrowded and technology changed, business leaders and scholars developed new strategic thinking and other tools. Peter Drucker's brilliant description of the *knowledge revolution* explained the changes that came with the advent of the computer and other advanced technologies. Clayton Christensen's ideas on *disruptive innovation* offered a template for how firms could understand change and respond when a new technology or approach disrupts a formerly indomitable incumbent. Royal Dutch Shell's *scenario planning* helped companies do strategic planning in a much less predictable environment. W. Chan Kim and Renée Mauborgne's *blue ocean strategy* helps companies and entrepreneurs develop new markets altogether instead of entering or intensifying the competition in established arenas.

Recently, Porter insightfully described how technology has, in its successive waves, reshaped traditional competition and strategy.[1] The first wave automated business activities and standardized business processes, unleashing the knowledge revolution. The second wave allowed companies to coordinate and integrate global supply chains to enhance productivity. The third wave, in progress now, transforms the products themselves. Porter makes many valuable contributions, but he maintains that the rules and principles of competition and competitive advantage endure.

As different technologies and markets developed, strategic thinkers and advisers have revised their theories to help managers operate in an increasingly fast-changing environment with new technology. Despite the updating, these analytical tools have not abandoned the core characteristics of the industrial economy—linear, planned, inwardly optimized, and outwardly competitive. Or they have developed different strategic frameworks for traditional versus digital businesses. For example, platform strategy powerfully incorporates network effects, thus advocating some principles similar to those we use at Alibaba. But discussions of platform strategy do not extend the implications for general business practice. In addition, the literature on platform strategy focuses on the content of strategy but offers little insight on the process of strategy.

Today's business strategists seldom anticipate that the entire business landscape, traditional and digital, will be reconstructed as a network. No longer linear, planned, and controlled, a network has very different characteristics. The tools necessary to analyze and improve performance are very different, as I will describe shortly. Strategic thinkers rarely consider how these changes will alter the nature of competition. In the new paradigm, the productive factors of the future are available to everyone—anyone can get online and coordinate—and data, algorithms, and computational power are available in the cloud at variable cost. Change happens much faster, communities aggregate and disaggregate quickly, and individuation is valued. In this environment, much of the traditional strategy tool-kit will become irrelevant.

This book has offered a unifying theory to close the gap between internet companies and all other businesses. These new forces are forcing companies to evolve, and that the future of every business is to become smart, that is, to use data intelligence and network coordination to dynamically meet customer desires.

The Economics of Information and Networks

In referencing many economic concepts, this book reflects my approach to strategy, an approach informed by my background in both industry and academia. It has highlighted how smart business uses different approaches to handle fundamental economic dynamics. On a deep level, the strategy of smart business is concerned with mediating economic relationships (network coordination) and designing the mechanisms that quantitatively optimize those relationships (data intelligence). Though most businesspeople know that an understanding of computer science is crucial for innovative entrepreneurship, fewer people recognize that a familiarity with economic theories and concepts is increasingly important for technology-driven business. In other words, it is important for all business.

Throughout this book, I have explained from an intuitive perspective why data and networks rely on each other and create a mutually reinforcing cycle of value. The broader your network, the more live data that is produced, and the more that data intelligence operates throughout the network, the more effectively all participants can coordinate. My metaphor of the double helix suggests why smart business is so competitive in practice. However, I can go a step further and use economic theories to discuss the logical reasons that smart business makes sense.

Smart business starts with information shared on networks. The immense value of information and data networks builds on the unique economic properties of information, which is quite different from a physical product. Unlike the marginal cost of reproducing a physical good, the cost of reproducing information is near zero; you can send information repeatedly and cheaply without exhausting the information. When information is shared simultaneously across an entire network, information asymmetries—a fundamental cause of market inefficiencies and market failure—are dramatically reduced. As a decentralized, distributed, and peer-to-peer network, the internet is ideally suited for processing information.

Moreover, while the consumption of physical goods consumes a finite stock of value, the consumption of information creates value. If this contrast doesn't make intuitive sense, remember the example of MYbank earlier in the book. The more sellers that take out loans and reveal their preferences for risk, the more accurately risk algorithms can calculate an optimal loan product for these sellers. In other words, the lender's operating data is more valuable to the sellers and the platform after it has been used. This positive feedback loop is why I have emphasized the importance of rich interactions in a network. As Thomas Jefferson famously said, "He who receives ideas from me, receives instruction himself without lessening mine; as he who lights his taper at mine receives light without darkening me."[2] Feedback creates more information; it surfaces knowledge, so to speak.

Finally, the value of information is hard to predict, and its value is different for different people. As described in chapter 5, whenever Big-E offers a preview of a new batch of clothes, she has no way of knowing who will like which skirt or top, so her goal is to share them across the largest possible network. The value of information is maximized if it is passed through heterogeneous channels to meet as many people as possible. The idea is similar to the concept of collective intelligence. Sharing information across an expanding network creates the most value and the greatest potential for increasing returns. This property of information, and businesses that traffic in information, is a key reason why smart business has built-in network effects and strong first-mover advantages. We can also predict that the economic advantages of an internet-based network structure for business activity should create great economic gains for all of society.

Mechanism Design

As discussed in chapter 8, the organization must create mechanisms that not only make software development more efficient, but even incentivize certain behaviors within the company. Both this approach to organizational engineering and its associated academic discipline are called *mechanism design*.

The idea of mechanism design emerged from economics and game theory to describe principles for engineering strategic or economic interactions. When an interaction is conceptualized as a game, the rules of the game can be designed to achieve desired outcomes, such as fairness, best price, or most efficient allocation. In essence, mechanism design describes how the playing field, the rules, and the team positions affect the game and the game's results within the "sport," that is, the industry or the firm.

With the spread of the internet, scholars have successfully applied mechanism design to online social networks and, progressively, to human situations. In *Social Physics*, Alex Pentland, professor of information technology at Massachusetts Institute of Technology, describes how he and his coworkers have used technology to scientifically test different arrangements of workers.[3] To identify practices that are more creative, efficient, and intelligent, Pentland and his colleagues examined how workers are physically located, how their breaks are staggered, and how they interact online. In his experiments, online stock traders may need less real-time communication and fewer information updates to dampen their impulsivity and crowd response. In other settings, collaborative teams may want to set up a system where all team members get an equal time to talk, to surface all ideas and concerns. In retrospect, the consequences of such mechanism designs may seem obvious. But it took many decades of research in related fields to show the importance of designing business mechanisms for best results. For example, computer scientists have studied how the alteration of screen displays or the interaction rules built into email systems affect results or usage.

There are many ways that organizations can thoughtfully incorporate mechanism design into their operations at all levels, from physical architecture to technological infrastructure to incentive structure. A relatively simple structural fix is to place more meeting areas where people can interact with each other, even relocating passageways, offices, or gathering places that funnel the right people, as disparate as they may be normally, into the same place. For example, the ranking method for AdWords, Google's brilliant automated advertising service, originated from a casual game of pool, during which five employees from different departments began discussing complaints that Larry Page had made about AdWords. They decided to take on the challenge of improving it and helped work out the new if basic model of bid ranking over that weekend.[4]

This seemingly serendipitous gathering did not occur by accident. Tremendous effort had been put into place for this free-flowing discussion to happen spontaneously. (Google's cafeteria is assigned a product manager to optimize the "game" of eating.) Most of Google's free benefits not only save time, but they also help boost interaction. Pool and table tennis are so popular in Silicon Valley because participants who may not know what they have in common can easily start playing. The facilities of Google, Facebook, Alibaba, and others are called *campuses* for good reasons.

Microsoft offers another early example of a more complicated mechanism. The software behemoth is well known in the industry for directly incentivizing sharing and collaboration through its clever design of employee performance metrics. Microsoft's internal database keeps track of edits to code and software and thus can record and evaluate an individual engineer's contribution to the business. However, the company does not reward engineers for writing more lines of code. Instead, it rewards the engineers whose code is reused by more and more employees. This example of mechanism design has radical implications for the organization. Thanks to a virtuous incentive structure, engineers instinctively want to write code that is useful for more people. Redundant work and internal competition all decrease, merely because of reasonable design of evaluation mechanisms.

Most internet companies ply approaches similar to Microsoft's to encourage globally optimal behavior. At Google, for example, some employees get what amounts to a demerit for code that has never been reused by any other teams. If your work product is good, why wouldn't other people use it? Mechanism design for more effective interaction and collaboration within the firm can significantly improve organizational efficiency more than simply motivating the individual. The results of mechanism design are more salient where innovation is needed, e.g., in knowledge-intense and high-level intellectual environments.

Mechanism design can increase innovation and collaboration in almost any environment but for Alibaba, our challenge was less about clever rules that encourage sharing and more about creating an efficient platform for collaboration. As the Aone example showed in chapter 8, if your code is not created and updated in the cloud, others will be unable to track who is making and sharing what. To engineer incentives through mechanism design, you first need a technological basis for implementing those mechanisms. With the Aone platform, we at Alibaba can now experiment with mechanism design across more and more sections of our many businesses. The company is imagining new and exciting synergies when employees working on vastly different problems start to interact.

We at Alibaba are only in the early stages of the practical applications of ideas grounded in research from fields like network theory, social physics, and complex systems. In academia, however, at the intersection of physics, economics, biology, and sociology, these esoteric-sounding disciplines are quite established.

Analyzing Smart Business

To illustrate and quantify the dual forces of networks and data in business models and in the analysis of companies, I often use the graph in figure C-1. By plotting network coordination and data intelligence for business models, we can locate the strategic position of

FIGURE C-1

Strategic positioning of businesses

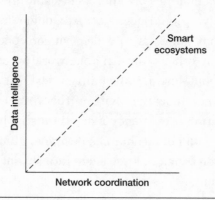

any particular firm and begin assessing its strengths, weaknesses, models, and products.

The largest and most promising companies are clustered at the upper right, while more traditional firms reside in the lower left. At the origin lies many so-called traditional companies, whose operations do not rely on complex coordination or data-driven optimization. Toward the upper right are the revolutionary companies that will redefine industry after industry. The world's internet companies are moving aggressively forward along the dotted line plotted in this map, creating equal capabilities in both network coordination and data intelligence. Of the top ten companies with the largest market cap, six are internet companies.

What can we learn from this graph? Winning is a function of strength in both networks and data.

You gain an extra advantage from using both networks and data in your business model, because the advantages accrued from each force often build on one another. The theme of this dual advantage has run implicitly throughout this book, most notably in the many Alibaba examples that straddle network and data. For example, MYbank's microloan service relies on live data from a vast network of sellers to continuously determine optimal credit ratings and interest rates, and Taobao's search and recommendation products similarly make effective connections between networks of buyers and sellers. But even if companies cannot be as large or sprawling as Alibaba, firm after firm is still moving in the same direction. Ruhan's Layercake infrastructure, for instance, aims to coordinate the data and processes from retail platforms, social media, and manufacturing networks.

In practice, both network coordination and data intelligence require similar foundational work, such as softwaring all activities, putting business processes online, and ensuring data flow through APIs. Furthermore, the two forces feed into each other. In a very real sense, the growth of the network requires data intelligence. If a network of numerous actors is not coordinated by data intelligence, it will quickly dissolve into a morass of inefficiency. Remember the hundred billion product recommendations generated on Singles Day 2016. That is the intelligence needed to support a vast network of products, sellers, and users. The reliance of networks on data intelligence is why business models and organizational forms involving networks at such a scale and with such a complexity have not been practicable in the past without the breakthroughs in computational power and machine learning. Almost 43 percent of China's population participated in the Singles Day sale in various ways; such complex coordination could only be done automatically through data intelligence.

But at the same time, data intelligence often has little value without vast and varied data. Ant Financial relied on triangulation from different kinds of data to arrive at empirically robust measures of credit. In many applications, what brings value is less the size of the data per se but more its richness and freshness. Hence, the term *live data*. The value skyrockets when live data comes from varied but equally fresh sources. Mobile recommendations on Taobao are that much more effective than those in a PC environment because user activity is deeper and more robust in a mobile setting. The time, place, device, and other apps that the potential consumer is using all constitute distinct streams of data. Now, imagine the same principle applied to business processes themselves. What if Ruhan could base its design choices on streams of live data, generated from retail platforms like Taobao, about the preferences of apparel consumers? And from broader trends in the industry, generated from social media such as Instagram? And from the current capabilities of the entire supply chain, from fabric to patterning to manufacturing? The design process would not only look completely different than it does now, but would also be immensely more effective.

Just as search networks demand data intelligence, adding data intelligence to a network of information about users and their activity makes the network stronger and more valuable. Recommendation engines produce better results with input from a broader network, and the network in turn drives the recommendations to get smarter and smarter. We have discussed the two forces of network and data separately in this book to help firms more effectively implement them. But the strong, mutually reinforcing relationship between the two forces creates a virtuous circle. That circle represents the quintessence of smart business.

Enabling: The Logic of Networked Business

The relationship between the platform (or plane, as described in chapter 6) and other players in the network requires careful attention. Who makes the business decisions on the platform? Is it the platform itself, in a sort of planned economy? Are the so-called point players and line players completely free to act of their own accord? The trade-off between command-and-control and laissez-faire is common to every ecosystem and platform business. After years of operational and even philosophical struggle at Alibaba, we have come up with a simple guiding principle: the platform's role is to enable the players on the platform, not manage their actions.

In the economics literature on the industrial economy, there is a clear dichotomy between markets and hierarchies. They are the two ends of a continuum. Markets rely on decentralized information-based mechanisms, such as auctions, to make decisions, whereas hierarchies rely on centralized decision making, the command-and-control style of management. Hierarchies internalize many functions that might have been operated as a market—where two or more parties can interact and transact—to reduce coordination or transaction costs and exploit economies of scale. As a hybrid of the market and the hierarchy, a network was once considered a special case in traditional organizational economics. Organizational networks have been ill defined, with examples and best practices hard to find.

With the penetration of the internet, coordinated networks such as Taobao are becoming widespread and will be the norm of the future. As infrastructure is built and more knowledge becomes widely accessible through APIs and other tools for sharing, contributors in the internal network see their ideas compete for attention and resources. As mentioned earlier, some companies give a sort of demerit to software engineers if no one reuses their code. In other words, the infrastructure creates an internal market in many respects, as well as an automated response to the external market. If a product's sales are growing and require more engineering or other inputs, resources are allocated. The system has been constructed so that those projects or products that come out on top on the performance rankings are funded in order until resources run out. Human design improves this system and continues to find tweaks to create the best systemwide results, similar to the way Taobao continued to adjust its search methodology described in chapter 4 to find what served the entire ecosystem best. In this way, resource realignment happens automatically as market acceptance grows. In essence, a firm is no longer a means by which hierarchical management internalizes some part of a value chain. It is becoming more of a market in itself.

Firms of the future will use data intelligence and network coordination to mimic market mechanisms. Moreover, as the network expands beyond the boundaries of the organization, it pushes the envelope for an increasing number of market-like interactions. The firm, and the firms with which it works, are becoming more like an open-source community. A network business is not a traditional business, and running networks is a different process from traditional management. Running a network requires enabling your players much more than it requires managing them.

Unlike a traditional retailer or brand owner with franchises or branches, the Taobao platform does not manage the millions of independent brands on its website. It bears no outright financial relationship with the businesses themselves, other than levying a commission on certain transactions. Overall, the platform looks like a service provider with scattered organizing functions and a certain measure of control.

The history of Taobao is that of new, emerging ISVs and the gradual introduction of the tools and infrastructure that these vendors need to do business. Through such a steady transformation, the platform emerges from a series of vertical applications; the ecosystem evolves from the interplay of new roles and new entrants to the network. Yet we at Alibaba struggled for many years with the absence of an established model for these relationships, much less a framework for how those relationships should be organized. As the resident intellectual, I expended a lot of gray matter on this conundrum.

A platform can be understood as the central hub of a network. But what is the exact relationship between the platform and the sellers on the platform? What should the platform do? As described in chapter 6, the platform (the plane) cannot exist without sellers (line players). Yet the plane does not manage the work of line players in the traditional sense of the term *manage*.

Viewing sellers as the customers of the platform's services doesn't solve the problem, either. Sellers are clients of the platform, but they also serve the platform's other clients, namely, consumers. Nor are sellers subsidiaries of the platform. In the retail context, the platform looks like a virtual shopping mall, but it has significant control over its "tenants" by creating incentives and performance metrics that determine which sellers might participate in sales or earn promotion and accolades from the platform. (These are examples of the mechanism design I mentioned in a previous section.)

No existing model could help us understand the relationship between platform and merchant that was fundamental to our business model. After months of discussion and soul-searching in 2012, our strategy team arrived at a word that seemed to capture the essence of the association between platform and merchant: *enable*. (The term was originally directly expressed in English, only to be back-translated by our team into Chinese as *fu neng*, literally "to endow with capability.") I have mentioned the term throughout chapter 8 in the organizational context. To recap, the work of enabling consists of providing infrastructure and solutions to decrease the costs of doing business; crucially, most of these solutions are software as a service (SaaS) products that run on data.

Enabling defines the boundaries and division of labor between platform and seller and the philosophy for governing the ecosystem. In an enabling relationship, Taobao and merchants are partners in a very real sense, working in cooperation to provide consumers with products and services. These offerings themselves are created by the merchant, but Taobao's application interfaces (like the Mobile Taobao app or Singles Day sales) deeply affect the consumer experience. The platform and the seller jointly serve the consumer.

In practice, Taobao as a platform stands behind the merchants, supporting them in their selling and branding and creating the infrastructure for their success. Within any ecosystem, platform firms mainly provide the infrastructure that undergirds the merchants' operations. Infrastructure comprises two key ingredients for enabling business: tools and rules. Tools are the products and functionality that enable connection and collaboration, like API technologies or the Taobaoke affiliate marketing platform. Rules are the mechanisms that facilitate healthy partnership and competition, such as Taobao's reputation systems or search algorithms. Rules are extremely important, as they directly influence how a market is run. Infrastructure mediates the relationships on the platform and provides members of the ecosystem with the needed resources and proper incentives. Infrastructural services across the ecosystem act as public goods in the rigorous sense of the term, creating externalities and network effects that make business in the ecosystem more efficient. These services consist of providing the capabilities of network coordination or data intelligence. This is why the Chinese translation of *enable* means "to endow with capability."

Enabling is the best way to conceptualize relationships within a business network. Because the network is halfway between a market and a hierarchy, it mandates a different logic than that used in traditional theories for building a market or managing a hierarchical organization. The platform does not manage sellers, per se, but its decisions and strategies are deeply implicated in their business. Sellers do not exist "at arm's length," as described by classical market theory. Sellers cannot exist without the platform, but at the same time, the platform is nothing without sellers. If sellers do not prosper, the platform runs the risk of being outcompeted by competitors or new entrants to the market. The rules for the act of enabling are new, and old definitions don't apply cleanly or neatly.

As networks pervade the business world, the boundary between firm and market is less and less clear. External markets outside of individual firms (e.g., financing platforms) are becoming more like a network. Inside many organizations, rigid hierarchical structures are giving away to more-flexible networks. And the flow between internal and external networks is also much more fluid.

Overall, the logic of enabling broadly applies to all business networks, be they in the industry (chapter 6) or within the firm (chapter 8). My discussion of building network coordination in chapters 2 and appendix B in itself explained how enabling actually works, while chapter 4 provided insights on how to enable network parties on the technical level.

Ultimately, the highest forms of enabling consist of facilitating network coordination and data intelligence. Whether they are platforms or firm, all organizations must speed the growth and spread of these two fundamental forces.

NOTES

Introduction

1. Conversions from RMB to dollars in this book use a standardized rate of 6.5 RMB to 1 USD.

2. "Inside VISA," https://usa.visa.com/dam/VCOM/download/corporate/media/visanet-technology/aboutvisafactsheet.pdf, accessed March 24, 2018.

3. Beginning in 2016, the popular business press seemed to wake up en masse (if maybe five years too late) to the idea that the Chinese technology sector can, in fact, innovate. For a small smattering of articles on the topic, see Paul Mozer, "China, Not Silicon Valley, Is Cutting Edge in Mobile Tech," *New York Times*, August 2, 2016; Jonathan Woetzel et al., "China's Digital Economy: A Leading Global Force," *McKinsey Global Institute*, August 2017; Louise Lucas, "China vs. US: Who Is Copying Whom?" *Financial Times*, September 17, 2017; and Christina Larson, "From Imitation to Innovation: How China Became a Tech Superpower," *Wired*, February 13, 2018.

4. Out of sixty-four companies, Alibaba was voted the top ten-year "buy-and-hold" company by clients and followers of CB Insight, an investment tools and research site. Alibaba captured 63 percent of the tally, beating out second-place finisher, Amazon. CB Insights, "What Is the Best Company to Invest In and Hold for Ten Years?" *CB Insights*, n.d., accessed March 10, 2018, www.cbinsights.com/research-company-investment-bracket.

5. Jack's creativity with coming up with titles within Alibaba is an important part of our company's culture. *Zong canmouzhang* literally translates to "general chief of staff," and indeed, the word *canmouzhang* is used in the Chinese translation of the Pentagon's "joint chiefs." The reason why Jack did not directly dub me chief strategy officer is because, in his opinion, the chief executive officer must serve as the firm's chief strategy officer.

6. Sun Tzu, *The Art of War*, trans. Lionel Giles (Blacksburg, VA: Thrifty Books, 2007).

7. The Chinese term *wang hong* is an abbreviation of *wangluo hongren*, literally "internet celebrity," and is sometimes translated that way in the Western tech media. This book prefers the pithier translation "web celeb." The term *wang hong* dates back to 2013, when social media influencers first emerged as a phenomenon on Weibo and other Chinese social media websites. *Wang hong* has since become a common moniker for young women who ply an image of stereotypical feminine beauty (often with the help of plastic surgery and photo editing software) in their quest for fame and fortune online. Not surprisingly, in common parlance, *wang hong* carries a slightly pejorative

connotation. This book uses "web celeb" neutrally, restricting discussion to *wang hong* in China's e-commerce space with a focus on the innovation of the underlying business model.

8. Taobao takes no cut from businesses like LIN Edition, which normally operate on Taobao as opposed to Tmall. Taobao's revenue is based on an advertising model, where businesses can pay for placement and better-quality traffic within the marketplace. Tmall, Alibaba's marketplace for branded merchants, operates on commission, generally taking a 0.4 to 5.0 percent commission on transactions depending on industry and product category. Foreign merchants operating through Tmall Global are further assessed a 1 percent transaction fee to cover the currency exchange handled through Alipay. For more information on Alibaba's different platforms and businesses, see appendix A.

Chapter 1

1. The term *network coordination* is the translation of a similar Chinese term (*wangluo xietong*) that I coined for internal strategic work within Alibaba in June 2007. The concept draws on theories from classical economic disciplines such as industrial organization, as well as newer interdisciplinary fields such as network science. For more background on network-based business models, see David Easley and Jon Kleinberg, *Networks, Crowds, and Markets: Reasoning About a Highly Connected World* (Cambridge: Cambridge University Press, 2010).

2. The seminal paper on this structuring of businesses was Ronald H. Coase, "The Nature of the Firm," *Economica New Series*, 4, no. 16 (1937): 386–405 (Blackwell Publishing). Subsequently, he published another very influential article: Ronald H. Coase, "The Problem of Social Cost," *Journal of Law and Economics* 3 (October 1960): 1–44. Significant additional work in the field of organizational economics has been done by many economists, including the Nobel laureate Oliver E. Williamson.

3. The term *data intelligence* is the translation of a similar Chinese term (*shuju zhineng*) that I coined for internal strategic work within Alibaba in 2014. It describes a certain strategic approach to applying machine-learning technologies. As I will explain in chapter 3, unlike related terms such as *machine intelligence*, *data science*, and *big data*, data intelligence focuses more on the practical use of data and algorithms to produce adaptive business results. For good background on machine learning and data science, see Pedro Domingos, *The Master Algorithm: How the Quest for the Ultimate Learning Machine Will Remake Our World* (New York: Basic Books, 2015).

Chapter 2

1. For more background on the Chinese economy in 2003 and the rise of e-commerce, see Porter Erisman, *Alibaba's World: How a Remarkable Chinese Company Is Changing the Face of Global Business* (New York: St. Martin's Press, 2015).

2. The evolution of Taobao was a classic exercise in building a platform through network externalities, catering to both buyers and sellers as the two sides of the

market built off one another. More sellers brought more buyers, bigger sellers needed more services, and so on. In economics, the spillover effects of an action are called "externalities." These externalities are unrelated or are tangential to the goal of the action, and can be positive or negative. Alibaba's experience has taught us that fostering and harnessing externalities is the key job of a platform business—see appendix C for more detail. In the case of Taobao's incubation, these waves of externalities were very positive, successfully incubating the platform. These externalities even spilled over off the platform, as sellers created informal offline organizations to improve Taobao's business environment.

3. The new focus within economics and management on platform strategy represents the rethinking of strategy in a network context. Alibaba operates at the forefront of these disciplines, and this book, especially chapter 6, reflects many ideas within that body of research. For an excellent treatment of the topic, see Geoffrey G. Parker, Marshall W. Van Alstyne, and Sangeet Paul Choudary, *Platform Revolution: How Networked Markets Are Transforming the Economy and How to Make Them Work for You* (New York: W. W. Norton & Company, 2016).

4. There are many origin stories for APIs, but an important contributor was computer scientist Roy Fielding ("Architectural Styles and the Design of Network-Based Software Architectures" [PhD diss., University of California, Irvine, 2000]) and his subsequent work.

5. In the field of sociology, these gaps are called "structural holes." In his book *Structural Holes: The Social Structure of Competition* (Cambridge: Harvard University Press, 1995), Ronald S. Burt analyzes the importance of these gaps in competitive networks, and analyzes the strategies of entrepreneurs that occupy these holes to create new forms of value. At Taobao, we have found that the evolution of the network amounts to a continuous cycle of new structural holes emerging, after which the platform helps entrepreneurs to "plug" the holes effectively.

6. The Wikimedia Foundation (www.wikimediafoundation.org) has considerable information about Wikipedia, including its history and operations. The Linux Foundation (www.linuxfoundation.org) maintains the open-source Linux environment, chronicles the history of Linux, explains how the operating system works, and provides training. Netscape was sold to AOL in 1999. Netscape's browser and other open-source tools were later spun off into a separate company, the Mozilla organization, in 1998, and then the Mozilla Foundation in 2003, when ties to AOL were cut. The foundation has a wholly owned subsidiary, the Mozilla Corporation. Information about the foundation and its other tools can be found at www.mozillafoundation.org.

Chapter 3

1. Data-mining startup Scrapehero indicates Amazon and Walmart offer over 500 million products and nearly 17 million products respectively. As nonofficial statistics, these should be understood as lower bounds. See "Number of Products sold on Amazon vs. Walmart—January 2017," January 26, 2017, https://www.scrapehero.com/number-of-products-sold-on-amazon-vs-walmart-january-2017/; and "How Many Products Does Amazon Sell?—January 2018," January 11, 2018, https://www.scrapehero.com/many-products-amazon-sell-january-2018/.

2. These applications of machine learning to business questions involve more technology and domain knowledge than computer science. Machine learning relies on recognizing hidden patterns through statistical analysis of big data, which is not always a cost-effective approach to solving business problems. Most modern machine-learning methods should have limited constraints on finding patterns: this lack of constraints allows computers to find deeply hidden patterns invisible to human experts. But the lack of constraints greatly enlarges the algorithm's search space, making the computational and data costs of finding patterns very large.

Thus the technology industry's most cutting-edge applications of data intelligence, including many mentioned in this chapter, do not just use machine learning. They combine computer science with two other academic disciplines: economics and optimization. Economics provides the basic mathematical models of human behavior, which greatly restricts the search space of hidden patterns. Machine-learning methods can then be used to obtain and clean the relevant data, and calculate the correct parameters for the model with respect to the business problem in question. Optimization methods (also called mathematical programming) can be applied to ensure that the models and methods of calculation are efficient given time and budgetary constraints. Entrepreneurs must remember that though the probabilistic methods of machine learning represent a revolutionary change to tactical decision making, machine learning in and of itself is not a golden bullet.

3. Data available from Amazon's SEC filings, http://phx.corporate-ir.net/phoenix.zhtml?c=97664&p=irol-sec&control_selectgroup=Annual%20Filings.

4. For background on Augury, see Klint Finley, "Augury's Gadget Lets Machines Hear When They're About to Die," *Wired*, November 4, 2015, www.wired.com/2015/11/augury-lets-machines-hear-when-theyre-about-to-break-down; and Ethan Parker, "Augury Secures $17 Million Series B Funding Round to Power the Future of IIoT," *Business Wire*, June 19, 2017, www.businesswire.com/news/home/20170619005161/en/Augury-Secures-17-Million-Series-Funding-Power.

5. For background on the state of financing for China's private enterprises (nonlisted, nonstate), see Franklin Allen, Jun Qian, and Meijun Qian, "Law, Finance, and Economic Growth in China," *Journal of Financial Economics* 77 (2005): 57–116; and Meghana Ayyagari, Asli Demirgüç-Kunt, and Vojislav Maksimovic, "Formal versus Informal Finance: Evidence from China," *Review of Financial Studies* 23, no. 8 (2010): 3,048–3,097. Together, these papers indicate that financing methods other than banks could account for up to 80 percent of firm financing, of which a significant portion comes from informal or underground channels. Ayyagari et al. in particular suggest that China's smallest firms rely the least on bank financing. I am grateful to Tang Ya, assistant professor of finance at Peking University, and PhD student Li Huixuan for their advice and for providing information on SME financing in China.

6. According to the State Council Leading Group Office of Poverty Alleviation and Development, China's "key counties for poverty alleviation and development work" (previously, "counties suffering from extreme poverty") are selected based on numbers of impoverished residents, income levels of farmer population, standard of living, and status of poverty alleviation and development work, with appropriate weight given to GDP and fiscal revenue per capita. Key counties are reassessed each decade: in both the periods from 2001–2010 and 2011–2020, 592 counties (out of nearly

3,000 county-level administrative units) across China qualified as key counties. ("Regulations on national poverty alleviation and development work regarding key counties," February 23, 2010, http://www.cpad.gov.cn/art/2010/2/23/art_46_72441. html).

7. Information on MYbank comes from the bank's website, mybank.cn, and from MYbank's 2016 operating statement (in Chinese): MYbank, "2016 Annual Report," May 2017, https://gw.alipayobjects.com/os/rmsportal/FzRFwOIBDOvSAeMuZewN.pdf.

8. These three building blocks—data, algorithms, and adaptable products—are my own formulation. For more background on machine learning and algorithms, see Pedro Domingos, *The Master Algorithm: How the Quest for the Ultimate Learning Machine Will Remake Our World* (New York: Basic Books, 2015); and John MacCormick, *Nine Algorithms That Changed the Future: The Ingenious Ideas That Drive Today's Computers* (Princeton, NJ: Princeton University Press, 2011).

9. I first read about Shigeomi Koshimizu's work in Victor Mayer-Schönberger and Kenneth Cukier, *Big Data: A Revolution That Will Transform How We Live, Work, and Think* (Boston: Houghton Mifflin Harcourt, 2013). Additional information is available at the website of the Advanced Institute of Industrial Technology (www.aait.ac.jp).

Chapter 4

1. For more background on the history of China's bike-sharing boom, see "Chinese Startups Saddle Up for Bike-Sharing Battle," *Wall Street Journal*, October 25, 2016, www.wsj.com/articles/chinese-startups-saddle-up-for-bike-sharing-battle-1477392508; Didi Kirsten Tatlow, "In Beijing, Two Wheels Are Only a Smartphone Away," *New York Times*, March 19, 2017, www.nytimes.com/2017/03/19/world/asia/beijing-bike-sharing.html; and John Lipton, "Bike-Sharing Boom in China Pedals to New Heights," *CNBC*, July 18, 2017, www.cnbc.com/2017/07/18/bike-sharing-boom-in-china-pedals-to-new-heights.html.

2. Marc Andreessen, "Why Software Is Eating the World," *Wall Street Journal*, August 20, 2011, www.wsj.com/articles/SB10001424053111903480904576512250915629 460.

3. This chapter's discussion of softwaring and APIs brushes an enormous quantity of technical detail under the rug. Structuring a business's technical stack to support on-demand operations (modularizing the core processes of the firm and ensuring that information flowing between them is coordinated through network calls as opposed to local calls) is a considerable technical challenge. I am not an engineer, and this is not a book for a technical audience, but readers interested in the technical aspects of softwaring business are encouraged to consult the ample literature on microservices and service-oriented architectures.

4. The story of Jeff Bezos's decision to mandate internal API use has not been formally told publicly, though it is obliquely foreshadowed in Brad Stone, *The Everything Store: Jeff Bezos and the Age of Amazon* (New York: Little, Brown and Company 2013), 209–210. The account comes from former Amazon employee Steve Yegge's rant about current employer Google, but Yegge's comment has since been deleted after its original posting on Google+. (An archived version can be found at Rip Rowan, blog on Google+, October 12, 2011, https://plus.google.com/+RipRowan/

posts/eVeouesvaVX.) For the pertinent excerpts, see Staci D. Kramer, "The Biggest Thing Amazon Got Right: The Platform," *GigaOm*, October 12, 2011, https://gigaom. com/2011/10/12/419-the-biggest-thing-amazon-got-right-the-platform.

Chapter 5

1. C2B stands for Customer-to-Business, not Consumer-to-Business. Due to Alibaba's background in the retail industry, I often use the term "consumer" in this and other chapters, but the reader should understand that a C2B mindset applies equally to all businesses, whether or not they are consumer facing. Any business that creates value in service of a client (i.e., all businesses) would benefit from this C2B theory. Indeed, this is why internet firms often prefer the neutral term "user," which covers the full breadth of possible beneficiaries of the firm's services. Readers less familiar with the lingo of the tech sector can view "customer," "user," and "client" as synonymous.

2. Nicole Shen, interview with author's team, Hangzhou, China, July 14, 2016.

3. KPMG, "Seeking Customer Centricity: The Omni Business Model," KPMG International, June 2016, https://home.kpmg.com/be/en/home/insights/2016/06/ seeking-customer-centricity-the-omni-business-model.html.

4. Big-E's strategy for establishing multiple touch points to gauge consumer demand and fine-tuning production schedules in an iterative fashion is an excellent example of the contributions of game theory frameworks to business operations. By turning a "single-shot game" (i.e., a business's guess about consumer demand) into a "repeated game" (a series of incremental decisions), the production choices of the supplier are mathematically much more likely to converge on consumer demand. Game theory tells us that, in the presence of incomplete or hidden information (e.g., consumer demand), repeated games are more likely to result in an optimal outcome for all players involved.

5. For an English-language article on the company, see Jane Ho, "China's Suit Maker Red Collar Blazes Trail for Mass Made-to-Measure," *Forbes*, August 15, 2016, www.forbes.com/sites/janeho/2016/08/15/chinas-suit-maker-redcollar-blazes-trail-for-mass-made-to-measure/#2e87a4fb5470.

6. Information on Shangpin comes from Ming Zeng and Song Fei, "C2B: Hulianwang shidai de xin shangye moshi" (C2B: The new business model for an internet age), *Harvard Business Review China*, February 2012.

7. Figures come from "Shangpin Home Collection's Sales in First Half of 2017 Break Two Billion, Net Profits 65.8701 Million RMB," *Yiou Wang*, August 29, 2017, baijiahao.baidu.com/s?id=1577030207271487167; and "Custom Furniture C2B Exemplar Shangpin Home Collection's Market Cap to Double by 2020," *ifenxi*, from ifenxi.com/archives/1745.

Chapter 6

1. Michael E. Porter, *Competitive Strategy: Techniques for Analyzing Industries and Competitors* (New York: Free Press), 1980.

2. In this discussion of point, line, and plane strategies, I often refer to "firms" as a basic analytical unit, with the implication that each firm needs to choose a singular strategic position. For smaller firms, this is a reasonable assumption, but speaking

more rigorously, it is more accurate to say that these strategies apply on the level of an individual product or service. It is perfectly reasonable for a single firm to work on two different businesses, one of which operates like a line and one operates like a plane. (A simple example is Amazon. Products sourced and sold by the company reflect a line strategy, while the third-party Amazon Marketplace exhibits a plane strategy.) Alibaba is a rare example of a company for which a majority of our products and services are positioned as planes from day one.

3. Inman is a casual women's apparel brand founded on Taobao in 2007. The brand's natural colors and fabrics like cotton and linen very quickly gained a strong following among young urban women. In 2008, founder Fang Jianhua became one of the first merchants to open a flagship store on Tmall. Since then, Inman has become one of the most popular female apparel brands on Tmall, ranking in the top 10 as measured by GMV in multiple years of Singles Day sales. On Singles Day, 2017, Inman's parent company, the Huimei Group, did 210 million RMB (US$33 million) in gross merchandise volume (GMV). As of November 2017, it has begun to expand from its online roots into offline retail, operating over four hundred brick-and-mortar retail stores in over 150 cities across China and planning to continue its expansion.

HSTYLE is a fast fashion online brand founded in 2006, operated by the Handu Group. Handu began as an online buyer for South Korean women's apparel, and in 2008 incubated the brand HSTYLE. Handu then continued to evolve into an online brand operator, incubating and managing over seventy apparel brands, including womenswear, menswear, childrenswear, and sportswear. HSTYLE is one of the largest women's apparel brands on Alibaba's platforms. On Singles Day 2012 to 2017, the Handu Group ranked (respectively) 3rd, 2nd, 1st, 2nd, 4th, and 5th in the women's apparel category. On Singles Day 2017, all of the Handu Group's brands did a cumulative 516 million RMB (US$ 2.5 million) in GMV. As of February 2018, the Handu Group is planning a public listing on the Shanghai Stock Exchange.

4. The past few years have seen an explosion of interest in platform strategy in popular business literature. See, for example, Ming Zeng, "Three Paradoxes of Building Platforms," *Communications of the ACM* 58, no. 2 (2015): 27–29. For more reading on the topic, see Geoffrey G. Parker, Marshall W. Van Alstyne, and Sangeet Paul Choudary, *Platform Revolution: How Networked Markets Are Transforming the Economy and How to Make Them Work for You* (New York: W. W. Norton & Company, 2016); David S. Evans and Richard Schmalensee, *Matchmakers: The New Economics of Multisided Platforms* (Boston: Harvard Business Review Press, 2016); and Andrew McAfee and Erik Brynjolfsson, *Machine, Platform, Crowd: Harnessing Our Digital Future* (New York: W. W. Norton & Company, 2017).

5. In the years since Baozun's IPO, the stock has consistently delivered exceptional growth in the small cap category. For background in English, see Aparna Narayanan, "Small E-Commerce Firm Sizzles As It Brings Western Brands to China," *Investor's Business Daily*, July 2, 2017, https://www.investors.com/research/the-new-america/this-small-e-commerce-gem-sizzles-as-it-brings-big-western-brands-to-china/.

6. For details on the WhatsApp acquisition, see Reed Albergotti, Douglas MacMillan, and Evelyn M. Rusli, "Facebook to Pay $19 Billion for WhatsApp," *Wall Street Journal*, February 19, 2014, www.wsj.com/articles/facebook-to-buy-whatsapp-for-16-billion-1392847766.

Chapter 7

1. This chapter draws heavily on concepts and frameworks from Martin Reeves, Ming Zeng, and Amin Venjara, "The Self-Tuning Enterprise," *Harvard Business Review*, June 2015. I am grateful for Reeves's lead in developing that article and helping me reflect on and refine my experience at Alibaba.

2. Aside from military and political strategies, the concept of business strategy didn't really get started until the twentieth century with the advent of Frederick Winslow Taylor and the science of management. It was at this time that most MBA programs were started and management began to be a role that was trained and professionalized. Corporate executives accepted that strategy was their domain shortly thereafter, as demonstrated by Alfred P. Sloan Jr., the CEO of General Motors, and his classic book, *My Years with General Motors* (New York: Doubleday, 1963; reprint Currency, 1990). Business strategy as a discipline took shape and produced powerful new insights and tools, such as the experience curve effects and growth share matrix pioneered by Boston Consulting Group's founder Bruce Henderson, and Michael Porter's five forces analysis outlined in *Competitive Advantage: Creating and Sustaining Superior Performance* (New York: Free Press, 1985). Since then, refinements and elaborations have been many and powerful. For developments in technology, see Andrew S. Grove, *High Output Management* (New York: Random House, 1993); and Clayton Christensen, *The Innovator's Dilemma: When New Technologies Cause Great Firms to Fail* (Boston: Harvard Business School Press, 1997).

3. Jack Ma and eight other leading Chinese entrepreneurs and scholars founded Hupan ("Lakeside") School of Entrepreneurship in 2015. Their goal in establishing Hupan was to draw on Alibaba's experience with innovative business models and organizational strategies and to identify and train entrepreneurs who will shape the Chinese economy and even play a key role in the global business arena. Ma serves as president, and I act as dean, overseeing curriculum and teaching.

Chapter 8

1. Eric Schmidt and Jonathan Rosenberg's book *Google: How Google Works* (New York: Grand Central Publishing, 2014) calls this kind of worker a "smart creative" and details such a person's qualifications and mindset. Though I do not explicitly use Schmidt and Rosenberg's terminology in this chapter, Google's lessons on people and hiring are very consonant with my experience at Alibaba.

2. Paraphrase from Elon Musk, interview with Kara Swisher and Walt Mossberg, at the Recode Conference, June 2, 2016.

3. As of early 2018, Anna Holmwood has translated the first of these wildly popular books by Hong Kong author Jin Yong. The iconic series has been called "the Chinese *Lord of the Rings*," inspired a nearly infinite assortment of television and movie adaptations, and remains beloved by hundreds of millions of Chinese readers of all ages. Jin Yong and Anna Holmwood, *A Hero Born: Volume I of The Legend of the Condor Heroes* (London: Quercus Publishing, 2018).

4. Alibaba's *huaming* (literally, "flower name," but here translated as "martial-arts name") is a unique and enduring element of our culture. Though the practice

began as a silly custom meant to inspire the imagination of early employees at Taobao, to this day the martial-arts nicknames help foster an egalitarian culture that is markedly different from that of most Chinese firms. Like most Asian languages, Chinese uses an elaborate informal system of terms for strangers and colleagues. These terms differ depending on the age, gender, and relationship of speaker and listener. Alibaba dispenses with these deeply ingrained cultural habits to give every employee—from the rank-and-file up to senior vice presidents—a unique and baggage-less moniker, which all colleagues are encouraged to use directly. (Of course, these nicknames can result in some humorous situations. There are many stories of Alibaba employees accidentally booking hotel reservations for colleagues under their martial-arts nicknames, only to cause profound confusion at check-in. And for employees who also use English names and regular Chinese nicknames, team members might well need to memorize four if not more designations for the same person.)

5. *Infrastructure* is another of those easily dismissed buzzwords that is indispensable to strategy discussions at Alibaba. My definition in this chapter appears to differ slightly from that of other places in the book, notably in chapter 2, when it refers to the tools and mechanisms that undergird a business network. Yet these tools and mechanisms too are basic services. The goal of technological infrastructure is merely to provide public capabilities across the platform ("infrastructural" services). Therefore, different uses of the same term in the platform and organizational contexts reflect the same core idea.

6. Zhang later served as CEO of Taobao and is now the chief technology officer of Alibaba Group.

7. All users on Alibaba's online forum, called "AliWay," accumulate "sesame seeds" as a way to reward activity. Users gain sesame seeds by engaging with colleagues on the forum, e.g., through commenting, and a user's total stock of seeds is displayed every time they make a post. Any post by any employee, up to and including management, can be rewarded with sesame seeds depending on the user's rank within the forum (not within the company). More amusingly, users can *dock* posts that they do not like, subtracting sesame seeds from the poster's total stash and sharing the reason for their dislike. Thus it is common to see users with negative sesame seed scores, often as a result of highly visible public discussions. For more examples of these mechanisms, see Tony Hsieh's excellent book on building company culture and a consumer-driven business at Zappos, *Delivering Happiness: A Path to Profits, Passion, and Purpose* (New York: Grand Central Publishing, 2010).

Chapter 9

1. Joseph Schumpeter's well-known book in which he fully develops his theory of creative destruction is *Capitalism, Socialism and Democracy* (London: Routledge, 1942).

2. There are many books on the market that talk about ecosystems, but not many that really get the strategy right. Despite its prolix style, Kevin Kelly, *Out of Control: The New Biology of Machines, Social Systems, and the Economic World* (New York: Basic Books, 2009), remains to this day one of the best resources for deep reflection

about the strategic mindset needed to shepherd (rather than plan) the growth of a business ecosystem.

3. I use the term *creativity revolution* in reference and homage to Peter Drucker and his masterpiece of understanding changes in the business world, *Management Challenges for the 21st Century* (London: Routledge, 2015). Drucker first described the knowledge worker in his *Landmarks of Tomorrow* (New York: Harper & Row, 1959).

Appendix A

1. For more background on the Chinese economy in 2003 and the rise of e-commerce, see Porter Erisman, *Alibaba's World: How a Remarkable Chinese Company Is Changing the Face of Global Business* (New York: St. Martin's Press, 2015).

2. Henry Chin and Alan Chow, "The Case for China Retail: Issues and Opportunities," Prudential Real Estate Investors, March 2012, p. 14, http:// dragonreport.com/Dragon_Report/Corp_China_files/PRU_China_Retail_0312.pdf. Readers should know that 2011 numbers have most certainly increased significantly since 2003, when Taobao entered the market. As of this book's publication, China's infrastructure has improved immensely, but many per capita statistics still lag (well) behind developed nations.

3. Information on MYbank comes from Alibaba Group's press release "Official Launch of Ant Financial Services Group Brings New Financial Ecosystem to China," October 16, 2014; MYbank's website mybank.cn; MYbank's 2016 operating statement (in Chinese): MYbank, "2016 Annual Report," May 2017, https://gw.alipayobjects. com/os/rmsportal/FzRFwOIBDOvSAeMuZewN.pdf; and also from Shu Zhang and Ryan Woo, "Alibaba-backed Online Lendor MYbank Owes Cost-Saving to Home-Made Tech," Reuters, January 31, 2018, https://www.reuters.com/article/us-china-banking-mybank/alibaba-backed-online-lender-mybank-owes-cost-savings-to-home-made-tech-idUSKBN1FL3S6.

Appendix B

1. The transaction process on Taobao, and by extension all Chinese e-commerce platforms, requires the buyer to explicitly confirm physical receipt of product through the platform. In this way, transactions on Taobao are different from those on US e-commerce platforms. Before the buyer confirms they have received what they bought (and that their product matches the seller's original description), the order is not considered final. Not only is payment from the transaction held in escrow; from the platform's perspective, the merchant has not even made a sale. (Only when the consumer asserts receipt of goods, money changes hands, and the transaction finishes does the sale count toward the merchant's sales history.) This small change in logic affects many complicated aspects of Taobao's operations and platform rules, most of whose complexity is beyond the scope of this book. To give one example, in Taobao's arbitration department, orders contested after payment but before buyer confirmation (midsale) are handled differently from orders for which payment has not been posted (presale) or from orders where the buyer has already confirmed receipt (postsale.) Each of these three types of arbitrations follow a completely different set of rules and regulations.

Appendix C

1. Michael E. Porter and James E. Heppelmann, "How Smart Connected Products Are Transforming Competition," *Harvard Business Review*, November 2014.

2. Thomas Jefferson to Isaac McPherson, August 13, 1813, in *The Founders' Constitution*, ed. Philip B. Kurland and Ralph Lerner (Chicago: University of Chicago Press, 1987), writings 13:333–335, available at http://presspubs.uchicago.edu/founders/documents/a1_8_8s12.html.

3. Alex Pentland, *Social Physics: How Social Networks Can Make Us Smarter* (New York: Penguin, 2014).

4. Eric Schmidt and Jonathan Rosenburg, *Google: How Google Works* (New York: Grand Central Publishing, 2014).

FURTHER READING

Alibaba

Clark, Duncan. *Alibaba: The House That Jack Ma Built*. New York: Ecco, 2016.

The authoritative outsider account of Alibaba.

Erisman, Porter. *Alibaba's World: How a Remarkable Chinese Company Is Changing the Face of Global Business*. New York: St. Martin's Press, 2015.

The story of the founding of Alibaba and Taobao as told by one of the company's earliest foreign vice presidents.

Tse, Edward. *China's Disruptors: How Alibaba, Xiaomi, Tencent, and Other Companies Are Changing the Rules of Business*. New York: Portfolio, 2015.

One of the rare books on Chinese business that gets it right. Ed Tse was formerly the head of first the Boston Consulting Group and then Booz Allen Hamilton's practices in China.

Network Coordination

Barabasi, Albert-Laszlo. *Linked: The New Science of Networks*. New York: Basic Books, 2014.

An accessible and comprehensive introduction to the theories of network science by one of the giants in the field of complex networks.

Easley, David, and Jon Kleinberg. *Networks, Crowds, and Markets: Reasoning about a Highly Connected World*. Cambridge: Cambridge University Press, 2010.

An undergraduate textbook that condenses the complicated concepts and theories behind network coordination into digestible, intuitive ideas and applies them to real-world situations.

Shirky, Clay. *Here Comes Everybody: The Power of Organizing without Organizations*. New York: Penguin Books, 2008.

Classic thinking on how to organize behavior and work without hierarchies or central management.

Data Intelligence

Domingos, Pedro. *The Master Algorithm: How the Quest for the Ultimate Learning Machine Will Remake Our World*. New York: Basic Books, 2015.

> One of the best broad introductions to machine learning and algorithms for a nontechnical audience.

MacCormick, John. *9 Algorithms That Changed the Future*. Princeton, NJ: Princeton University Press, 2011.

> An in-depth but accessible look at how the most important algorithms in computer science are used to utilize data intelligence across society.

Mayer-Schönberger, Victor, and Kenneth Cukier. *Big Data: A Revolution That Will Transform How We Live, Work, and Think*. Boston: Houghton Mifflin Harcourt, 2013.

> The classic book that popularized the term *big data* is still worth reading for its observations about the changes to business and society brought on by new technologies for collecting and processing data at a massive scale.

O'Neil, Cathy. *Weapons of Math Destruction: How Big Data Increases Inequality and Threatens Democracy*. New York: Broadway Books, 2016.

> Alarmist tone aside, this book presents the flip side of Mayer-Schönberger's predictions about big data, explaining how a badly designed feedback loop can go wrong and how to design these loops effectively.

Platform Strategy

Evans, David S., and Richard Schmalensee. *Matchmakers: The New Economics of Multisided Platforms*. Boston: Harvard Business Review Press, 2016.

> A comprehensive look at the economic principles behind multisided markets (what I call plane firms in chapter 6) and the challenges of getting them started.

Kelly, Kevin. *Out of Control*. New York: Basic Books, 2009.

> Despite its prolix style, still one of the best in-depth looks at the strategic mindset needed to shepherd (rather than plan) the growth of a business ecosystem.

Mitchell, Melanie. *Complexity: A Guided Tour*. Oxford: Oxford University Press, 2009.

> A clear and accessible introduction to the science of complex systems.

Parker, Geoffrey G., Marshall W. Van Alstyne, and Sangeet Paul Choudary. *Platform Revolution: How Networked Markets Are Transforming the Economy and How to Make Them Work for You*. New York: W. W. Norton & Company, 2016.

> A deeply practical and grounded breakdown of platform business models, their core components, and how to jump-start specific tactics and strategies.

Information Economics and Its Business Applications

Anderson, Chris. *The Long Tail: Why the Future of Business Is Selling Less of More.* New York: Hachette Books, 2006.

One of the earliest and most lucid books on how internet technology affects business models, strategy, and operations.

Chandler, Alfred D., and James W. Cortada. *A Nation Transformed by Information: How Information Has Shaped the United States from Colonial Times to the Present.* Oxford: Oxford University Press, 2003.

Though this book is less well-known than Chandler's *Scale and Scope*, business historian par excellence Chandler is equally at his best in this recounting of how information technology changes business and society.

Shapiro, Carl, and Hal R. Varian. *Information Rules: A Strategic Guide to the Network Economy.* Boston: Harvard Business School Review Press, 1998.

Every smart business traffics in information goods to some degree; even after two decades, this classic of information economics is still required reading for those who wish to understand the counterintuitive principles of information's value creation and transfer.

Addressing the Future

Drucker, Peter. *Management Challenges for the 21st Century.* London: Routledge, 2015.

One of Drucker's last and best books on the comprehensive changes to management and organizations caused by technological change.

Kelly, Kevin. *The Inevitable: Understanding the 12 Technological Forces That Will Shape Our Future.* New York: Penguin Books, 2016.

This book presents some of the future's most important technological trends abstracted so that they apply to all readers.

Tegmark, Max. *Life 3.0: Being Human in the Age of Artificial Intelligence.* New York: Knopf, 2017.

A guide to working and living with, not just despite, AI.

INDEX

ACKNOWLEDGMENTS

The first person I want to thank, of course, is Jack Ma. I am deeply grateful for his invitation to join Alibaba on its wonderful journey and for all his guidance and support over the last eighteen years. He has greatly influenced my thinking about the future and strategy. Many concepts presented in this book, such as customer-to-business (C2B) and network coordination, coalesced in the endless discussions we had.

I have benefited enormously from the interaction with thousands of colleagues across Alibaba's many businesses, from Yahoo! to e-commerce, from cloud to finance. Almost everything I know about the internet is because of the education they have given me. I cannot name all these colleagues individually, but I am eternally grateful for their insight and energy.

I have been working on this book for the last four years. My strategy team has been true collaborators during this time as we worked through the ideas described in the book. Yu Li, as my deputy, has been of great assistance. Li Junling, Zhang Xiaofan, and Yang Renbin have contributed many original ideas to our conversations.

Nick Rosenbaum, my assistant for the last three years, has played an indispensable role. He has participated in every stage of this book. His competence and purposefulness have always exceeded my expectations. Rita Koselka contributed greatly in editing the book, especially in putting the final draft together. Melinda Merino, my editor at Harvard Business Review Press, was very quick to grasp what I was trying to say in the first rough draft. She pushed for a concise framework that really put my work into focus. Without her capable guidance and the hard work of everyone behind the scenes at HBRP, especially our heroic copyeditor Patty Boyd, the book not only would have taken much longer, but would also have been much less accessible to readers.

They say it takes a village to raise a child; in my case, it takes an ecosystem to write a book. Without the many tens of millions of people who have built China's e-commerce industry from little more than their own grit, this tiny book could not exist. Over the years, I have had the honor of talking with innumerable sellers, lecturers, Taobao partners, delivery personnel, web celebs, independent service vendors, and more. These people have done far more than enrich my own understanding: they are pioneers in the wilderness. Their tenacity, diligence, and optimism have created a vibrant oasis on what was once barren ground. Our revolution from the periphery is a success.

On a last note of gratitude, I have been lucky enough to work and engage in stimulating discussion with hundreds of adventurous businesspeople in China and elsewhere over the last twenty years. They have created businesses large and small, experienced setbacks and even failure. Their efforts to use business to improve the world around them have inspired and challenged me. I hope this book will be of some assistance to them and to you.

Finally, it is my job and calling in life to find, analyze, and assist you, the entrepreneurs and thinkers who are creating the future. Your work can be hard and lonely. Wherever you are in the world, if this book and its ideas resonate with you and your dreams of the future of business, please continue the conversation through e-mail via zengming@aliyun.com. I would be delighted to engage with you.

ABOUT THE AUTHOR

MING ZENG first worked as a strategy adviser for Alibaba Group from 2003 to 2006, joining the company full time in August 2006 as Zong Canmouzhang (similar to chief strategy officer) from 2008 to 2017. Working closely with Jack Ma, Dr. Zeng has played an important role in the phenomenal growth of the company. He is now chairman of the Academic Council of Alibaba Group, fostering innovative research both within and outside Alibaba.

Dr. Zeng began his career in academia in 1998 as a professor of Asian business at INSEAD in France. In 2002, he returned to China to help found the Cheung Kong Graduate School of Business, the first private business school in China. In 2014, he became the dean of the Hupan School of Entrepreneurship, located in Hangzhou and established by Jack Ma and a few other farsighted business leaders in China.

Dr. Zeng is one of the most respected strategy thinkers in China and has published widely on strategy, e-commerce, and Chinese business. His book *Winning by Strategy* (in Chinese, 2003), was voted the best business book of the year. *Dragons at Your Door: How Chinese Cost Innovation Is Disrupting Global Competition* (with Peter Williamson, Harvard Business Review Press, 2007) was one of the first books studying emerging global multinationals from China.

Dr. Zeng obtained his PhD in strategy and international business from the University of Illinois at Urbana–Champaign in 1998 and his BA in economics from Fudan University in Shanghai in 1991.